A WESTERN HORSEMAN BOOK

RODEO LEGENDS

20 Extraordinary Athletes of America's Sport

By Gavin Ehringer

Edited by Gary Vorhes

RODEO LEGENDS

Published by
WESTERN HORSEMAN®magazine
3850 North Nevada Ave.
Box 7980
Colorado Springs, CO 80933-7980

www.westernhorseman.com

Design, Typography and Production
Western Horseman
Colorado Springs, Colorado

Cover photography by
Dan Hubbell

Back cover art by
Dave Merrick

Printing
SFI, Inc.
Englewood, Colorado

©2001 by Western Horseman
a registered trademark of

Morris Communications Corporation
725 Broad Street
Augusta, GA 30901

All rights reserved
Manufactured in the United States of America

Second Edition: May 2003

ISBN 1-58574-710-6

FOREWORD

RODEO HAS always been a contest filled with human drama, the kind sportswriters like to ponder in their columns and to which people are naturally drawn. After all, there's something about a 135-pound cowboy trying to ride a 1,600-pound bucking bull that gets your attention.

The really interesting part is finding out how a guy got into the situation in the first place. If he started out as a youngster named Tuff Hedeman - a slender lad with little natural ability to ride - you can't help but cheer when the underdog becomes world champion. There's also a lesson in courage for anyone who watches a competitor like Tuff overcome crippling injuries and go on to win again.

Exhibiting grace under pressure is another aspect of the sport, and a theme writers like to explore. The crowd at the 1985 National Finals gasped when 15-year-old barrel racer Charmayne James dashed into the arena on her horse Scamper - and the horse's headstall fell away! Rather than panic in a situation caused by a lost screw in the bridle, she ran the pattern with confidence that flowed through to her horse, who wore the bridle like a necklace. Charmayne kept her head and won the go-round.

Rodeo is more than a sport; it's a way of life for some, and maybe an art form for the purist. The action takes place in an arena, of course, but the real stories often involve things like work and commitment, mental and physical preparation, desire and self-control. In the final analysis, this game is probably a contest not so much between an athlete and an animal, but more a personal contest the individual has with himself.

Herein lies a wonderful collection of true stories - written by Gavin Ehringer, a veteran rodeo writer - that chronicle the lives of 20 of the all-time best rodeo athletes, including Tuff Hedeman and Charmayne James. Start with the piece on bareback riding champ Joe Alexander, and read why the late Red Smith, dean of the sportswriters, couldn't help but dub him "Alexander the Great."

Continue on through legends like Larry Mahan and Ty Murray, ironman Jim Shoulders and unforgettable Casey Tibbs. Then wind up reading about the phenomenal Fred Whitman, the big-event player of pro rodeo who says he's the greatest and makes you believe it.

— Randy Witte
Publisher
Western Horseman

INTRODUCTION

THIS BOOK began as a proposal from the editors at *Western Horseman*. We decided to use the format of the very successful Legends series on horses to create a book that would celebrate rodeo's greatest champs of the last 50 years.

The original book was to have been ready for the 1999 NFR, but as the months dragged into years, I still hadn't finished. Stretching deadlines like rubber bands, I finally came up on a wall of scowls around the *Western Horseman* offices. Clearly, it was time to get things done.

But I can say this, I am glad I procrastinated. Because the lives of my subjects proved to be very dynamic, and things kept happening.

For example, many people thought that when Charmayne James retired her horse Scamper, who had carried her to 10 straight world championships, her career would dry up and wither like an old boot on a fence post. But after making it back to every NFR aboard average-caliber barrel horses that Charmayne coaxed and cajoled into NFR contention, she finally came up with a fitting replacement for her ProRodeo Hall of Fame "super horse."

Had I finished the book on time, I certainly would have missed mentioning Cruiser, the horse who may well put Charmayne back on the throne of women's barrel racing.

Likewise, I would have missed Fred Whitfield's 2000 calf roping world championship, an event that literally had me biting my nails at the NFR that year. I'd spent the better part of the week with Whitfield, and I'd staked a magazine feature story on his winning the world title.

When Fred won it in the final round, staving off attacks by two other very determined cowboys, I think I was even more relieved than Fred himself. His story would not have been complete without that great example of tenacity and confidence in his own ability.

But the one event I would have most regretted missing was a gathering that took place at the ProRodeo Hall of Fame on August 9, 2001. On that date, nine of rodeo's greatest all-around champs came together for the dedication of the Hal Littrell World Champions Pavilion in the hall's beautiful garden area. They represented a living history of rodeo in the last half of the 20th century.

Oldest among them was Gerald Roberts, the two-time world all-around champ of the 1940s. Gerald, whom I didn't include in this book but maybe should have, was instrumental in recruiting cowboys for the

Rodeo Cowboys Association back in the 1940s. He helped to shepherd in a new generation of competitors that included Casey Tibbs, the legendary saddle bronc rider and prankster who would claim a record six bronc riding titles from 1949 to 1959.

Also there for the party was Jim Shoulders, "Ol' Sixteen Times," the city-born son of an auto body mechanic who proved to be rodeo's dominant champ of the 1950s. Shoulders earned his nickname by winning 16 world titles, a record that seemed insurmountable until only recently, when Guy Allen piled up world title upon world title in steer roping. Allen is destined to tie Shoulders in 2001—a milestone that most thought would never be reached by anyone, let alone someone in a single event.

At the dedication ceremony, Larry "Bull" Mahan, the great rough-stock cowboy who in 1973 bested Shoulders' record of five world all-around cowboy titles, was doing what he does best: working the crowd and making each person feel like the most interesting and important individual he had ever met.

Not far from Mahan was his heir, Ty Murray, who'd grown up with one goal his entire life: to beat Mahan's record. "The Kid," as the older champs referred to him, did indeed do just that, winning his seventh world all-around title in 1998. Holding firmly to Murray's arm was Jewel, the lovely folk singer, who wore a rattlesnake skin jacket that she claimed was patched together from hides taken on Ty's ranch in Stephenville, Texas.

Had I not procrastinated, I might not have been able to include the photo I snapped of the exceptionally talented couple, nor would I have had the chance to sit in the stands at Madison Square Garden with Jewel, discussing her life, her career, and her attraction to rodeo's greatest cowboy.

I could go on and on about the many benefits of not having done this book on time. I could continue singing the praises of the champion cowboys enough to fill another entire book. But that wasn't really what I had in mind here.

What I want to say is that, having spent so much time with rodeo's greatest champs, I don't really look at them as heroes or role models—although many of them are both, I guess. I just think of them as interesting people leading purposeful and interesting lives.

In this book, I've tried to talk about their great arena accomplishments, for sure. But I also tried to talk about how they stumbled and fell, then picked themselves up and dusted themselves off.

Joe Beaver is a good example of that. After nearly expiring from a drug overdose, the calf roper pulled his life together for the sake of his newborn son, Brody. Because I waited, Joe reached a point in his life where he was willing to share the story with me, in hopes that it would inspire future rodeo cowboys not to make the same mistake. Thank you, Joe.

I also tried to dig up the funny incidents, the stories told again and again behind the bucking chutes and on all-night drives from one rodeo town to the next.

Such as the time Casey Tibbs slipped Harry Tompkins a couple of pills to help cure a case of nausea just as the two took off in a small chartered airplane. The pills were, in fact, laxatives, and Tompkins spent the entire flight battling their effects.

To my mind, stories like these (some of which appear nowhere else) are the stuff of legends every bit as much as world titles and 90-point rides.

In choosing the subjects for this book, I had to make some hard decisions. I am sure to get letters from people saying, "So, why didn't you pick so-and-so. After all, he won everything there was to win!"

My response is, I chose people not only for the number of world championships they won, but within other criteria as well. Did they somehow revolutionize some aspect of rodeo? Did their charisma capture the imagination of rodeo fans, the press, and the general public?

I know that there will be people who say, "You're biased." My response: guilty as charged. But fret not: If you don't find a personal favorite in this book, perhaps you'll see him or her in a sequel.

Why, you may ask, did we focus only on cowboys who competed after World War II? Well, there are several answers.

First, the system for choosing world champions wasn't established until 1929, meaning that any claims to "world" championships prior to that are nebulous at best.

Furthermore, rodeo records and biographical information on cowboys who competed prior to the 1940s are frequently incomplete or nonexistent. For the first few years of its existence, the Professional Rodeo Cowboys Association, formed in 1936 as the Cowboys' Turtle Association, operated out of the trunk of a car. Even if a great deal of information were available about rodeo's earliest days, I would still be inclined to limit this book to the last half of the century.

It's my opinion that the first generation of truly professional rodeo hands emerged in the late 1940s and early '50s. During the postwar boom, rodeo surged in popularity, enabling competitors to make a decent living if they had the talent, ambition, and drive to do so.

The public was exposed to rodeo through magazines, newspapers, and for the first time, television, giving the people a chance to see rodeo as more than simply a wild west show or a circus whose performers wore broad-brimmed hats and boots.

A debate has raged for years in the sports departments of daily newspapers as to whether rodeo cowboys are athletes or something else—entertainers, perhaps. Rodeo is still relegated to the lifestyle and news sections of many newspapers and is often absent from the sports pages, where it rightfully belongs.

Once you read about the practice routines of these cowboys—how Roy Cooper tied calves until his hands bled, or how 13-year-old Ty Murray rode his new bucking machine until his thighs were rubbed raw—I think you'll know where I stand.

Most of all, I hope the stories told here serve as an inspiration to you, the reader. Whether you choose to become a rodeo cowboy, an astronaut, a doctor, or a school teacher, I think you can look at the people in this book and see the unquenchable desire they possessed to be their very best.

If you get discouraged because you don't have the slickest horse at the National Little Britches Finals, or you don't have a new truck to drive now that you are 16, or you missed the chance to attend college because you didn't make the grades, just read the chapter on Dean Oliver and how he rose from utter poverty to become the greatest calf roper to swing a loop. If that doesn't inspire you to make the best of life, well, I don't know if anything ever will.

Now, get to reading. Time is a wastin'.

CONTENTS

	Page
JOE ALEXANDER	8
JAKE BARNES & CLAY O'BRIEN COOPER	18
JOE BEAVER	28
LEO CAMARILLO	40
ROY COOPER	52
TOM FERGUSON	62
BRUCE FORD	72
MARVIN GARRETT	82
DON GAY	96
TUFF HEDEMAN	106
CHARMAYNE JAMES	118
BILL LINDERMAN	128
LARRY MAHAN	136
TY MURRAY	150
DEAN OLIVER	162
JIM SHOULDERS	174
CASEY TIBBS	184
HARRY TOMPKINS	194
FRED WHITFIELD	204
AUTHOR PROFILE	214

JOE ALEXANDER

IT WAS the legendary *New York Times* sports columnist Red Smith who dubbed him "Alexander the Great." And although a mere 5 feet 8 inches and 155 pounds, he was great in the estimation of both his peers and rodeo history.

A native of Wyoming, Joe Alexander was not considered the best rider of rank horses among his generation. He never managed to win the average at the National Finals, despite competing there 13 times. And in his rivalry with one of the rankest horses of his day, a mare known as Three Bars, he won only one bout of six.

But if it wasn't his ability to ride anything with hair on it, what made Alexander a legend? How was it that he became the first bareback rider in rodeo history to win five world titles, a feat so far matched only once by Colorado cowboy Bruce Ford?

The answer lies in Joe Alexander's deep well of determination. Joe was a tireless road-warrior who crisscrossed the nation in planes and fast cars, rarely letting a chance to compete pass him by. If there was a day's wait at a rodeo, Joe would hop a charter or drive 500 miles to get on a horse in another town.

But there was more to his game than merely outcompeting the other cowboys: Alexander was a great stylist with a knack for timing his spurring with a bareback bronc and making a showy ride that drew

Alexander's upright style of riding was a throwback to the earlier generation of bareback riders.

the admiration of judges, fans, and fellow bareback riders. Most who saw him compete would agree—there's never been a more stylish bareback rider.

"(Joe) has a spurring lick virtually unequaled today; he's always in complete control of the bucking, pitching horses clear up to the 8-second whistle," said one of his rivals. That, combined with the determination to pile up money at a prodigious rate, helped him rewrite the rodeo history books. Alexander first matched, then exceeded 1950s bareback kings Jim Shoulders and Eddy Akridge. And he did it by winning titles back-to-back-to-back during an intense period of rodeo competition stretching from 1971 to 1975.

Having surpassed those two riders in the record books, he then went on to win two additional PRCA championships in 1976 and 1977, when a new system of determining world titles at the National Finals Rodeo was implemented. Had the old system remained in place, he would have an even more impressive seven world titles to his name. All the while Joe was setting earnings records in his event and building up more than a half-million dollars in arena earnings over a career that ultimately landed him in the ProRodeo Hall of Fame.

Joe Alexander grew up in the northwest corner of Wyoming, not far from the world-renowned resort town of Jackson. His parents, Bud and Dorothy, were ranchers who operated a 10,000-acre spread outside tiny Cora, which was even

High School he competed in basketball, football, and track.

It is a surprising fact that Joe didn't start riding bonafide bucking horses until he was 17. But with his natural athleticism and a lifetime of horse sense, he mastered bareback riding quickly. At the time he also enjoyed riding bulls, wrestling steers, and team roping.

Such versatility was of key importance in fielding a college rodeo team at that time, and Joe's talent as a multievent competitor helped him to hook a rodeo scholarship at Casper College, a junior college that was well known for its rodeo teams. Joe's rodeo coach, Dan Stiles, was impressed with the goal-setting ability of his incoming freshman.

"I want to finish school and I want to be a champion," Joe told his coach when the two met at fall registration. In only his first year in college rodeo, Alexander won the regional title in bareback riding (a title he would successfully defend for the next four years) and qualified for the 1966 National Intercollegiate Rodeo Association's finals. There he won the national bareback riding title and led his team to the men's national championship. In 1967 he was the reserve national champ in his specialty event.

After the two-year program at Casper, Alexander transferred to the University of Wyoming. His downward slip in the collegiate national rankings continued. Alexander finished third in the nation in 1968, and fourth in the nation in 1969. Still, being a top-five finisher each year among the collegiate riders was a worthy accomplishment, and one that any rider at that level could look to with a great deal of pride. After four years of rodeo competition and academics, Joe achieved his goal of graduating, leaving the University of Wyoming at age 24 with a degree in agriculture.

Like many of that era's college-educated cowboys, Joe defied the stereotype of the hard-drinking, hard-living, hard-luck rodeo rider of old. He didn't smoke and

less than a one-traffic-light outpost in the Jackson Hole valley.

Like most ranch kids, Joe was horseback by the time he had mastered walking. He and his two brothers, Ross and Kip, were pursuing the sport of team roping in grade school, and it was a favorite pastime in a place where the nearest mall was a good 15 miles away. In such a remote rural setting, the boys had to make their own entertainment.

"Winning to me is everything," he said early on in his professional career. "It's my life, my business."

Dorothy Alexander was a former schoolteacher who made sure her boys stuck hard to their homework. To get her boys to the schoolhouse, she drove a mile and a half to the school bus stop. In winter, when the snows drifted too deep for their mother to get out, the boys rode horses through the deep snow, leaving their mounts in a barn put there just for that purpose.

Joe was a good student who excelled in academics as well as sports. At Pinedale seldom visited the bars. He could often be found doing calisthenics behind the chutes, and he would take long runs to keep his wind strong. From the word go, he was an athlete, with an athlete's will to win.

"Winning to me is everything," he said early on in his professional career. "It's my life, my business."

Like many of the cowboys of the time, he was impressed and influenced by the businesslike approach of all-around champ Larry Mahan. When the rodeo season ended, Alexander was determined to have at least a portion of his earnings in the bank. That desire to get ahead and stay ahead in a sport where an athlete's career could end tomorrow was one reason Alexander felt he had to rodeo so hard. And Alexander had the advantage of greater maturity than most rodeo rookies of earlier eras, who typically joined the rodeo circuit straight out of high school.

Nearly everything about rodeo was in a state of transition in 1970, Joe's first full year of competing in the professional ranks. This was especially true in the bareback riding event, which had undergone a revolution in riding style throughout the 1960s.

During the preceding years, cowboys had stiffened the once soft and pliable handhold of the bareback riggin' with fiberglass, metal, and finally rawhide. With a stiffer "suitcase" handle to grip, the riders could take greater liberties, leaning way back and spurring with great style, flair, and ferocity.

Alexander represented the ideal transitional rider: He did not ride upright, with rigid legs stretched out in front of him like Jim Shoulders, Eddy Akridge, and Harry Tompkins had done in the 1950s and early 1960s. But neither did he ride fully laid back along the horse's spine, as did the Mayo brothers, Clyde Vamvoras, and others who are said to have originated the new style.

Since the judges were often from the older generation of rodeo cowboys, many of them still liked to see the style that they, themselves, had used or at least watched

CAREER MILESTONES

Joe Alexander

born: November 4, 1943
Jackson Hole, Wyoming

Five-time World Champion Bareback Rider (1971-75); Two-time PRCA Champion (1976-77).

1982 Injured in the third round, Alexander sits out seven NFR rounds, then bucks off his final horse. Having surpassed the goal of contesting in 12 NFRs, he semiretires at his California ranch and raises purebred beef cattle.

1981 After announcing his retirement from competition, Alexander aims for a record 13th trip to the NFR. There he bucks off the horse Gypsy Velvet in round one, reinjuring his broken thumb. Sidelined for the remainder of the rodeo, he finishes the year ranked sixth in the world.

1980 Injuries plague Alexander at the NFR. An encounter with the horse Three Bars in round four nearly results in paralysis, but Alexander comes back to win the next round. However, another mishap in round eight forces him to sit out the final two rounds.

1979 Alexander joins the first class of inductees at the ProRodeo Hall of Fame.

1978 Alexander finishes fourth overall in the NFR average, but the world title goes to Jack Ward. Bruce Ford, heir to the bareback throne, earns the PRCA championship. For the first time in eight seasons, Alexander is not the top money-earner in his event.

1977 Again, Alexander has more regular-season earnings than any bareback rider, but comes up short at the NFR. Jack Ward wins the world title; Alexander again wins the PRCA championship.

1976 Alexander falls victim to a new system for naming world champs; Chris Ledoux wins the gold buckle. Alexander is named PRCA champ, winning the most money that year, more than $50,000, a record in the bareback riding event.

1975 In October Joe marries Cindy Dodge, Miss Winston Rodeo, and a former competitor in barrel racing, team roping, and bull riding. One sponsor rep remarks, "Joe won $26,000 from us in the last three years (in Winston bonus earnings) and now he has taken our queen!" At the NFR Alexander places in five rounds, tops ten head, and finishes second in the average, the best NFR showing of his career. He also clinches his fifth bareback title to set an enduring record in the event.

1974 Alexander captures his fourth bareback title, drawing even with Jim Shoulders and Eddy Akridge in bareback world championships. At Cheyenne Frontier Days he earns 93 points on Beutler & Cervi's Marlboro, the highest score in bareback riding to that time.

1972-1973 Alexander successfully defends his world title, setting earnings records of $32,126 and $37,021.

1971 Alexander wins the bareback riding world title in only his second full year as a professional. At the NFR he struggles through one of the worst bareback riding averages of his career.

1970 His first full year of professional competition, Alexander qualifies for the NFR, finishing fifth in the world. At the Grand National Rodeo in San Francisco, he scores 89 points, one of the highest-marked bareback rides in rodeo history up to that time.

1968 Alexander finishes second in the nation in NIRA bareback riding.

1967 Alexander joins the Rodeo Cowboys Association while a freshman at Casper (Wyo.) Community College. He wins the first of four consecutive regional NIRA bareback titles, wins the NIRA's bareback riding title, and leads his team to the national men's championship.

Alexander making the bell on Sippin Velvet in the first round of the 1979 NFR.

JAMES FAIN

when they came up in the sport. Joe, therefore, appealed to their prejudices when it came to marking points. But he was such a smooth rider with such excellent timing and a clean spurring lick, he also appealed to younger judges who favored the new, let-it-hang style.

Alexander's more conservative approach to riding was evident from the moment he started competing hard in the pro ranks. In a biographical sheet that was given to each cowboy, the riders were asked "Who do you consider the toughest man in your event?"

Joe picked Gary Tucker, Ace Berry, and Australian Jim Dix — all of whom practiced the older style of bareback riding. Alexander even wore conservative gray hats and understated shirts that contrasted to the wilder, flashier style that was coming into vogue among his generation of riders.

Although Joe had competed in his first pro rodeo while still a freshman in college, he waited until he had completed his degree and gained some experience in the college

ranks before concentrating his efforts on professional rodeo.

In 1969 he claimed nearly $5,000 during a six-week run, and decided that he was ready to commit to a career as a bareback rider. His first full year as a pro rider was, by nearly every measure, an excellent debut.

As the 1970 regular season drew to a close, Alexander capped the year off with an 89-point ride at the Grand National Rodeo in San Francisco. The ride, aboard a bronc named My Pet, was among the highest-scored bareback rides in rodeo up to that time, and it helped make Joe the fifth-ranked bareback rider in the world standings going into the National Finals.

He'd need that final boost. After an inspiring regular season, Alexander turned in a performance at the NFR that was anything but inspiring. After bucking off in the first round, he placed second in round two.

Then things simply fell apart for the Wyoming cowboy. He failed to make the whistle on six of his remaining eight horses, finishing the rodeo far out of the average. In fact, were it not for injuries that took two riders out of the competition, Joe would likely have finished dead last in the bareback average. Freshman jitters aside, however, Alexander did manage to hold on to his fifth-place ranking in the world standings.

Joe began the 1971 season with the intention of making it back to the NFR. Certainly the prospect of a world title was on his mind, but not foremost.

But in midsummer he was chided by his friend "Cody Bill" Smith to push himself harder. That sent Alexander on an Independence Day winning spree that propelled him to the lead in the world standings.

Joe continued winning throughout the remainder of the summer, strengthening his lead in the world standings to the point that it was as impregnable as a missile silo. There was no hope for any rider to surpass Alexander at the National Finals, yet Joe still poured salt on their wounds by winning rounds seven and eight. The Wyoming hand who had celebrated his 28th birthday in November got a belated present: the gold-and-silver buckle proclaiming him the bareback champion of the world.

Evidently Alexander liked the feeling and the buckle, for he went on to claim the world championship for the next four years.

In 1974 Joe began the season with an exceptional winter, winning the Denver National Western Stock Show, Fort Worth, San Antonio, and Houston. Sweeping that run of major rodeos might be compared to winning four majors on the PGA Tour, or perhaps winning each of the Grand Slam tournaments in tennis.

That summer he continued on a rampage, cashing checks at rodeos from Calgary to Prescott, Arizona. All told, the rider placed at an amazing 52 rodeos. He went into the NFR that December with his fourth world title virtually assured.

As Alexander built up to his record-tying season, he finally decided it was time to wed the woman he'd been courting.

Cindy Dodge was the daughter of famed cutting horse trainer Don Dodge. Although she grew up in the show arena, by the time she graduated high school, she had abandoned that world in favor of rodeo.

She started out working for Cotton Rosser's Flying U Rodeo outfit in 1969, around the time Joe was winding up his college career and making plans for the pros. The two first met at a rodeo in Seattle, Wash., and began a courtship that would last several years.

In 1974 Cindy applied for a position as Winston's marketing rep on the rodeo circuit and won the job of Miss Winston Rodeo. The job entailed traveling the rodeo circuit, riding horses in the grand entries, and chasing cattle out of the arena while taking care of the various responsibilities of a corporate rep.

Due to federal regulations, the tobacco companies had been forced to take their advertising funds out of television and magazine advertising. With no outlet to promote their brands, they applied that money to selected sports. Rodeo was among the beneficiaries, and Joe was among the most successful at grabbing the lucrative bonuses that the Winston folks poured into the sport.

When Joe and Cindy announced their plans to get married just before the 1974 NFR, Richard Dilworth of RJ Reynolds

Unimpressed by Alexander's record and unaware of his new status as a domesticated man, Three Bars dumped the rider in the opening round.

remarked, "Joe won $26,000 from us in the last three years and now he has taken our queen." Graciously, Joe received his $5,000 Winston bonus check at the world champions' banquet, thanking the sponsor for "helping to pay the tab on the wedding we just had."

In spite of a few spectacular wrecks, Alexander suffered few serious injuries during his rodeo career.

COURTESY PRCA

Cindy wasn't the typical stay-at-home "rodeo widow." She traveled nearly as much as Joe during her eight-year reign as Miss Winston Rodeo, and she even competed in rodeos herself.

As a member of the Women's Professional Rodeo Association, Cindy had teamed with bareback rider J.C. Trujillo's wife, Margo, to win the 1973 women's team roping national championship. She also finished second in the women's bull riding standings that year. When possible, she and Joe competed in mixed team roping events or jackpot roping contests, winning a fair share of those events.

When they had a chance to take some time off, they relaxed at a small ranch that they bought together in Marysville, California. Joe liked living in the Golden State, as he'd taken on a fondness for warm, mild winters. In the summertime, however, the two often returned to Wyoming to stay on Joe's family ranch, where he liked to fish and hunt.

Joe and Cindy's honeymoon at the 1974

NFR was rudely interrupted by the first horse he drew, a rank mare named Three Bars who would prove to be one of the greatest challenges of his career. Unimpressed by Alexander's record and unaware of his new status as a domesticated man, Three Bars dumped the rider in the opening round.

"I had Three Bars six times (in my career) and that was her best trip. She really bucked," remarked Alexander of the ride. "I think I'd have been 90 points on her if I could have lasted a couple more seconds. But about six seconds into the ride, she stumbled. That set me up, and popped the back of my hand out of my riggin'. Then all I had … were my fingertips."

Despite trying to grab hold with his legs, Alexander got spit off the horse when she threw one last mighty kick. It would not be the two champs' last meeting at the National Finals.

In the ensuing contest the cowboy managed to place in three rounds, but he also was goose-egged twice more, leaving Okla-

This ride, however, aboard New Deal at Calgary took him out of action at a crucial time during the '77 season.

homa City with only $843. Still, the world title had been decided even before he slung a leg over Three Bars. Alexander had tied Jim Shoulders and Eddy Akridge, becoming only the third bareback rider in rodeo to earn four world titles.

Now Joe set his sights on winning a fifth world championship. This time, though, he would arrive at the NFR with the championship anything but decided. For the first time in five years, Alexander had a challenger for the title: bareback rider Rusty Riddle, one of the most consistent young riders of the era.

For the past three years Riddle had completed the season as the reserve world champ behind Alexander. He had actually done better than Alexander in two of the three previous NFRs, but simply could not win enough money to overtake him. Now Riddle was within shooting distance of Alexander. To claim his fifth world title, Joe was going to have to outperform Riddle by placing not only in the go-rounds, but in the 10-round average.

Alexander kicked off with a 76-point ride aboard Beutler & Cervi's Devils Dream, placing second in the round and setting the pace for the remainder of the competition. Riddle answered by placing in the next two rounds, but Joe managed to make qualified rides, maintaining a place at the top of the average.

Riddle's riding went stale in the fourth round, and though he continued to make qualified rides in five through eight, none of them earned him a paycheck. Meanwhile, Alexander continued to place, racking up fourth-place finishes in rounds four and eight. Round nine proved to be the showdown between the champ and his would-be successor.

Rusty drew the good Calgary Stampede horse Moon Rocket, posting an impressive 79 points to lead the go-round. But Joe answered with a 77 on the Alsbaugh Rodeo horse Sparkplug to place second in the round. Both riders had successfully ridden nine horses, but Alexander had the lead in the average. If he could maintain that edge,

Riddle had no chance of overtaking him in the world title race.

In the final round Joe sealed the deal with a winning 80-point ride aboard Little Dan of the Beutler & Cervi string. After a run of mediocre National Finals, he finally topped off all of his horses and placed second overall in the average — the best NFR finish of his entire career. But the important thing was that he had won $4,176 to retain the lead in the world standings, finishing the year with $41,184 to Riddle's $38,767. Alexander was, once again, the undisputed champion of the bareback riding event.

Having accomplished more than he had ever dreamed of in rodeo, Alexander found that his drive to be No. 1 was flagging. Younger riders were coming up, and they were hungrier and more willing to rodeo hard to win the world title. Still,

At the peak of his career, Alexander makes a solid ride on Dark Canyon at Tucson in '75.

the rodeo game had afforded the Wyoming cowboy a nice living, and he was torn. By 1977 he was already contemplating retirement. He conceded that, at 34, he no longer felt like he had when he came into the sport a decade earlier.

"I still feel good, but I get too sore if I try to go hard," he said. "As you get older, it gets tougher. Most of the guys who are going six times a week are ten years younger than I am."

At this point in his career, Alexander had already surpassed the $400,000 earnings mark. He was assured of a home in the ProRodeo Hall of Fame.

And yet, something kept him from hanging up his rigging. Call it habit, or pride, or what you will, Alexander felt that he had to stay on the road, although somewhat less than he had in the years leading up to his world championships. It wasn't as though he needed to keep competing. Joe had planned for the future and had two western-wear stores and a burgeoning cattle ranch in California. But the allure of competition remained strong.

Throughout most of his pro career, Alexander had managed to avoid serious injury. His excellent physical conditioning combined with great agility and good fortune had allowed him to compete non-stop since his pro debut way back in 1967. But in 1977 Joe was competing at the famed Calgary Stampede when he injured his collarbone and pulled a back muscle. He was forced to turn out his last horse and to take time off to recuperate.

Second behind Bruce Ford in the standings, he dropped to fourth, then fifth as the weeks passed. Although he'd been sidelined only 10 days, he was ineffectual afterward. Meanwhile, Ford was stretching his lead, while other riders were pushing Alexander farther and farther away from the lead position.

Despite rallying to challenge for the world title, as the season drew to a close he was simply too far off the pace to catch Bruce Ford. Still, the 1978 Finals was a memorable one: Joe placed in seven of the eleven rounds, including an 82-point win in round seven aboard Bay Muggs of the Barnes Rodeo Co. string. His fourth-place finish in the 11-round average had been his best since 1975 when he had finished second at the finals.

Heartened by the strong finish, Alexander

put aside his plans to leave the rodeo game behind, and 1979 saw him once again out on the road.

As one year turned into another, Joe remained one of the top competitors in his specialty event. Between 1976 and 1980, he had never dropped below fifth in the world standings. He continued capturing berths at the National Finals Rodeo, and that helped him to summon the determination to begin each new year.

At 37 Alexander had one more goal to achieve before he hung up his riggin' for good. He stated at the time that the world championship was no longer his goal. "I don't need another gold buckle," he said. "I got plenty of 'em." What he wanted was to return to the NFR one last time and thus set a record for the most qualifications in his event.

The 1981 season progressed exceptionally well, and by summer Joe was trailing world standings leader J.C. Trujillo by a mere $1,000. But a bad turn of luck at a rodeo in Prescott, Ariz., effectively took him out of world title contention. After dismounting from his bronc, Alexander landed on the ground — with the horse's hoof in his face.

"I was right there behind the leader, J.C. Trujillo, when I got hurt," Joe recalled. The accident left him with a broken cheekbone and a broken thumb. The injuries took him out of action for seven weeks, the longest vacation he'd had in his pro career.

He returned to action with a screw holding the bones in his cheek in place. Despite falling more than $10,000 behind Trujillo, Alexander was secure in his ability to get to the National Finals for the 12th time. As he had done throughout his career, Joe had put in a request for NFR tickets for his family before the season even began.

But the event was anything but joyous for the Alexander family. In the first round Joe's injured thumb caused him such pain that he was forced to withdraw. The result was that he finished the rodeo having won not a penny. That left Alexander ranked sixth in the world at season's end, his worst

COURTESY PRCA

Alexander rejected the image of the wild cowboy, preferring a more businesslike approach to the rodeo game.

finish going back all the way to his rookie season. Clearly that was not how the champ wanted to leave the game.

Joe took one more run at the NFR, stretching his string to a record 13 straight qualifications in 1982. But in a near repeat of the previous year's unfortunate outcome, Alexander, now 40, again suffered an injury, this time in the third round. His riding hand became painfully swollen, causing him to withdraw in round four.

He rallied to ride in the 10th go-round, but sadly, the record books will forever record a no-score for Alexander the Great's final ride at the NFR. On a positive note, however, he did surpass the $500,000 mark in career earnings in 1983 with a win at Denver in January, becoming the first cowboy in rodeo history to do so.

Looking back over his long and exceptionally distinguished career, Alexander has no regrets. Often he remarked that a rodeo career "beats a desk job or packing a lunch basket." History will long remember him as the greatest bareback rider of his era and, with five straight titles and an asterisk indicating that two more world titles should be appended to his record, perhaps the greatest of all time.

Jake Barnes &
Clay O'Brien
Cooper

THERE ARE sports records that seem to be surpassed every year or every few years. Then there are those that seem eternal: Joe DiMaggio's 56-consecutive-game hitting streak in 1941 and Wilt Chamberlain's 100-point basketball game in 1962, for example. One of those enduring records belongs to Jake Barnes and Clay O'Brien Cooper, the greatest team-roping unit in rodeo history.

The year was 1994. The event, the National Finals Rodeo in Las Vegas. Barnes and Cooper were chasing their seventh world title in team roping, which, when accomplished, would constitute another record. In the first round Barnes slipped his loop on the steer and made the turn, but Cooper picked up just one foot, and the two earned a 5-second penalty. After that, the two ropers were flawless. Through eight consecutive nights of roping, neither hit a barrier, missed a catch, cross-fired, or threw a figure eight. On three of those nights, they won first place. On another they placed second. Then came the final night with the world title on the line. All they had to do was catch their final steer, and the title was assured.

"Jake and I didn't need to say a word to each other about it," recalled Clay O'Brien Cooper. "I watched his head loop go on, then I roped the steer and dallied, and he faced. I looked up at Jake's face, and he was

Barnes and Cooper set the standard to which all roping teams are compared.

looking right at me. Time stopped for just a moment, and we could feel what we'd just done through the other guy. I could see it in his eyes, and he could see it in mine."

What they had done was obliterate the NFR record for the fastest time on 10 head by more than 18 seconds. Their time: 59.1 seconds.

One minute. Ten steers. Impossible.

Even Jake Barnes found it hard to believe.

"If someone had put a gun to my head and told me we had to rope 10 steers there in 59.1 seconds, I'd have said we couldn't do it," he said.

Doing the impossible just seemed to be an everyday thing for Barnes and Cooper, the most successful pairing ever in the team roping game. The two really did have an almost telepathic understanding of each other, never having to guess what the other was about to do and rarely having to communicate their thoughts and feelings. It's said that Jake and Clay often roped 100 steers in a practice session and scarcely spoke a word to one another. The two were simply on the same wave, pursuing the same dream with the same intensity.

Jake Barnes and Clay O'Brien Cooper grew up under similar circumstances. Both were from the Southwest, and both wanted from an early age to become world champions. "Both of us have been roping since we were little kids," said Barnes, who was raised on a ranch just outside Bloomfield, New Mexico. "I met Clay at the World Junior Team Roping Championships in 1974 in Oklahoma. We went to a lot of the

Relentless practice gave Barnes and Cooper the ability to anticipate each other's responses in any rodeo situation.

same rodeos, and we roped together a little bit back then."

At that time O'Brien Cooper had already lived a unique life that might easily have led to another career—as a film actor. Clay's

> **"Ever since I picked up a rope and started competing, I've always been trying to figure out how to win, and always do better."**
>
> — *Clay O'Brien Cooper*

stepfather, Gene O'Brien, had been a movie wrangler, working on various projects throughout Hollywood in the 1960s and 1970s. One of those projects was a John Wayne film, *The Cowboys.* The storyline told the tale of a rancher forced to hire a crew of school kids after adult cowhands left the area to try their fortunes in the gold fields.

When it became apparent that the child actors were seriously deficient in riding and roping skills, Clay, who was on the set helping his stepdad, offered his help. The director noticed the boy's considerable skills and decided to add the 10-year-old to the cast.

Smaller and younger than the other boys, Clay played a key scene in the movie. At one point Wayne's character, Will Anderson, comes to the one-room schoolhouse and tells the boys that he's prepared to hire them for the long drive ahead. Cooper's character, Hardy, the smallest and presumably youngest of the boys, asks tentatively, "All of us?"

Anderson calls the boy up to the chalkboard and marks a line just above his head, telling the schoolboys that anyone over that height can have a job. Obviously disappointed, Hardy looks despondent until Anderson leaves. At that point two of the other boys come forward and lift the chalkboard off some books that had been set under the legs to raise its height. Hardy's tearing eyes give way to a big grin as he realizes he's about to set off on the trail to Belle Fourche.

During the filming of *The Cowboys*, Wayne took a liking to the young boy, who in many ways was like the character he portrayed. When he was only 5, Clay decided it was time he saddled his own horse. He led his horse to a large olive tree next to the tack room and climbed a 3-foot wall, then struggled to get the adult saddle above his head and onto the horse's back.

"I'm sure it was good watching, the way I juggled it around and pushed it up with my head, but when you've got to do it, you figure it out," he said.

That kind of can-do spirit made an impression on Wayne, who made a point of singling out Clay whenever he talked about *The Cowboys*, letting reporters know what a good job the boy had done. That led to additional work in the John Wayne film *Cahill: US Marshall*, a part in *Macintosh and T.J.* with Roy Rogers, and the Disney productions *The Apple Dumpling Gang*, *Climb an Angry Mountain*, *One Little Indian*, and *Alvin the Magnificent*. Clay also found work on the small screen, appearing in the television shows *Gunsmoke*, *Little House on the Prairie*, *Marcus Welby M.D.*, and a short-lived series called *The Cowboys*, which was based on the original film.

As much as Cooper enjoyed meeting and working with big screen legends, he had no desire to go down that career trail.

"It was a great opportunity to work with people like John Wayne and Roy Rogers, and it gave me a good start in life financially," he said. "If I had continued acting, I might have made it, and I might not have. It was just my dream to rope."

Almost from the day he could swing a rope, Clay was a competitor.

"I started matching the other kids for money when I was 5," he said. The contests, called penny pots, involved roping steers on foot, and Clay took them very seriously. "Ever since I picked up a rope and started

competing, I've always been trying to figure out how to win, and always do better."

Jake Barnes grew up in the hinterlands of New Mexico, about as far from the Hollywood lifestyle as a person could get. But he shared Clay's same passion. As a kid he followed his father around the

CAREER MILESTONES

Jake Barnes/Clay O'Brien Cooper

born: Jake
April 4, 1959
Huntsville, Texas

born: Clay
May 6, 1961
Gilbert, Arizona

Seven-time World Champion Team Ropers (1985-89, '92, '94).

1998 Barnes and Cooper reunite, roping together at the National Finals Rodeo.

1997 Barnes and Cooper are inducted into the ProRodeo Hall of Fame in Colorado Springs. During that year, the two split to pursue individual interests.

1994 At the NFR, the team ropes 10 steers in 59.1 seconds, fully 18 seconds faster than the previous record. In so doing, they clinch their seventh world championship.

1992 With $40,349 in NFR earnings, the duo earns their sixth world championship, stretching their own record. At the finals, they rope half their steers in under 5 seconds.

1989 Barnes and Cooper enter the NFR in second place behind the team of Dennis Gatz and Bobby Hurley. They finish second in the 10-round team roping average to clinch their sixth world title with earnings of $90,455.

1988 By winning their fourth world titles, the partners draw even with Leo Camarillo as winners of the most team roping world championships.

1987 En route to their third world title, the team wins a record $35,122 at the NFR. In round one, they beat their own record for the fastest NFR time, pulling tight in 4.1 seconds.

1986 They capture world title No. 2 with earnings of $89,498. They also set a then-record time for team roping at the NFR: 4.3 seconds.

1985 Barnes and Cooper team up. That year, they win the average at the NFR and earn their first world title with then-record earnings of $99,047.

1983 Barnes ropes with Leo Camarillo, helping the Californian to win the world title. Barnes finishes second in earnings behind Camarillo that year.

1980 Jake Barnes joins the PRCA, teaming with Allen Bach.

1978 Clay O'Brien Cooper joins the PRCA, roping with his brother-in-law.

Barnes spent a season heading for Leo Camarillo, helping him to win a world title before joining Clay O'Brien Cooper.

Indian reservation in Dulce, N.M., where Raymond Barnes worked as a livestock agent. Jake helped gather cattle and performed other tasks, serving, he said, as "Dad's right-hand man."

The Barnes family moved to Bloomfield when Jake was 10. On weekday evenings his dad held amateur roping events, and Jake began taking his turns in the box. He also participated in other sports—mainly baseball and basketball—but in his part of New Mexico, roping was king. Moreover, it was in Jake's blood. He took his name from his father's uncle, Jake McClure, the 1930 world champ calf roper. His mother's brother, Junior Vaughn, was also a professional roper.

"Roping has always been a part of my family," said Jake, looking back. "I think I was born to rope."

From the jackpot ropings at home and kid rodeos nearby, Jake graduated to high school rodeo, then college. As a team roper attending college in Portales, N.M., Barnes began to make a name for himself throughout the region as a first-rate jackpot roper. In 1980 he decided to try his hand in the professional ranks, and it was not long before he received an unexpected call from Allen Bach, the reigning world champ.

"Hi, I'm Allen Bach, and I'm looking for a partner," said the champ.

"Yeah, right. Who is this really?" Barnes replied.

On the advice of his friend, Tee Woolman, Barnes decided to take Bach up on his offer. The partnership lasted three years, with Barnes and Bach qualifying for three straight National Finals. They enjoyed their best season in 1981 when they finished fourth in the world.

In 1983 Barnes teamed up with roping legend Leo Camarillo, who had just dissolved his relationship with Tee Woolman after several successful years. Barnes helped Camarillo to win the world title that year. At the finals Barnes and Camarillo combined to finish second overall in the average. Jake came in second to Camarillo in the team roping world-title race, finishing just $1,473 behind "Leo the Lion," who graciously credited the young roper with putting him back on track in the world championship chase. "Roping with Jake has made me feel progressive, productive again. He's what you look for in a whole new game plan," he said.

But Jake chafed under the yoke of the overbearing, older roper. He wanted to rope with someone who was more like him — quiet, humble, and willing to share equally in the ups and downs of the rodeo game.

Clay O'Brien Cooper had been partnered with his brother-in-law Bret Beach when he first joined the PRCA. Then he roped with Tee Woolman. But from time to time, he'd share the road with Barnes and rope with him when either of his regular partners couldn't go. According to Clay, there seemed to be some chemistry between the two.

"Jake and I always did really well together and got to be good friends. We had the same goals, so we hooked up in 1985," said Cooper.

Roping with Camarillo and Allen had given Barnes a deep and complete understanding of the fundamentals of roping. Clay also was a tireless roper with good technique and exceptional ability at horse handling. Growing up in California, where big roping contests often required that a team rope eight or ten head, Clay had great respect for heelers who could catch consistently. And he patterned his roping after theirs.

"The emphasis was on being able to catch more in a row, not necessarily on speed, but consistency. The guys who were considered the elite in heeling at the time were the guys who could catch every time," he said. Throughout his formative years, Clay had been able to study the elite team ropers — Leo Camarillo and his brother, Jerold, Allen Bach, Walt Woodard, and others, emulating their consistency and technique. By the age of 8 or 9, he was already able to mimic their style.

"I was, I guess, good at watching and mimicking what the good ropers did. So I started trying to develop my skills, and the dream started forming in my mind — what I wanted to be and what I wanted to do."

In the spring of 1985, Clay moved to Arizona, not far from Jake. The pair invested in 33 head of practice cattle and quickly formed a routine. They roped the steers three times apiece in each daily practice session, which typically lasted four to five hours.

"We practiced nonstop," noted Clay. "That's all we did: eat, sleep, and rope."

That routine helped them to gel as partners and is cited by both as the key to their championship success. "Clay and I were so versatile that if we had to make a 4-second run, we were able to do it. If we just had to catch the steer, we could. Our fundamentals were that good," said Barnes. "We had every base covered. Some guys can only rodeo-rope and try to make fast runs; some guys are more conservative and lean more toward the average side. We were able to go both ways. I credit a lot of it to our persistence practicing."

In only their first year together, the two quickly established themselves as a domi-

JAMES FAIN

Barnes and Cooper clasp hands upon clinching the 1989 world championship at the NFR.

nant team. At that time it was somewhat unusual for two ropers to remain paired at every rodeo. Because the world title was awarded to the individual who won the most money in the event, a partner often had to make a choice. He could sacrifice his title chance so that his partner might win or find another partner at the National Finals and rope in opposition to the guy who had helped him get there. Barnes and

Clay O'Brien Cooper, the most consistent heeler in rodeo history, taking up slack at the '94 NFR.

Cooper decided that they wouldn't put themselves in that position; either they roped together, or they wouldn't rope at all.

That strategy carried them into the 1985 NFR with equal earnings—and the chance to share the world title at the end of the season. At the NFR the two quickly established themselves as the most cohesive unit—they were in the truest sense a team. Two men, two horses, one goal.

Barnes and Cooper jumped to the lead in round one, drawing their steer tight in 6 seconds flat. Then they won again in rounds three and four, each time roping faster than before. Despite a few penalties mid-rodeo, they still managed to maintain the lead in the 10-round average, winning that year's NFR in the time of 87.8 seconds on 10 head. Due to their amazing consistency throughout the year and the NFR, Barnes and Cooper won their first world title, having earned half-again as much as the second-place team. All told they earned $99,048 for the year, a team roping record.

Cooper, who also contested in calf roping throughout the season, also came tantalizingly close to Lewis Feild in the all-

around cowboy race that year. As many will point out, Cooper very likely would have won that title were it not for the fact that team ropers competed for one-third less money at the National Finals than did the single-event competitors in calf roping, bronc riding, steer wrestling, and bull riding.

The following year Barnes and Cooper once again carried a comfortable cushion of money between themselves and their nearest competitors going into the National Finals. This time around, though, they faltered early in the rodeo and had to go for wins night after night in order to stay ahead of Tee Woolman and his new partner Bob Harris. In the middle rounds, the duo won four first-place checks, and another check for second place. With the huge amount of added prize money available after the NFR's move to Las Vegas, Barnes and Cooper were able to bank a whopping $27,710 each. This gave them a $5,000 advantage over Woolman and Harris despite the fact that they didn't collect a nickel in the 10-round average competition. Among Jake and Clay's accomplishments was a 4.3-

second win in round eight, the fastest arena time in NFR history up to that point.

In 1987 Barnes and Cooper had the chance to become the first team in rodeo history to win three consecutive world titles. Again the duo entered the NFR as the leading team. And again they put together an outstanding show. Jumping out to an early lead with a win in round one, the partners strengthened their hand by placing in rounds two and five. But in between those paydays, they had gone long on two steers, losing their opportunity once again to make a mark in the 10-round team roping average. Gunning for the win every night, the two captured first place in two of the remaining five rounds and tied for the win in the final round to rack up an NFR-record $35,122 apiece. The two were elated to have gone down in the record books as the first team with three straight world titles.

"Every world title is special," said Barnes. "This third consecutive one makes me feel good because it put us in the history books."

Barnes noted that the two titles earned in 1986 and '87 had not come without some anxiety. Both years Tee Woolman and partner Bobby Harris had challenged the pair at the NFR, and Barnes wasn't yet willing to concede that he and Cooper were the best ropers going down the road.

"There are 15 teams out there with a chance to replace us," he noted after clinching the 1987 world title. "It just depends on who wants it worse. Next year could be anybody's year."

Equally humble, Cooper added, "We don't feel we are anywhere near being the best we can be. We can get faster and more consistent. There's lots of room to grow."

But the following December the two were again virtually untouchable when they pulled into the parking lot at the 1988 NFR. Despite a spoiled run in the first round that resulted in a horrendous time of 31.5 seconds, they quickly bounced back, tying for the win in the second round. They continued having an up-and-down finals, finishing the rodeo in ninth place. Still their '88 world championship earnings totaled $84,578, more than $30,000 better than the second-place team.

Many rodeo insiders thought that 1989 would be the year that David would finally slay Goliath. For the first time since teaming up, Jake and Clay did not lead the world standings at the end of the regular season. That honor belonged to Bobby Hurley, a hot young Arkansas roper, and his partner, Dennis Gatz. But at the NFR Barnes and Cooper once again proved why they had come to be regarded as the greatest team in the world.

In the first half of the rodeo, Barnes and Cooper jumped to the lead by placing four times, including wins in two rounds. A mistake, however, in round five cost them their advantage in the average competition, and by round eight Hurley and Gatz had closed the gap to less than $300. When neither team managed to place in the ninth round, the world-title competition essentially came down to a one-head rope-off.

Though Hurley and Gatz put in a speedier

> ## "After a couple of championships, I believed that I had to do everything on my own. But there was something missing."
> — Jake Barnes

run, placing second in the round, Barnes and Cooper managed a fourth-place finish, maintaining a position in the average competition. Their second-place finish in the 10-round average paid $10,908, enough to give them the lead in money won at the finals. And, of course, their fifth world championship.

"That was the toughest steer I've ever roped," said a relieved Cooper following the final round.

Although the two were hardly complacent following that fifth win, they did feel exhausted and burned out from so much time spent on the road. As the most celebrated team ropers in rodeo history, both were in great demand as product endorsers. They also put on numerous roping schools and clinics over the course of a season, another commitment that kept them from home.

Increasingly, they found it more difficult to summon the will to rodeo hard over the entire season, and they roped at fewer competitions and concentrated mainly on the big-money events. In 1990 their names didn't even appear among the top 15 in the world. In 1991 they finished in eighth place. Many rodeo pundits began to assert that Jake and

Barnes and Cooper seldom had to exchange words in the roping box, since each knew what to expect from his partner.

DAN HUBBELL

Clay's days as the most feared team in rodeo were past.

But then, a surprising thing happened in 1992. Having qualified as the second-ranked team going into the finals, Barnes and Cooper returned to their previous form. In the first round they leaped out to share the win with their former rivals, Dennis Gatz and Bobby Hurley. Then Jake and Clay continued grabbing checks in the subsequent rounds, including two for their back-to-back wins in rounds six and seven.

By the tenth round, the two were within striking distance of leaders Charles Pogue and Steve Northcott. All Barnes and Cooper had to do, once again, was catch their final steer. And, of course, they did, drawing tight in 6.6 seconds. That helped them maintain their third-place position in the average, which put them over the top in the world standings. When their winnings from the NFR were totaled, Barnes and Cooper had set another record with $40,349 each. They needed nearly every dollar; their margin of victory over Northcott and Pogue basically came down to a single go-round check.

"It's a miracle that this happened," said Jake Barnes of the world title victory. "We had to rope a great finals. We came here hoping to have a good moneymaking week. It was by the grace of God that we won this."

That last comment was telling, for both Barnes and Cooper share not only a bond of friendship, but also a bond of Christian spirituality. Both cowboys had been raised as Christians, but the two admitted to having strayed in the early days of their careers. Clay had sought out the Pro Rodeo Ministry and found that a renewed faith helped him to feel better about himself and his career. It made him a better roper and a better person.

Soon Jake began joining his partner at the impromptu church services held at the various rodeos they attended. "After a couple of championships, I believed that I had to do everything on my own. But there was something missing. I was trying to do everything myself, and I wasn't

DAN HUBBELL

At the '94 NFR, the duo snared 10 steers in less than a minute to set the all-time record for the fastest average in rodeo history.

happy. Clay helped me out a lot. We started going to the (church) services together."

In addition to being the model for success in the arena, Jake said, he began to see his mission in life as being a positive role model in the lives of the younger rodeo cowboys, who strive to emulate his success. "My goal is that some of the younger guys will see what we are doing and accept the Lord as their savior," he said.

Perhaps God wasn't through with the pair just yet. As had been the case in four of their previous six world championships, Jake and Clay's battle to win the 1994 crown came down to an exceptional performance at the National Finals. Of course, their 59.1-second record time was as close to perfect as any ropers have ever come at the NFR.

As Clay is quick to point out, there were many times at the NFR when the world title teetered on a single steer. But again and again, the two proved that when the pressure was greatest, they stood tall and roped clean. Although their record for world titles may one day be surpassed, their team roping average bested, the two men will always be remembered as giants in the sport. They established the benchmark for what could be accomplished in a team-roping career, says fellow roper Speed Williams, also a multiple world champ who honed his craft catching for Clay O'Brien Cooper after Barnes went into semiretirement.

"They worked as hard or harder than anyone in the business. It takes a lot to push yourself like they did, to get up and go when you really don't feel like it. I have nothing but admiration for both of them. They set that standard for team ropers, the mark by which all other great teams will be judged."

JOE BEAVER

MANY AN NBA basketball player has honed his skills on the hot asphalt courts of the inner city, where a foul isn't a foul unless blood is drawn.

Joe Beaver wasn't raised on the mean streets, but in the hot, dusty rural arenas of Texas amateur rodeo. But there, the competition was every bit as rough as on the toughest playgrounds in the inner city.

"When I was coming up, David Nygard was known as 'the King of Texas Match Ropers.' He was like Minnesota Fats — a hustler. And we'd rope together all the time. At least three times a month, we'd match other guys for at least $1,000," recalls Beaver, who was all of 16 at the time. "He'd tell me, 'You'd better learn to swim with the sharks, or they'll eat you alive.'"

By the time Beaver was 18, he says, it was nothing for him to compete at 250 rodeos in a year, and he figures he earned anywhere from $60,000 to $100,000 a season. When Beaver hit the pro-rodeo trail in 1985, his rookie season seemed like a vacation. "One hundred rodeos my rookie season? I thought it was a day in the park."

Beaver's reputation as a no-holds-barred amateur roper and an easygoing personality earned him a lot of friends coming up, and as a result, he spent his first year in the Professional Rodeo Cowboys Association traveling with the savviest veterans of the day.

At the beginning of the 1984-85 season, he ran into Roy Cooper at a benefit roping and said he wanted to jump in the truck with him. Coop told Joe that he'd take the young roper under his wing if he got his full PRCA card, which would entitle him to compete at all the major events. That fall, Beaver entered three permit rodeos, smaller rodeos where rookie riders often compete in order to gain full membership status. At his first event in Wichita Falls, Tex., Beaver won the calf roping, and he was off and running.

"That first season, I was with Roy Cooper, John Rothwell, and Raymond Hollabaugh. Roy taught me planes, trains, and automobiles, and from Rothwell and Hollabaugh, I learned to get to the rodeos in a series," says Beaver. "A lot of guys strike out their first year not knowing how to rodeo and they get themselves in a bind." With details like travel schedules and the intricate system of entering handled by the more senior riders, Beaver was able to concentrate solely on winning.

But it wasn't all champagne and roses for Beaver, for after that first win, he went into a brief slump. Roy's brother, Clay Tom Cooper, took him aside and reminded him that he didn't have to rope to impress the other cowboys — he just had to get out there, be himself, and his formidable talent would get him through. Soon after, Beaver was at the National Western Stock Show in Denver, one of the biggest winter rodeos and, therefore, one of the most competitive. With the ink barely dried on his PRCA

At the 1996 NFR, Beaver snared rodeo's most coveted title: that of the world champion all-around cowboy.

card, Beaver roped and tied a calf in the Mile High City in the time of 7.6 seconds — not only the fastest time that year at the rodeo, but the fastest time then recorded in that arena. After that, paychecks began to fill his wallet with regularity.

Although Roy Cooper could point to several innovations such as the fast tie and the practice of handling his slack to keep the calves on their feet in helping him to leap to the front of the pack as a

"We weren't rich people. We worked for everything we got. And if I didn't win, I didn't go."

rookie, Beaver was simply more aggressive than anyone else.

His formula for success was always to have exceptionally fast horses who would charge the barrier and give him the best chance to catch the calves in the shortest possible distance from the roping box. Once out of the box, Beaver was lightning fast in bringing up his loop and making his throw.

Often, Beaver's horse would barely leave the box before his rider would tag the

horse, the signal to apply the brakes. Beaver could do this because he wasn't afraid to reach with his rope, sometimes throwing the loop almost to the limits of its length.

If there is one signature Beaver style, it is his horse pulling up and stopping right in front of the chute — at about the same place where most calf ropers are still readying their ropes for a toss.

That formula helped Beaver to not only win the Resistol® calf roping rookie of the year and overall rookie titles in 1985, but also set him up for his maiden trip to the National Finals Rodeo. That year, 1985, marked the end of an era. The NFR was slated to leave its home of 21 years, Oklahoma City, for the bright lights and all-night action of Las Vegas.

Some of the cowboys complained about the new home, saying that the converted basketball court of the Thomas & Mack Center was simply too small and too tight for calf roping. But Beaver liked the challenge the arena presented, as well as Vegas' growing reputation as the sports entertainment capital of the West.

"Yeah, the other cowboys griped. But I said, 'I'll rope in the parking lot for $3,000 a go-round,'" said Beaver with a laugh.

Beaver's can-do attitude would serve him well. He came to the rodeo a decided underdog as the sole rookie in any event as well as the youngest calf roper in the field. He faced a major obstacle in Roy Cooper, who'd dominated the world championship title for five straight years. Cooper, in fact, led all others going into the season-ending NFR and had an $11,000 margin over the stout, 6-foot 2-inch Beaver. But none of that seemed to daunt Joe as he backed into the roping box for his go-round.

Piggin' string clenched firmly in his teeth, Beaver gave an almost imperceptible nod of his head, brought the loop up in a single swing, and snared his calf before it had even hit full stride. Hustling down the rope, Beaver flopped the calf over on its side, slipped the string over a leg, and with the fast hands of a card shark, bound the calf tight and lifted his arms high. There was silence, then a rousing cheer when it was announced that Beaver had taken the lead. History would record that Beaver, all of 20 years old, had won the first round of his NFR debut.

Cooper, roping last by virtue of his lead going into the finals, failed to capture his calf, and Beaver felt a surge of hope.

"I was down $11,000 (to Roy Cooper) so I couldn't expect too much. I couldn't expect a miracle. But when I won the first round and Roy missed his calf, I knew I had a chance," Beaver reflected.

As with any game in Las Vegas, Lady Luck would have her say in the outcome. Throughout the rodeo, Beaver drew calves that gave him a chance to win — nice, manageable animals that neither kicked nor dodged. He made the most of his good fortune, placing in four rounds and closing out the rodeo with another win in round ten. All told, the rookie had won $42,824, roughly 45 percent of his entire year's total. And, he'd bested the best, defeating Cooper by just over $10,000.

But if Beaver had any illusions of greatness, he wasn't advertising them. Of his victory over Cooper, who'd also won the world title his rookie year, Beaver said, "I'm not stepping into his shoes. Everyone has his own way. Maybe I am just starting my own."

Beaver's overnight success had been 15 years in the making. Born in Victoria, Tex., on Oct. 13, 1965, Joe remembers roping off a Shetland pony at age 5. He was born into a rodeo family. His father, Walter, was a roper and his mom, Bonnie, raced barrel horses. Both parents made many sacrifices for their son. Walter worked in the oil fields, and the job of taking Joe to youth rodeos fell to Bonnie, who Joe figures "drove me to at least 1,000 competitions."

Bonnie also gets a good deal of the coaching credit, according to Walter.

"Joe's mother was the one who recognized that Joe had real talent. She can't rope a lick, but she's a good critic. She hauled him to rodeos when I couldn't and turned steers out for him in the practice pen. When Joe was in high school, he headed home for the roping pen almost every day after school, and his mother was waiting. I can count on one hand the times he went with friends to have a Coke® rather than rope."

Joe roped in his first contest at age 8, and by 10 he'd won the year-end age group title among Texas Youth Rodeo Association competitors. "They kept track of points all year, and when they were added up, I'd won. And I thought, 'This is the best feeling, to be the best at the end of the year,'" he

CAREER MILESTONES

Joe Beaver

born: October 13, 1965
Victoria, Texas

Three-time World Champion All-Around Cowboy (1995-96, 2000); Five-Time Calf Roping World Champion (1985, '87-'88, '92-'93).

2000 Wins inaugural Wrangler® Pro Tour Finale in Las Vegas, then goes on to claim his third all-around cowboy title at the National Finals in December.

1996 Despite breaking a wrist in mid-season, Beaver comes back to qualify for the National Finals in December. At the finals, he wins $78,770 to surpass Herbert Theriot in the all-around standings to claim the world champion all-around cowboy award.

1995 With money earned in team roping, Beaver wins his first world champion all-around cowboy title. He had been runner-up to Ty Murray in 1991, 1993, and '94.

1994 Surpasses $1 million mark in career earnings.

1993 Successfully defends previous year's calf roping world title.

1992 World champion calf roper.

1988 Beaver qualifies for the National Finals Steer Roping for the first time in his career and repeats as calf roping world champ.

1987 Beaver claims the National Finals Rodeo average title in calf roping, his first of four such titles. With the victory, Beaver also claims his second calf roping world championship.

1986 Sets PRCA record for the fastest time (6.7 seconds) in calf roping under PRCA revised rules. Claims the PRCA Pro Tour calf roping championship.

1985 At 20, wins PRCA overall and calf roping rookie of the year titles; qualifies for first National Finals Rodeo; wins first PRCA world title in calf roping.

1983 Wins the Smith Bros. roping "world championship," considered one of the most prestigious non-PRCA-sanctioned roping awards. Also wins the Texas Calf Roping Association championship and the Gulf Coast Rodeo Association all-around and calf roping titles.

RICHARD LEVINE

Beaver stringing a calf at the California Rodeo in Salinas.

says. As a youth roper, Joe won enough saddles to stock a dude ranch. Although they made him proud, he was much more interested in their monetary value than in piling up a gaudy display in the barn.

Naturally, when Joe got his first chance to match-rope another competitor for money, he begged his parents to let him. Walter said no, but Bonnie persuaded him to let Joe rope. From that point forward, Joe's focus was on putting money in the bank. By high school he'd graduated from youth rodeos to amateur competitions and weekend jackpot ropings.

"We weren't rich people. We worked for everything we got. And if I didn't win, I didn't go," remembers Joe. "All the kids who came up with me — Fred Whitfield, Brent Lewis, Troy Pruitt, Ricky Canton, Matt Tyler — none of us were born with silver spoons in our mouths. We had to win, and we expected to win."

Joe won nearly every prestigious amateur event in Texas. In 1983 alone, he claimed wins at the Smith Bros. World Championship of Roping, and championships in the Texas Calf Ropers Association and the Gulf Coast Rodeo Association (both all-around and calf roping). He also competed in the International Professional Rodeo Association, and had qualified to compete at their 1984 Finals, but declined to go so that he could compete in the rival Pro Rodeo Cowboys Association. At the time, the PRCA rules did not allow a contestant to compete in other rodeo organizations. That rule was later challenged in court, and the PRCA was forced to drop its restrictive policy.

Joe, in fact, became so accustomed to finishing first that he thought little of winning the world championship during his rookie season. "I was 20 years old, I had the gold buckle, and I thought all this was easy," he recalls. Going into his second year as the reigning world champ, Beaver was automatically drafted into the prestigious Pro Tour, a series of team rodeo competitions that included $100,000 purses backed by major corporate sponsors including Kodak and Coca-Cola®. Joe figured he'd pick up some big paychecks at the Pro Tour events and not worry about the rest of the rodeos or the world championship.

Joe says he would get up for the Pro Tour competitions, but that he slacked off at the regular season rodeos. He hit a career milestone, however, at a mid-sized rodeo in Jordan, Utah. There, Beaver caught and tied a calf in 6.7 seconds, establishing the new benchmark for the fastest arena time in calf roping history. (A 5.7-second time was credited to Lee Phillips at a Canadian rodeo, but he had roped the calf without his horse ever leaving the roping box. A rule change would later invalidate such runs.) As of the 2001 season, Beaver's record has yet to be matched, much less broken.

But for the most part, Beaver lagged. Although he did make his goal of winning the Pro Tour championship, he was mired deep in the calf roping standings as fall approached. After scrambling to qualify for the NFR, Joe roped only marginally and finished a disappointing seventh in the world standings.

"That was a learning year for me. In this business, if you dog it, they'll make you a dog," he concluded.

After that desultory season, Beaver vowed to keep his eye on the world title race and raise the level of his game, regardless if he was roping for $10,000 or $300. He began traveling with Ricky Canton, a childhood roping friend who would go on to win the rookie title, and Jerry Jetton, another Texan with a booming laugh and a reputation for tough-to-beat horses. The trio worked well together, and come December, all three made the National Finals with Beaver leading the pack in the world standings.

In Las Vegas Beaver again triumphed, absolutely outclassing the other 14 ropers. He won the rodeo's 10-round average for the first time and amassed $51,822 in NFR earnings en route to winning the world title with $108,500. That amount was an astounding $35,000 more than the reserve champion, D.R. Daniel of Florida, and the biggest margin of victory in any of the seven NFR rodeo events.

"When I came to the National Finals, I wanted to win it all and show that my lead wasn't a mistake," said Beaver. "I hope those people who called the first title a fluke were at Las Vegas to see me win."

Joe felt that he was back on top of his game. All of 22, he'd won nearly $300,000 in just three years, had two world championship buckles, and was looked on as a serious threat in the all-around race. Reflecting on his amazing successes, Beaver said something that seemed innocent at the time. Calculating his future — as a leading rodeo champ, Beaver said "I should have 10-12 good years left in me." Then he added oddly, "But if I make it to 25, I'll feel lucky."

Beaver would repeat as world champ in 1988, and add another notch to his gun handle by qualifying for the National Finals Steer Roping, the championship-naming event for single-steer roping. It was an amazing feat, considering that he was competing on an ever-worsening knee injury that he'd incurred as a teenage roper.

The constant dismounting, coupled with the pounding runs down the rope, were taking their toll. Beaver was in nearly constant pain. At one point in the summer, orthopedic surgeon J. Pat Evans told Beaver that he wouldn't make it through another week. Beaver replied, "I'm tougher than that."

Beaver, in fact, made it through to the NFR, winning the 10-round calf roping average for the second consecutive year. After collecting his third gold buckle, Beaver flew to Dallas and went under the knife to repair his torn and scarified knee ligaments.

Rodeo is rife with stories of cowboys toughing out injuries that would sideline other athletes. The rodeo cowboys even have an encouraging phrase for such

SUE ROSOFF

Joe followed in Roy Cooper's bootsteps by winning both the rookie of the year and world champion titles in a single season.

pain-be-damned heroics: cowboy up. What is seldom mentioned is that cowboys often use painkillers to mask the pain.

Beaver was no different. He not only began to rely on painkillers in order to compete, he admits getting caught up in the recreational drug and drinking scene in the party atmosphere that travels from town to town, wherever a rodeo competition takes place. As his knee condition worsened, Beaver became more and more dependent on painkillers to keep going.

"When I started to rope, J. Pat (Evans)

Dad credits son Brody with helping him steer clear of life in the fast lane.

told me that I needed to take more time off. But I wouldn't. To keep going, it took more and more," Beaver says. Following his knee surgery, Beaver was forced to take three months off. During that time, he says, his drug and alcohol abuse worsened.

He tried to make a comeback at Houston in February, against Dr. Evans' advice, and both of the calves he tried to tie ran right over him. Humiliated and still recovering, Beaver didn't return to competition until June of '89. He picked up roping with David Bowen, an amiable Texan who had won the calf roping rookie title in 1986. With such a late start, Beaver failed to qualify for the NFR for the first time since joining the PRCA. Bowen, however, made the finals and won the calf roping average, solidifying his reputation as an up-and-coming challenger.

1990 proved to be a turning point for Beaver. Despite his substance problems, he managed to pick up enough checks to get "on the bubble" for an NFR berth. He and his girlfriend, Jenna, were married at rodeo announcer Bob Tallman's ranch in June in a gala party that was a who's who of professional rodeo.

Beaver knew that he was in trouble. His weight had ballooned to more than 230 pounds — he'd weighed 190 his rookie season — and his health and his roping suffered. He resolved to clean up, to get back in control of his life. Then, tragedy struck.

On July 2, 1990, Bowen and three other calf ropers had chartered a flight from a rodeo in St. Paul, Ore., to the Ponoka Stampede in Alberta, Canada. En route, they encountered cloudy weather just south of Seattle, Wash., and the small propeller plane crashed into Mt. Rainier, the tallest peak in the Cascade Range. All perished.

Beaver was deeply moved by the death of his good friend. The weight of responsibility pressed heavily on Beaver's shoulders, and he resolved to qualify for the NFR. He went to Dee Pickett, the 1984 World Champion All-Around Cowboy who had served as Beaver's best man at his wedding, and relied on Pickett's advice and encouragement to pull him through. Beaver managed to make the NFR, finishing 10th overall in the world standings — more than $30,000 behind that year's champion, Troy Pruitt.

By his side at the NFR were his new son, Brody, and his wife, Jenna. Brody's birth on November 11 had caused Joe to make yet another resolution to straighten out his life. Following the NFR, Beaver swore off the drugs and the partying, seemingly to good effect. At the first major rodeo of the year, the National Western Stock Show in Denver, Beaver captured first place. In February, he flew to El Paso, Tex., to compete at the Southwestern International Rodeo. There was a party at the hotel room, and Beaver fell off the wagon. After partying all night, he roped in the slack then headed for the airport with calf roper Fred Whitfield, who had forsaken the party in order to get some sleep.

When the two arrived at the airport, they both headed for a bank of phone booths. Whitfield was talking when he turned and saw Beaver crash to the ground.

"Joe was pale as a sheet, and his eyes rolled back in his head. He was jerking like an epileptic," said Whitfield. Beaver was rushed to the hospital, where his heart stopped in the emergency room. But Beaver already felt as if he'd passed into the netherworld.

"When I passed out by the pay phone, I remember seeing a guy lying on the floor and I was above him, trying to get back," he said.

Physicians were able to restart Beaver's heart. Joe was 25, and he'd very nearly fulfilled his odd prediction of early mortality. Later, in the hospital, Beaver thought about his family and all the people he'd hurt with his drug use.

Now, his resolve to change was hardened into steel. Forced to convalesce for a month due to a dislocated shoulder incurred when he passed out, Beaver went to see a coun-

selor, Ronnie Wilkinson, and told him that he intended to give up the drugs and booze. Wilkinson put a $100 bill on the desk and said, "You can't do it by yourself."

Beaver decided to prove him wrong. He attempted to make a comeback at a memorial roping dedicated to his friend

"When I passed out by the pay phone, I remember seeing a guy lying on the floor and I was above him, trying to get back ..."

Bowen, but his arm strength had abandoned him. He began a program of physical rehabilitation. He was so weak, his first exercise was to pick up socks, moving them from one pile to another, then starting over again. By May, he was back to practice-roping.

The Beavers were taken in by Lee Farris, who welcomed the family to his California home. "Lee was good to me at a bad time in my life," said Beaver of his friend's hospitality. Before the month was out, Beaver was back to competing.

Going hard throughout the summer, the sober and reinvigorated Beaver had nearly caught up to the leaders by November, when the season ended. Wins at the Reno Rodeo in June and Canada's Rodeo Royale helped re-establish him as a title contender, and Beaver promised himself not to squander another opportunity. He missed winning the world title, but just barely. His friend Fred Whitfield, who less than a year earlier had saved Beaver's life, simply outroped everyone at the NFR, becoming the first man in the rodeo's history to drop 10 calves in under 100 seconds. Beaver, however, finished second in the world behind Whitfield by a margin of less than $10,000. With the monkey now off his back, "the Beav" was back.

Beaver resumed his winning ways in 1992, dismissing the year by casually saying

"I had a good year with no major tests." That winter, he and his son took the stage in Las Vegas to claim Beaver's fourth championship buckle. A dedicated family man now, Beaver speaks openly about the damage that his substance abuse had caused him, in hopes that those who look up to him will steer clear of drugs and alcohol.

In addition to a new family, Joe had a new horse named Prime Time who had helped carry him to the NFR. Owner J.D. Tadlock told Joe to try the sorrel gelding, assuring him, "You'll run five calves on him and buy him." Beaver only needed to run three and he wrote out a check.

Beaver roped on Prime Time throughout the 1993 season, cruising into the NFR as the man to beat, with $67,179 won. But at Las Vegas, he did a funny thing: After the second round, he switched to his backup horse, Touchdown, a roan gelding he'd bought just a few months before from roper Doug Clark. It was a shocking roll of the dice, but when Beaver pulled off a tie for first place in round three, nobody questioned his judgment.

His family had truly become the center of his universe, and he looked at his calf roping career as a means to an end rather than an end in itself.

Riding Touchdown, Beaver stayed consistent if not spectacular. His roping might have suffered due to a bout with stomach flu, but he managed to battle off the nausea and to post a win in round eight. Sickness, however, was only secondary to the challenge posed by red-hot Troy Pruitt, who climbed the ladder of earnings from the 15th hole in the world standings to challenge Beaver for the world title in the final round. Also threatening Beaver's fifth world championship was Shawn McMullan, a fellow Texan who was neck-and-neck with Pruitt for the average

championship. As is often the case at the NFR, the world title came down to the final round.

McMullan needed only to wrap his final calf in 9.2 seconds to tie Pruitt for the lead in the 10-round average, which would have given him the cash he needed to overtake Beaver. But McMullan fumbled, drawing tight in 12.2 to cede the world title to Beaver. Despite his heroic effort, Pruitt missed unseating Beaver from the championship throne by a margin of $6,510. Beaver was gracious in victory, saying "Troy Pruitt ... roped exceptional (sic) this week."

In the post-victory interview, Beaver revealed his strategy in changing horses. Apparently his tack man had saddled the wrong horse prior to the third round, and after winning the round, Beaver simply stuck with the horse.

That following season Beaver sold Prime Time back to Tadlock, who was better able to keep the horse razor sharp, and worked his way back to the NFR on Touchdown. This time around, he faced yet another nail-biter in the tenth round. His roping hadn't really caught fire until June, and Beaver went into the NFR with a $30,000 deficit behind the season's front-runner, Herbert Theriot. A sensational season had swept the then-28-year-old calf roper from Wiggins, Miss., into the NFR with a $22,794 lead over his nearest competitor, but Theriot saw his lead melt away like ice cream in the Nevada desert.

Failure to rope his calves in rounds one, five, and seven caused Theriot to sink in the ten-round average competition. Fred Whitfield and Joe Beaver rose to challenge Theriot. But back-to-back calves that kicked and slowed Whitfield's efforts in the final rounds forced the cowboy out of world-title contention. Beaver had only to tie down his final two calves to place in the average and claim the world. But in round nine, he blew

MIKE COPEMAN

Beaver's prowess as a team roper and single steer roper proved crucial in his efforts to win the all-around championship.

through the barrier like an impatient teenager at a stoplight.

So, in a near-repeat of 1993, the calf roping race came down to the last calf. Roping late in the round, Theriot needed to place second in order to stave off Beaver's attack. Theriot either had to shoot for the 7.4-second mark set by 10th-round leader Brent Lewis, or at least wrap tight in 7.9 seconds to overtake Cody Ohl, who had tied his calf earlier in the round in 8 seconds flat. Theriot, who had been riding six-time calf roping world champion Roy Cooper's horses all season, looked to Cooper for advice. Cooper told him, "Keep the calf on his feet, and the title is yours."

Theriot lined the calf out straight and zinged his loop true, snaring the calf perfectly. He tied tight and threw up his hands, then anxiously looked at the scoreboard. The time was 7.9 seconds. When the season's earnings were totaled, Theriot had edged Beaver by $14.80 — the smallest margin for a world championship title in the history of the Professional Rodeo Cowboys Association.

But by now, Beaver knew how to take

disappointment. His family had truly become the center of his universe, and he looked at his calf roping career as a means to an end rather than an end in itself. But all that was to change, thanks to a phenomenal rough-stock rider named Ty Murray.

Since winning the world champion all-around title in 1989, Murray had dominated rodeo's most prestigious award. Murray, amazingly, had stayed relatively injury-free despite riding in all three rough-stock events, but his luck ran out at a Professional Bull Riding event held in Rancho Murietta, California. Murray tore the posterior cruciate ligament in his knee, and decided to have surgery on both knees. Beaver heard about the injury while competing at the Reno, Nev., rodeo. Beaver called Tom Moore, a talented heeler, and put two rigs on the road in a frantic effort to win the all-around title.

Up to that point, Beaver had conceded that world title to Murray. But now, the race seemed wide open. The all-around had been a total frustration: He'd lost previous bids to Lewis Feild, then Dave Appleton,

DAN HUBBELL

Joe acknowledges the applause after cinching the all-around championship at the 1995 NFR.

ending his speech with a thanks to Ty Murray. "Without him, I couldn't have done it," he said with a laugh.

Beaver scarcely thought about a title defense in 1996, as Murray returned to the arena. But again, Murray went down to injury (this time to his riding shoulder), and Beaver cranked up the machine once again, this time partnering with Tom Bourne of Murietta, Georgia. The entire Beaver family hit the road with two rigs. Finally, in October, Jenna craved home and pleaded with Joe, "That's enough!" Jenna and Brody returned home while Joe stayed on the road. In the final three months, he competed at more than forty rodeos.

Beaver needed every penny. Once again, he'd only qualified in the calf roping, while Herbert Theriot had qualified in both the calf roping and the steer wrestling. The previous year, Beaver had said that the all-around would go to the rider who qualified for the NFR in two events. Nobody had. But now, with Theriot competing in two events, Beaver knew his chances had been cut in half. When the final round came, Beaver and Theriot were once again locked in a battle for a gold buckle. This time, though, Beaver would not be denied. With a win in the final round, Beaver also won the calf roping average contest (his fourth, matching the record for NFR average wins in calf roping), and closed the book on the all-around title.

Beaver again attempted the all-around win in 1997, qualifying in both the team roping and calf roping. But this time he lost the title to saddle bronc rider Dan Mortenson, who somewhat ironically proved wrong again Beaver's dictum that the cowboy who competes in two events will win the all-around.

Knee surgery again sidelined Beaver for much of 1998, and Beaver took over in the ESPN television booth in a very popular stint as the NFR color man. Murray returned to full-time arena competition that year, garnering his record seventh all-around title. The following year, it was Whitfield who rose to the occasion, winning the calf roping and becoming the

and finally Murray, who Beaver acknowledged "beat me like a drum."

Beaver earned enough money to qualify for the calf roping at the '95 NFR, roping unusually cautiously to protect his lead in the all-around. When the money was totaled up, he'd captured the all-around title with $141,753 in combined earnings, defeating Roy Cooper by $33,000. At the awards ceremony, Beaver thanked many people,

first African-American to win the all-around championship.

Beaver's success as a color commentator might have pointed toward another career, and it seemed that as 2000 approached, the 35-year-old was indeed reaching the twilight of his athletic endeavors. Immensely popular among rodeo fans, Beaver might very well have considered bowing out. Assured of a place in the ProRodeo Hall of Fame, Beaver had parlayed his winnings and the money from commercial sponsorships and endorsements into a used car dealership. Brody was performing in school plays, acting in television commercials, and auditioning for film roles as a child actor. He showed no interest in following in his father's big bootsteps, and that was just fine with Joe and Jenna.

Nobody could have predicted what was to take place at the 2000 NFR — including Joe himself. Almost all year, Aussie bronc and bareback rider Scott Johnston had dominated the all-around title chase. Beaver had once again qualified in both the calf roping and team roping, but he was only 12th in the all-around standings as the rodeo commenced. After a disastrous first round in both events, Joe fell off the radar screen entirely. He walked past the media room to the elevator on the ground level at the Thomas & Mack Center, and said to the elevator operator, "Take me to the top." The man replied, "Concourse level?" And Beaver said, "No, the roof. I'm gonna jump off."

But the magic that Joe had brought to that arena year after year returned. Stepping up the intensity that had made him an NFR superstar, Beaver and partner Brett Gould turned in a stellar performance in the team roping. Joe was also rock-steady in the calf roping, piling up checks round after round. Gould and Beaver capped their 10-day run with a win in the final round. They had placed in seven rounds to win an event-record $68,845. When his calf roping money was added in, Joe had won $123,356 at the National Finals — the second most in the rodeo's history. That gave him the edge he needed to defeat Johnston by nearly $25,000. As he'd done many times in the past, he took the winner's stage with son Brody.

"I wanted to win this so bad," said Beaver. "Brody was so young before that he never realized what his dad had done. Now, he can realize what this experience is all about. I told Brody that this world title was for him." He strapped the buckle onto his young son's belt.

GAVIN EHRINGER

Texas pride: Cash Myers and Joe celebrate their victories at the first Wrangler® Pro Tour Finale with Cash's father, Butch.

LEO CAMARILLO

LEO CAMARILLO took team roping from a favorite weekend pastime of Californians to a full-fledged national event, equal in stature to bronc and bull riding, calf roping, and steer wrestling.

There were two reasons for this: The first was that Camarillo and his younger brother, Jerold, revolutionized the sport with a technique of catching a steer's heels (heeling) heretofore unseen in the rodeo arena.

And second, they were not merely fierce competitors out to drain every dime off their fellow ropers, they were artists. Masters of both rope and horse, Leo, Jerold, and their cousin Reg transformed team roping from a pokey arena interlude into a choreographed performance, a brief but powerful pas de deux.

Although the credit for team roping's appeal should rightfully be shared among the three members of the Camarillo clan, Leo's mystique was the stronger and his will to win greater. He, therefore, prevailed as a team roping icon.

His list of accomplishments is long. He won the most consecutive NFR team roping average titles (four) for the fastest time on ten head, he remains the only cowboy to win six team roping averages at the National Finals Rodeo, and in 1982 he and Tee Woolman lopped 10 seconds off the then-fastest average time at the NFR.

Notably, if Camarillo had competed under the rules used by the Pro Rodeo Cowboys Association today, he'd have won the same number of world titles as Jake Barnes and Clay O'Brien Cooper, the most successful team ropers in rodeo history. As it was, he still won four team roping world championships and prevailed as co-all-around cowboy in 1975.

But numbers alone hardly convey the impact this acerbic, even caustic man had on rodeo. Even as Camarillo slowed down and eyed his own retirement, the young ropers he had taken under his wing — Tee Woolman, Dee Pickett, and Jake Barnes, among others — continued to dominate the event into the new millennium.

Although some successful rodeo cowboys can lay claim to a proud ranching tradition within their families, the Camarillo clan could claim a heritage belonging to an entire culture — that of the Californios, the early Spanish cowboys who introduced many cattle raising and horse handling techniques to North America.

Around 1900 Leo's great-grandfather Cavianno Camarillo rode up from Sonora, Mexico, seeking work on the vast ranches of southern California. Roping, of course, was a key skill for a California vaquero, and the skill was passed from one generation to the next.

Cavianno's grandson Ralph never gave thought to any career but that of a cowboy. His first job away from home was as a cowhand for the vast Santa Marguerita Ranch, which stretched from San Juan Capistrano

Loop at the ready, The Lion poised to pounce.

work in the Santa Ynez Valley at the Hollister Ranch and the Peakes Ranch.

Despite her ranching background, Pilar was none too thrilled when her young husband began teaching his two boys, Leo and Jerold, how to rope. Family legend has it that Ralph gave the young boys small ropes and compelled them to rope pop bottles for hours on end in the family's living room. Although the Camarillos now relate this story with pride, it often drove their mother to tears at the time, for her husband was a demanding father.

It was understandable that Ralph wanted his boys, even at an early age, to work toward success in the rodeo arena. According to Leo, arena roping wasn't merely recreation for Ralph Camarillo, it was a means to a better life.

"Dad came up the hard way, and winning at rodeo represented a big bonus. He maybe earned $30 a month plus a place to live and a side of beef from time to time," recalls Leo. "To win $300 at a rodeo, that was a huge amount."

Leo remembers a time when Pilar desperately wanted a new washing machine; she'd been using a scrub board for years. Although Pilar was dead set against her husband slipping off to rodeos, he went far north to compete and returned home with $800—far more than a washing machine cost at the time.

"It was just like he'd won the lottery," said Leo. "Life was good for a long, long time."

Leo was about 10 at the time, and he began to see roping as a means to earn some walk-around money and help the family at the same time. At first the kids competed in playdays and kid rodeos, where the stakes were small. Even so, it gave the young boys a sense of independence and made them feel proud to contribute to the family's modest income.

"I took them to all the rodeos with me," said Ralph, "and I would tell them to come find me when they needed something to eat. But their pockets were full of money. They'd match the little kids with

to Oceanside, encompassing San Diego, Riverside, and Orange counties. While working there, he would ride the fence line of an adjoining ranch on the southeastern side, paying particular attention to its condition, and hoping to attract the attention of the rancher's daughter, Pilar.

"We had many happy times along that fence," said Pilar, who would later marry that attentive cowboy. Like the Camarillos, Pilar's family was steeped in ranching.

"We roped a lot of range cattle in tall pasture grass. And man, those cattle were wild, virgin."

Her great-grandfather migrated from France, eventually purchasing a ranch near San Luis Rey. He married an Indian woman from San Juan Capistrano, and Pilar gained her Hispanic heritage from her Spanish grandmother. As Pilar liked to boast, "Five generations on both sides of the family, and we've never left Orange County."

That, however, would soon come to an end as Pilar and Ralph moved north, finding

their ropes all day, and beat them out of all their money."

As teenagers, the boys graduated to adult jackpot events where serious money changed hands — usually in the direction of the Camarillos. They trained incessantly for the competitions, mindful of their father's admonition that the boys had "better practice every day and be at the top" if their goal was to earn a living. At one point he gave them a choice: rope or work. To his sons roping was infinitely more attractive than day work.

"At that time, working in an auction sales yard all day paid about 90 cents. Instead of doing that, me and Jerold would go to the weekend jackpot ropings and pay $2 to win $25 or $100. Then we'd use the money to eat in the school cafeteria or buy a new pair of sneakers," Leo recalls.

Despite being a talented athlete at Santa Ynez Valley High, Leo felt most at home at the rodeos. He never cared for school, describing himself as "a poor student," and his Hispanic heritage caused him to be looked down upon by the Anglo students. Making things doubly hard was the fact that he was a cowboy, an occupation held in little regard by his peers.

"We were raised in the shadow of white society. It wasn't overt racism, but we knew we were different. We didn't make it to the first row in the classrooms or the front of the school bus. Being a cowboy was like being a candlestick maker or a baker. It was a laborer's occupation," he says now. "And I'll admit, I felt a little embarrassed to wear a cowboy hat."

Sports were an outlet that offered acceptance, and Leo excelled at basketball, football, and track. But the roping arena was never far away. There, race was never an issue. Only speed and talent mattered, and Leo had both in abundance.

But there was something else, too, that made Leo and his brother very desirable as heelers, for they seldom roped together. It was a trick they'd learned roping steers in the open pastures of the ranches where their father worked.

"We roped a lot of range cattle in tall pasture grass. And man, those cattle were wild, virgin. You couldn't stop them or slow them, like all the ropers did in the arena at that time. But if you led them off right, they would kinda hop across the grass. And I got to thinking, if a heeler could consistently catch those heels up in the air ... ."

CAREER MILESTONES

Leo Camarillo

born: January 25, 1946
Santa Ana, California

Four-Time World Champion Team Roper (1972-73, '75, '83); World Champion All-Around Cowboy (1975); PRCA Champion Team Roper (1976).

1997 Roping with his brother Jerold, Camarillo wins the Gold Card Team Roping World Championship at Reno, Nevada.

1988 Camarillo competes at his last NFR, stretching his record for NFR qualifications to 19 and drawing even with Jim Rodriguez Jr. for the most NFR qualifications in the event.

1984 Camarillo surpasses $725,000 in career arena earnings, trailing only two cowboys—Roy Cooper and Tom Ferguson—in lifetime earnings.

1983 Roping with Jake Barnes at the NFR, Camarillo wins his fourth team roping world title.

1982 Again partnered with Woolman, Camarillo stretches his NFR average title record to six, a record that has yet to be surpassed. Their time of 80.8 seconds is the fastest NFR average time recorded to that date.

1980 Roping with Tee Woolman, Camarillo wins his fifth NFR average in team roping.

1979 Camarillo becomes one of the original inductees into the ProRodeo Hall of Fame in Colorado Springs.

1975 Camarillo is declared the world champion all-around cowboy, a title that would be challenged by timed-event hand Tom Ferguson. Eventually the title conflict is settled by naming both men the all-around champions for 1975. It would be the only time the all-around title was shared by two individuals. Camarillo also wins the team roping world title, his third.

1973 Camarillo returns to win a second-straight team roping world title.

1972 Camarillo captures the first of four world championships in team roping but sets off controversy when he raises a gloved hand in victory during one of the Oklahoma City go-rounds.

1969-1971 Roping with his cousin, Reg, Leo successfully defends his NFR average win, marking a streak of four average wins that will not be bested through the end of the millennium.

1968 Camarillo joins the PRCA, winning the rookie team roping title and the National Finals Rodeo average. He also sets the earnings record for a first-year contestant in the PRCA.

1966-1967 Roping in the California Cowboys Association, Camarillo wins the year-end all-around cowboy title, which he successfully defends the following season. Camarillo also wins the steer wrestling championship—20 years after his father, Ralph, had won the CCA calf roping championship.

Leo's greatest contribution to team roping was in catching the heels on the hop, an innovation that was faster and more consistent than the technique then practiced by most team ropers.

Leo and Jerold perfected the technique of timing their throws to coincide with a steer's hopping hind legs, using rhythm to anticipate the optimum time to slip the loop and make the catch. This contrasted with the heelers of the time, whose technique involved placing the loop just in front of the steer's feet and, as Leo said, "setting a trap."

Not only was the Camarillo innovation faster, it was also more consistent. As Leo points out, when he was coming up, all it took to win a roping event was to catch both hind feet on all of your steers. So few ropers could do it consistently that the Camarillos began to clean up.

The Camarillo boys had another advantage not afforded too many cowboys raised in modest circumstances: good horses. Ralph Camarillo had worked for Channing and Catherine "Katy" Peake, owners of Rancho Jabali in Lompoc. The Peakes were savvy horse breeders, intent on raising outstanding roping and ranch horses. The foundations of their breeding program were a band of mares by One-Eyed Waggoner, another band of mares out of Sonora, Mexico, and a stallion known far and wide among rodeo competitors—Driftwood.

A bay stallion who had first made his name as a match racer, Driftwood proved to be an outstanding roping horse. Legend has it that at a rodeo in Payson, Ariz., in 1941, the stallion was ridden in every single timed event—and carried his riders to the pay window in every single one. Then he won the stock saddle cow horse race down the length of the arena.

Once the Peakes added Driftwood to their breeding program, the reputation of his get quickly spread throughout the West Coast roping community. Needless to say, being around such fine caliber horses gave the Camarillos an education in and appreciation for quality horseflesh.

"At the Peakes' ranch, we had Roan Hancock, Driftwood, Speedy Peake. We had a half-dozen studs standing and some quite adequate mares, Lucky Blanton mares and those mares from the King Ranch," says Leo of those days. "Driftwood produced both speed and cow sense. Although bred for ranch horses, they were exceptional performance horses."

Leo's father was very exacting in the rodeo horses he rode, and so were his sons. "In those days cowboys thought of horses as tools for ranch work, not as specialists raised to perform in arenas. But that idea came early in my dad's experience, and I was raised the same way. I was fortunate, 'cause today it is clear that if you have a really good horse, you are at a great advantage," said Leo.

As he reached the end of his high school education, Camarillo never even considered college. His path in life had been chosen years before, when his dad had handed him a rope, a pop bottle to aim at, and a means to get out of "the ghetto," as Leo once called the poor ranching communities in which he'd been raised.

It was a reference his mother took umbrage at, but one that had a certain logic to it. Life had taught Leo that roping was a ladder on which to climb out of rural poverty, just as basketball and football were looked on as ladders of opportunity for poor inner-city youth.

Leo remembers that in his senior year of high school, his cousin Reg showed up at the ranch and asked him what his plans were. "I'm gonna go rope," said Leo.

"Well, that's kinda why I am here," Reg replied.

Reg, Leo, and Jerold hit the road in January, headed for a team roping in Riverside, California. They got there a week early, and Leo figures they had $7 between them. They matched the other ropers in informal competition, eventually building up the $100 stake needed to compete.

The main contest required the ropers to catch 10 steers, and when it was all over, Reg and Leo had won first place, and Jerold and his teammate were third or fourth. Their net: just over $3,000. "After that, I thought to myself, 'Never a poor day,'" said Leo, with a laugh. "We'd just announced, 'We are the Camarillos, and this is what we do.'"

As a ranch-raised kid who'd never ventured far from home, Leo loved the life of a rodeo gypsy. Each new town was an adventure, each new event a challenge. Soon the boys' reputations preceded them, and Leo began using their notoriety to his advantage.

"There was always a bit of gamesmanship. What do they call it today? Trash talking? Back then, it was just friendly conversation. But I had a knack for getting in people's heads. I might come up to a guy and say, 'Hey, that steer you drew likes to duck off.' And because of my reputation, he'd take it for gospel. Or a guy I knew well, I might remind him to be careful of the barrier. And he'd get to wondering, 'Why did Leo say that?' It might have been well-intentioned, but it still set them to thinking. It was pressure."

Leo thrived on such pressure. Later, when he competed at the National Finals Rodeo, he would comment, "In those days, most of the guys didn't rope full time, or they only roped at local events in Chowchilla, or wherever they were. And they would get to the NFR and they couldn't even talk, let alone catch. Me, I loved it."

Camarillo had that confidence because he'd already been challenged by many of the best ropers of his day. In the early 1960s California was the hotbed of dally roping. Only about one-sixth of all (Pro) Rodeo Cowboys Association-sanctioned rodeos even held team roping competition, and the majority of the big events were in California and the neighboring state of Arizona. And so the Camarillos often faced off against ropers who'd been to the National Finals and perhaps had won world titles.

"Before I went pro, I'd proven I could beat the pros. Jim Rodriquez, Ken Luman, the list goes on and on. World champs. And we would meet at these major jackpot events, and the way they measured your talent was in calcuttas. When the bidding got under way, I would always bring the most money. And I used that to intimidate the other ropers," said Leo, a devilish grin growing on his face. "I was like Muhammed Ali. I would ask them, 'You here to get your ass whipped by me today?' And more often than not, they did."

As the years went by, Camarillo's reputation for cockiness, gamesmanship, and a pen-

"We showed people all over the country what team roping was all about."

chant for biting criticism would grow, much to the chagrin of the older, humbler cowboys.

"He's not a lovable character," one of them would remark. "He's demanding and intimidating. But I'll say this, he's the best damn heeler in the world."

That fact became apparent virtually from the beginning of his pro career. Camarillo joined the PRCA as a full-fledged rookie in 1968, at the age of 22. The previous two years, Camarillo (who was also talented in steer wrestling and calf roping) had won the California State Rodeo Association all-around crown, and in 1967 he'd won the state's steer wrestling title too.

Now it was time to broaden his horizons. Because many rodeos at the time didn't hold team roping, he often entered the other timed events, even clocking a 3.8-second run in the steer wrestling at a rodeo in Phoenix and tying a calf with a winning time of 9.5 seconds at Moses Lake, Washington.

But it was as a team roper that he qualified for his first NFR, which took place in Oklahoma City in December of 1968.

Roping with Billy Wilson in the nine-round contest, Leo handily won the average competition. His brother Jerold, also a first-time contestant, was second in the average and second behind his brother in prize money earned. For the next 18 years, Leo Camarillo would never fail to qualify for the finals, a streak surpassed only by roper Jim Rodriguez Jr., who competed in every finals from 1959 to 1977.

Camarillo also began another streak that year that would endure. After winning the 1968 NFR team roping average, he went on to win that title for the next three years. In 1969 Jerold captured the world championship while Leo and cousin Reg won the nine-head average title. In 1970 and 1971 Reg and Leo successfully defended the average win.

Although Leo claims that winning the world championship wasn't his goal immediately, he was clear about wanting to win as much money as he possibly could—which, because world titles are based on money, meant the same thing in the end.

The Camarillos were traveling farther and farther from home, entering rodeos throughout the United States and piling up money. It soon became apparent to the other ropers that if they hoped to beat the Camarillos, they, too, would have to pursue a more rigorous travel schedule.

With more interest in team roping and more traveling cowboys to accommodate, the individual rodeos began adding team roping to their competitions. That was just fine with the Camarillos.

"We traveled all over the country, pioneering the team roping event. We showed people all over the country what team roping was all about. And we brought to the event a lot of consistency, which made team roping more interesting and exciting," said Leo.

"I'm not saying it was like bull riding, but there was a certain magic to seeing a guy catch both heels. To the fan, it didn't seem possible at first. And remember, at most rodeos team roping was just getting a toehold, and it was novel and different."

Jerold was the first Caramillo to win the world championship, in 1969. When Leo's chance came three years later, he captured the title in memorable style.

"I had won the last four NFRs, and 1972 was the year I'd gotten serious about running for a world title in that event," recalled Leo.

When he arrived at the Jim Norick Arena in Oklahoma City, Camarillo had statistically locked up the world championship before he even roped his first steer. He was looking forward to relaxing and enjoying the competition. Leo and Reg captured two go-round wins and a second-place finish, but a pair of no-times ended their streak of average wins. Still Leo was exuberant in victory, and that exuberance would cause him some unexpected problems with the conservative Oklahoma rodeo fans.

Due to the unusually cold weather, Leo had worn a black leather glove on his roping hand. After one winning performance, Camarillo lifted his gloved hand in victory. To fans, who recalled a similar gesture made by black track athletes at the 1968 Olympics, the raised hand represented an act of racial and political defiance. Camarillo was criticized by the press and by many of his peers. But, he says, it was all a misunderstanding.

"At the time, I was so into my roping that I never gave any consideration to political issues," he said in his own defense.

Like many of his contemporaries, Camarillo was simply a more demonstrative and emotional competitor than rodeo fans were accustomed to seeing.

Although he was far from being a California hippie, his hair was longer than the flat tops favored by most older cowboys. Certainly other cowboys of the time were more flamboyant—Larry Mahan, in particular. But Camarillo's Hispanic background made him more of an outsider, and his actions were subject to greater scrutiny.

"We were all more flamboyant than the cowboys who came before us. Not all of us had the beads, beards, and the flashy hatbands, but it was a more liberated time. People in general were expressing themselves in new ways, especially in sports. And I was no different. I am an emotional person, and I felt like I put a lot of effort into my roping, and I wanted to let my excitement out, to release my emotions. In the end, I think, we were a little defiant. We didn't want to fit the redneck cowboy stereotype, following every rule, driving 55."

Although the old-timers didn't like it, the younger generation lapped it up.

Many young cowboys came to emulate top stars such as Roy Cooper, Mahan, and Camarillo. And as team roping grew in prize money and status, Caramillo was right there, riding the wave of popularity he'd helped to create.

In 1973 Caramillo was once again the dominant roper of the year, again returning to the NFR with the title already locked up. Again he and Reg picked up checks in four of ten rounds, and again they chalked up several no-times, thus crushing their chances of winning the average.

The next year Leo was the reserve world champ behind Jerold's heading partner, H.P. Evetts. And in November Leo married flight attendant and barrel racer Sharon Meffan.

Perhaps it was the pace of rodeoing, or perhaps it was Leo's desire to contest in numerous events that led Reg to switch

REX DEAL

Leo (right) was the first winner of the "World's Greatest Cowboy Title," awarded to the winner of the Timed Event Championship of the World.

partners the following year, taking Jerold as his heeler while Leo teamed with H.P. Evetts. In any case, the new arrangement worked to the advantage of Leo, who returned to the NFR once again with the world title virtually assured.

At season's end the "breakup" proved to be a blessing, as Jerold and Reg captured the team roping average at the NFR, and

Though he was known as the best team roper of his era, Camarillo was an all-around timed-event hand adept at calf roping, steer wrestling, and steer roping too.

Leo claimed the third world championship of his career.

But again at the NFR, Leo landed in yet another difficult position. At the end of the rodeo, Leo was named the world champion all-around cowboy based on money won team roping, calf roping, and steer wrestling.

But the defending world champ, Tom Ferguson, challenged the title. When the books were audited, it was found that money that had been credited to Leo had, in fact, been won by Jerold. Similarly, money earned by brothers Larry and Tom Ferguson had been co-mingled. The books were such a mess that it proved nearly impossible to determine what money belonged in Leo's

column and what belonged in Jerold's, and what money was Tom's or Larry's.

So the PRCA struck a compromise: They would even up the prize money for both Ferguson and for Camarillo, and declare them co-champions. It is the only time in rodeo history that two cowboys shared the all-around title. (For more on this, see the Tom Ferguson chapter.)

Camarillo took the decision in stride, continuing to dominate his specialty event while Ferguson continued racking up all-around victories in the ensuing years, his streak intact.

In 1976 Camarillo faced a new situation at the NFR: World titles were no longer being decided by money won over the entire season, but instead by money won solely at the NFR. Still partnered with Reg, Leo handily won the year-end PRCA title as the team roper with the most money. But at the finals, he and Reg finished second to a pair of Californians who hadn't even qualified among the 15 top money-earners.

The next year Leo and Reg had a disastrous finals. In the first three rounds the duo never even crossed the 20-second threshold, effectively taking them out of the NFR average—and the world title race. Again, the PRCA year-end standings were dominated by the Camarillos, with Jerold taking first place, Leo second, and Reg third. Needless to say, the Camarillos weren't exactly pleased with the new system for determining world champions, and like many cowboys, they registered their discontent. The following year, the PRCA returned to its previous system of naming world champions based on money earned over the regular season plus money earned at the NFR.

But Leo was unhappy with Reg after the NFR, and he began casting about for a new partner. Dee Pickett, a talented young roper and a former star quarterback for Boise State University, was more than pleased to accept the invitation to rope with the sport's leading star. Explaining his decision to split with Reg, Leo said, "We're not used to being at the bottom. We're like the spirit of the Green Bay Packers and (coach) Vince Lombardi ... you either win or you lose."

Camarillo and Pickett did their fair share of both. Breaking in a new, young roper was difficult, and that difficulty proved especially apparent at the NFR, where the pair got off to a slow start. Despite placing in several later rounds, Camarillo was unable to close the income gap that separated him from eventual world champ Allen Bach.

As a new decade dawned, Camarillo was again looking for a new partner, and he felt he'd found the right candidate in a young talent he had spotted at one of his roping clinics. At that time, Leo had told the young man, "When you are ready for the pros, you let me know." In 1980 he did.

Like Camarillo, Tee Woolman was a versatile roper with an overwhelming desire to win. The combination of Woolman as header and Camarillo catching the heels proved an exceptional fit. Woolman relied on Camarillo for his managerial skills acquired over a decade of competition, while Camarillo found a young partner who energized him and made him excited to rope again. From the beginning, the two dominated their event.

But their success put Camarillo in the unaccustomed position of playing second fiddle to his young partner: As the NFR approached, Woolman actually had won more money than his mentor. If the two chose to rope together at the NFR, Leo would effectively give up any opportunity to win the world title, which at the time was awarded to the individual with the most money. (A rule change in effect since 1995 created separate world titles for the top-earning header and heeler.)

Woolman gave Leo the option of roping with someone else, but Camarillo waved him off. "When your team gets to the Super

"A good team roping duo is just like a marriage. You're going to have some attitude and personal problems to deal with."

Bowl, you don't trade your starting quarterback," Leo was quoted as saying.

The two put together a phenomenal finals, capturing first place in five of ten rounds, ensuring that Woolman would win his first world title in his rookie season.

In one particularly memorable interview, Camarillo declared that he and Woolman were "perhaps the most volatile team in history." It is unclear if he meant that the two were an explosive and masterful force in the arena, or that their strong and forceful personalities caused them to clash. Probably both.

In any case, things weren't working out for the two, and so in 1981 they decided to split. But neither fared well. At year's end Woolman finished ninth in the world, and Camarillo eleventh. The disappointing result of their split compelled them to team up once again for 1982, and Leo found himself in the uncomfortable situation of watching his young student again leading the world standings at the conclusion of the regular season.

Again, Woolman offered to rope with someone else and, again, Camarillo refused. The two had a phenomenal finals, placing

Camarillo's family ties to California extended back over five generations. Here, he bears the flag of the Golden State during the NFR Grand Entry.

COURTESY PRCA

in five rounds and setting a record time in the ten-round average (80.8 seconds) that was fully ten seconds faster than any in the history of rodeo's Super Bowl. When they were through, a mere $129 separated the two teammates in the world title race.

Woolman and Camarillo started off the 1983 season, but a certain amount of enmity again surfaced in their relationship. They weren't winning. The petty irrita-

tions that build, when two cowboys spend nearly all of their time together traveling from city to city, began to grow into full-blown confrontations. By August the two had agreed to go their separate ways, and Leo found a new partner in a quick-handed New Mexican named Jake Barnes, who had recently left his partner, Clay O'Brien Cooper. In an ironic twist, Woolman and Camarillo won the last rodeo they competed at together, the Colorado State Fair Rodeo in Pueblo. But the decision had been made, and both men abided by it.

Of the breakup Camarillo had this to say: "A good team roping duo is just like a marriage. You're going to have some attitude and personal problems to deal with. Tee and I seemed to be compatible for a while, but it was always a question of adjusting our personal feelings. We are two superstars, I guess. Most teams that have more than one superstar have a problem adjusting. Both people can be kind of selfish, so to speak."

With Barnes at the head, Leo returned to the National Finals intent on matching the world title record of his fellow California roper Jim Rodriguez Jr. Barnes and Camarillo were a strong, if not totally commanding, presence at the finals, capturing second in the average competition with a combined time of 104.2 seconds on 10 head and placing in 3 rounds, including 2 first-place awards. Camarillo needed every penny of the $8,103 the two won that week to defeat his former partner Dee Pickett and heeler Mike Beers.

It was Camarillo's 16th NFR appearance, and "The Lion," as he'd come to be called, now faced a whole new generation of young ropers who had grown up emulating him, his brother, and his cousin.

As rodeo historian Willard Porter noted, "(Leo) is credited by his peers for having speeded up the sport, for having eliminated the 'ho-hum, so-what' attitude, and adding class, pizzazz, and a touch of uncanny speed (to team roping)."

In the 16 years between winning his first NFR average and winning his final world title, average winning times at the NFR had fallen from just over 8 seconds to just above 5.6 seconds. Camarillo had played a key part in speeding up the competition and in training a generation of ropers via his frequent clinics throughout the country.

There was something of a "Frankenstein's monster" effect that had come into play: As Camarillo influenced an entire generation of young ropers, he increasingly found himself competing against more talented, harder-working rodeo athletes. He was not the dominating presence he'd been when he came on the scene.

But although he was no longer the only heeler who could consistently catch two heels, his greatness had not made him a has-been either. Camarillo continued roping occasionally with his old partner Tee Woolman, as well as a host of other headers. He went on to compete in the Pro Tour, a short-lived but very lucrative time for professional rodeo in which the cowboys were slotted into teams that appeared at select rodeo throughout the country. During the brief run of the tour, Camarillo was consistently the tour's leading team roper.

Though Leo's thirst for another world championship hadn't been quenched, it didn't gnaw at him either. As he closed in on 40, Camarillo began focusing more and more on giving back to the sport that had earned him a living and defined his life since his boyhood days growing up on the ranches of southern California. By 1984 Camarillo was heavily involved with his roping camps, and he had collaborated with then-*Western Horseman* editor (now publisher) Randy Witte on an instruction book called simply *Team Roping*. And as an instructor, he seemed to find his niche.

One of his students, David Gaines, said of Camarillo in a magazine article: "He is at his best when he's teaching. One on one with an interested student, Leo reveals an affectionate quality that belies his bad-guy reputation. His negative image is, to be sure, accurate. Leo is rude, temperamental, sarcastic. Still, Leo sheds his meanness when he puts on a coaching cap. With students, his outlook is positive."

If The Lion had mellowed in the latter years of his career, well, that was to be expected. For Camarillo, roping had always represented a means to a better life. At that, he'd been hugely successful. Leo qualified for his last NFR in 1985 at age 39.

At the time he was third in all-time arena earnings among rodeo cowboys — an amazing feat when you consider that throughout most of his early career, team roping had paid less and been held at far fewer venues than the standard rodeo events: calf roping, steer wrestling, bronc and bull riding. And, in the entire time he'd competed, a team at the NFR received only two-thirds the amounts paid to the individual contestants for a go-round victory or a win in the average.

Despite this, Camarillo managed to pile up close to $1 million in career earnings, and more if you take into consideration the bonus money paid out during the run of the Winston championships and the Pro Tour years.

All that Leo Camarillo accomplished in his career, he credited to his father, Ralph. His dad had been his teacher and his inspiration.

As a roper his father was no slouch. In 1945 he'd been the California Cowboys Association all-around champ and the CCA calf roping champ in 1947. But he always wanted his sons to be better than himself, and it made him exceedingly proud to have not one, but two sons who grew up to be not just world champs, but many-times world champs. When Ralph passed away at the age of 80, Leo gave the eulogy.

"Like John Wooden of basketball fame, Dad's place became a haven for young, aspiring horsemen to learn the [skills] of ranching and horsemanship. He had become a mentor to many young individuals, and his way of life would become a training ground for a new generation."

Principal among that new generation were his own sons, whose innovations modernized the sport of team roping. The competitive fire they learned from their father can best be summed up by Leo himself.

"We can appreciate that nobody likes to lose, but we like it even less."

PRORODEO

DAN HUBBELL

ROY COOPER

SOON AFTER the 1982 National Finals Rodeo, a group of coaches from Wake Forest University gathered to watch replays of rodeo's championship event. The coaches, all raised back east, marveled at the athleticism of the rodeo competitors, particularly the young calf roping champion Roy Cooper.

Cooper began the competition $15,000 behind the year-end leader and over the course of 10 days, he'd won more than $26,000 to claim the world title by a margin of $4,400. Cooper's formidable coordination, lightning-fast reflexes, strength, and agility impressed the coaches nearly as much as his desire to win.

One assistant football coach pegged him as a great quarterback or halfback prospect; an assistant basketball coach saw him as having the athletic makeup of a shooting guard. All agreed, had Cooper not grown up in the hinterlands of New Mexico, he might have had a career in one of America's marquee sports.

But Cooper would never start for the Celtics or catch passes for the Dallas Cowboys. Instead, he would carve out one of the most illustrious rodeo careers ever, earning $2 million by roping one calf at a time.

Despite growing up in the arid desert ranch country around Hobbs, N.M., Cooper did know a thing or two about basketball and football. As a teen, he

Cooper looped his way to a record fourth calf roping average title at the 1995 NFR.

played in both sports. Trouble was, he had asthma, and the respiratory disease kept him from pursuing either sport with the vigor of his rural classmates.

"As a kid, I had to rest more than my friends. I was able to play basketball, but not much football," he said. Asthma and related allergies — to horsehair, hay, and even dust — seemingly ruled out a rodeo career as well.

But even as a small child, Roy Cooper had an unstoppable desire to be a roper like his dad, Tuffy. And one day, he hoped, he'd be a champion too.

Roy Cooper was born in Hobbs on November 13, 1955. The son of Betty and Tuffy Dale Cooper, Roy was raised on a ranch 25 miles from town. His father had been a top calf roper but had given up the gypsy life to be at home where he could raise and teach his children.

Toward that end, Tuffy put a rope in his eldest son's hand about the time the boy began to walk. Given his father's enthusiasm and sacrifice, Roy felt a certain obligation to take up roping. "I had no choice," Roy once said, "I had to rope.

"I figure that my dad probably gave up his rodeo career so that my brother and sister and I could learn to rope. Me wanting to rope is probably one of the good things that has happened to my dad. He was good. I didn't really realize that until I got to know Toots Mansfield and Dean Oliver, and all the other guys he used to rope with. They told me that my dad roped really well," said Roy.

COURTESY PRCA

By the time he was in fourth grade, Roy was roping in earnest. When he got home from school, Tuffy was already waiting in the arena with the horses saddled and the calves loaded. First, Tuffy taught his children to follow and rate the calves so that they'd be in the optimum position to make a catch. Only then were they allowed to swing a loop.

Unbeknownst to Dad, Roy decided he was ready to tie his rope hard and fast to

"Practice doesn't make perfect unless you practice perfect."

his saddle. But since the tiny child's saddle he rode didn't have a back cinch, the first time Roy managed to snare a running calf, the saddle rose up in back and spanked him in the butt, sending him arms-akimbo over the horse's head. But there was a lot of try in the kid, and soon Roy was mastering the essential skills of his sport. And he graduated to a suitable roping saddle.

Later in life, Roy would make famous the phrase, "Practice doesn't make perfect unless you practice perfect." That philo-

sophy came from Tuffy, who always coached proper technique.

Once Roy roped correctly, his dad challenged him to catch the calf a little closer to the roping box, to speed up his run in some little way. And he did something else that every brilliant coach does. Rather than simply teaching Roy what he knew, Tuffy studied the other great ropers and incorporated their time-shaving habits into Roy's routine.

At age 4, Roy began practicing his tying skills on a Holstein calf. As his skills advanced, his dad showed him how to keep the calf's legs low and to tie quickly with a few short wraps, rather than using the wide, windmilling style common at that time.

Tuffy patterned the short tie on Olin Young's technique, keeping the legs low as Don McLaughlin did. He also admired Ronnye Sewalt's ability to finish the tie by pulling up hard and pushing with his legs, incorporating that into his son's routine.

By the time Roy began competing in the junior ranks, he was already a polished roper. Betty Cooper hauled her precocious 11-year-old boy to roughly 50 rodeos, where he competed in breakaway roping, ribbon roping, and calf roping.

The following year, he nodded his head at roughly 60 rodeos and missed catching just 4 calves. At age 17, Roy competed at 140 rodeos — an almost unfathomable number even for a professional roper.

At the time, he was competing with an outstanding group of Texas timed-event cowboys that included Steve Bland and Byron Walker. The group called themselves The Number One Rodeo Club, a testament to their cockiness and their confidence.

Not surprisingly, Roy began amassing junior titles. Roping in the American Junior Rodeo Association, he claimed the calf roping championship and the all-around award for four consecutive seasons, from 1972 through '75. In his final year, he served as AJRA president and was awarded the Alvin Davis Founders Award as the most outstanding individual in 25 years. In his senior year of high school, Roy also won the 1973 National High School Rodeo Association's calf roping title.

With such a long string of successes leading up to high school graduation, Roy was courted by all the top rodeo coaches, receiving offers from 20 colleges. But when it came time to decide, he picked tiny Cisco (Texas) Community College, a school with fewer students than his high school.

"I went there because of the coach, Tommy Pope. He was from New Mexico originally, and I liked him. I also liked the location. Cisco was between Abilene and Fort Worth, so I could rope every night in an indoor arena—and did." While at Cisco, Roy captured two regional calf roping titles, qualifying for the College National Finals both years.

Roy also competed often in amateur rodeos, which in Texas were amateur only in name. Texas is arguably the most competitive calf roping area of the country, a place where a cowboy who can't draw tight in under 9 seconds might as well not unload his horse. Roy thrived in that environment, watching the other ropers and picking up their techniques for shaving his own times. Those experiences would play a big role in Roy's debut as a professional some years later.

After two years at Cisco, Roy moved on to Southeastern Oklahoma State University in Durant. He was lured there by the university's president, Dr. Leon Hibbs, a roper who wanted to build a national-caliber rodeo program. With Roy as the backbone of a squad coached by 1973 calf roping champ Ernie Taylor, Southeastern captured back-to-back team championships in the National Intercollegiate Rodeo Association.

Hibbs prided himself on not only recruiting good rodeo athletes, but also on preparing them for life after college. Roy was not, however, a star pupil. Of Roy's academics, Hibbs smiled and said, "Well, he attended, anyway."

Roy never envisioned an occupation outside the rodeo arena. Of his academic career, he quipped, "All I knew was I wanted to major in calf roping and minor in steer roping."

In the former discipline Roy went to the top of his class, capturing the 1975 National Intercollegiate Calf Roping World Cham-

CAREER MILESTONES

Roy Cooper

born: November 13, 1955
Hobbs, New Mexico

Eight-Time PRCA World Champion, All-Around (1983), Steer Roping (1983), Calf Roping (1976, 1980-84). PRCA Calf Roping Champ (1976-78); American Junior Rodeo Association Boys Calf Roping Champion & All-Around Champ.

2000 First cowboy to surpass $2 million in arena earnings.

1999 Cooper qualifies for the National Finals Steer Roping, his 31st National Finals qualification.

1996 Wins his fourth National Finals Steer Roping average, becoming the only cowboy to win four finals averages in two events. Cooper's time, 131.5 seconds, establishes a 10-head record for single steer roping at the finals. In qualifying for the National Finals Rodeo in calf roping, Cooper stretches the record for the most qualifications in the event to 18.

1995 Wins his fourth National Finals Rodeo calf roping average, a record.

1993 Cooper wins his third NFSR average title.

1987 In May becomes only the second cowboy to surpass $1 million in arena earnings.

1985 Cooper repeats as NFSR average winner and wins his fifth straight calf roping title, matching the record for consecutive calf roping world championships established by Dean Oliver.

1984 Competing in the National Finals Steer Roping, Cooper wins the average in the then-record time of 146.7 seconds on 10 head.

1980 Regains the PRCA world title in calf roping.

1979 A severe injury to his right wrist puts Cooper's career in jeopardy. However, he recovers sufficiently to qualify for the NFR, winning the average in the then-record time of 107.9 seconds.

1977-1978 Cooper wins the PRCA calf roping championship for the most money won during the season. Under the rules in effect at that time, he was not awarded the world championship (world titles were, instead, awarded to the NFR winners).

1976 Cooper wins the PRCA overall rookie of the year title and is named calf roping rookie of the year, qualifies for his first National Finals Rodeo, wins the PRCA calf roping championship for the most money won during the season, and wins the world championship as the highest money-earning roper at the NFR.

1975 National Intercollegiate Rodeo Association calf roping champion (year end) and NIRA Collegiate National Finals calf roping winner.

1973 National High School Rodeo Association calf roping champion.

DAN HUBBELL

pionship and the College National Finals Rodeo calf roping title. His college rodeo squad was never defeated at a regular season rodeo or the CNFR.

Although Cooper had applied for his Professional Rodeo Cowboys Association permit at the age of 17, he put off competing seriously in the association until the age of 20. But he often got a taste of top-drawer talent by matching world champion ropers such as Phil Lyne and Dean Oliver.

At 20 Roy again applied for a PRCA permit, this time filling it by placing second at his first rodeo in San Angelo, Texas. (In order to compete as a full-fledged professional, a cowboy was required to win at least $1,000 in PRCA events. Roy won $1,002.)

With his newly printed membership card in his wallet, Roy burst onto the pro rodeo scene like a bombshell, cashing checks at nearly every rodeo he entered. It was soon apparent that the rookie had a good chance of winning a world championship, and even his academic mentor had to admit that Roy's future was in the rodeo arena.

Hibbs told Roy, "As long as you stay healthy, there's no one in the world who can beat you—not day after day."

What set Roy apart from other ropers was his ability to incorporate every time-shaving trick into an altogether new routine. In addition to the fast-tie technique honed by his father, Roy had learned to keep calves on their feet by holding his rope while he pitched the slack. As his horse ground to a stop, Roy would slide off the horse with his rope still in hand.

By doing this, he was able to control the calf and keep the pull of the rope from snapping the calf over backward. Thus, when he got to the calf, it was already on its feet, saving Roy the effort of lifting the calf up off the ground before tipping it onto its side. It was a technique that Roy had learned from the amateurs in Texas, and it became known as "switching."

"When I was 19 years old, 18 years old, I saw guys roping and dropping their slack and popping them around. I began playing with that, holding my slack, and I had some horses that I could do it on. A lot of guys were doing it in the amateurs. In 1976 no one in the pros was doing that. Maybe Butch Bode, a left-handed roper, was doing it back in 1976 too," notes Roy.

His technique caught the attention of veteran ropers.

"Every once in a while, a guy will come along and change things. Roy changed things. He revolutionized the event. The way he got off the right side of a horse holding his slack and kept calves standing—no one had done the things he was doing," said eight-time calf roping champ Dean Oliver.

Not since Elvis Aaron Presley swung down out of his truck and walked into Sun Studios had such a young man had such a great impact on his profession. Once Cooper came onto the professional scene, calf roping was never the same. His innovations quickly led to a tidal wave of change in calf roping as young, upcoming ropers and even some of the old-timers willing to learn a few new tricks copied Cooper's style.

"He had several innovations," noted many-time NFR calf roper Mike Johnson. "He dismounted faster than anybody, he held his slack, and he developed the fast-tie style that you see everyone use today. He even had long hair and listened to rock 'n' roll music."

Johnny Emmons, a third-generation calf roper and NFR qualifier whose family manufactures ropes, recalls, "He was a kid, he had a big feather in his hat, and he wore bell bottoms. He just caught your attention. I was probably only 9 or 10 years old, and he was my hero."

The Emmons family had more than admiration for Cooper. They also credit him with helping to promote their patented piggin' string. Always looking for an edge, Roy began using one of the Emmons strings, a stiff nylon loop markedly different from the soft, natural-fibered strings then in use.

"The strings had just come out (in 1976), and Roy showed how you could wrap a calf quicker with them," said Emmons.

Cooper came into the PRCA at a unique time in the association's history. For the first time, the world championships were decided solely on money earned at the season-ending National Finals Rodeo, rather than by money earned throughout the regular season plus the NFR.

Based on the old system, the cowboy would have gone into the '76 NFR with a $1,679 lead in the calf roping over his nearest rival, all-around hand extraordinaire Tom Ferguson. As it was, Roy started the Bicentennial NFR dead even with the other 15 contestants.

At first, it seemed like the rookie of the year would be bested by Ferguson, who put together two first-place runs and two second-place runs in the first four rounds. But Cooper stole the momentum in round five, and stayed consistent throughout the ten-round event, placing six times to Ferguson's five finishes in the money.

When it all wrapped up, the college senior had secured the NFR average for the fastest time on 10 head (133.1 seconds), to capture his first world championship with NFR earnings of $5,789. It was a spectacular year by any measure. Roy claimed the PRCA rookie of the year award, the PRCA national championship, the NFR average title, and the PRCA world championship.

The following season, the PRCA's new system for deciding the world title didn't fall in Cooper's favor. Despite winning the PRCA championship with regular-season earnings of $45,713, Cooper, then 22, failed to repeat his stellar NFR performance of 1976.

In the 10-round NFR, he only managed to finish third overall in his specialty event, giving up the world title to Jim Gladstone, who'd entered the competition ranked 14th in the world.

COURTESY PRCA

Some of the older cowboys disliked Roy's rock'n'roll lifestyle, but you couldn't deny his winning charm. Cooper claims the 1978 PRCA calf roping championship saddle.

The next year was a near repeat of 1977. Again, Cooper scored major victories throughout the regular season, winning San Antonio and cashing big checks at San Francisco's Cow Palace, Cheyenne Frontier Days, and the Calgary Stampede.

Again, he handily clinched the PRCA championship based on season earnings but watched his world title slip away at the NFR, where he finished 12th. Despite the disappointing finals, Cooper still managed to rack up $67,153 in the regular season, becoming the first man in rodeo history to cross the $60,000 threshold.

Dave Brock, who won the title that year, earned but one-third that amount.

Eminent rodeo historian Willard Porter was among those who called for the PRCA

Cooper shares face time with rodeo commentator Pam Minick at the 1983 NFR.

to abandon its new system for naming champs, serving up Cooper's losses as examples of injustice.

"Sticklers for details are apt to remind me that in 1977 and '78, he wasn't world champion but PRCA champion. Those were the years when the PRCA made a controversial ruling that a win at the NFR would decide the championship of the

world, despite what a hand had done all season long," said Porter.

Although Roy's name doesn't appear in the record books as world champ, Porter stubbornly counted those years among Cooper's world titles anyway. The PRCA returned to its previous system in 1979.

Alas, insult in the form of a lost world title turned to injury for Roy. In June of 1979, Cooper was practicing in the arena with his former coach, Ernie Taylor. The two had finished roping when Roy spotted a calf that had run back up the alley into the pen. Rather than turn the calf out, Cooper decided to rope it.

"I roped him real close and double-shuffled my slack—shot it up twice and went to tag my horse. And I stuck my hand right through a coil of that rope. It jerked me out of the saddle, and I was hung up. Finally, my hand came loose and just hung there at a funny angle, and I knew."

Roy's hand was nearly severed, but he still asked Taylor to take him home. Taylor wisely refused, convincing the cowboy that they needed to go to a Dallas hospital where surgeons did their best to reconstruct Cooper's wrist.

Taylor was nearly in tears, realizing that the career of this bright young talent had likely come to an end. Roy stayed in the hospital for eight days, receiving nearly a hundred calls from well-wishers during his stay. A testament to the respect Cooper engendered from the roping community was that nearly every roper contacted him to offer encouragement.

Amazingly, Cooper recuperated sufficiently to begin roping a mere two months later. He went on to qualify for the National Finals Rodeo. "I knew I couldn't try to be real fast and win any go-rounds, because my wrist was too stiff—it still had the pins in it. All I wanted to do at the NFR was tie down all my calves and hope to place well in the average." He did that and more. Roy set a fast-time record for the NFR average: 107.9 seconds on 10 calves.

"Winning the National Finals that year probably meant more to me than being world champion the first year," he reflected. "When I started roping again after the accident, I realized how much I loved to rope, how much I had missed it. I'll always rope because of that feeling."

The following year, the "Super Looper" would again assert his dominance in the calf roping event. Now 25 and at the height of his game, Cooper led the parade throughout the 10-round National Finals, placing in 5 of 10 rounds (including 4 first-place wins) and finishing third in the average despite missing his calf in the ninth round. With $77,026 in earnings, Roy won more money to claim his second world championship than any other single-event title winner.

Few people in the Cooper clan will forget 1981. That year's finals matched Roy against his cousin, Jimmie Cooper, in a nail-biting race for the all-around world title. Jimmie, the 1980 Overall Rookie of the Year, entered the NFR ranked fourth in the all-around title chase behind Roy, Tom Ferguson, and the previous year's winner, Paul Tierney.

Jimmie and Roy tied for third place in the calf roping average, with Jimmie winning the tilt on the strength of the tie-breaker for clocking the fastest time on a single run. Although Roy claimed the world title with a record-stretching $94,476 in winnings (again, the most of any single event competitor), Jimmie outdistanced his cousin in the all-around race by a mere $47!

Losing the all-around to his cousin probably didn't sting as hard as if he'd lost to someone else, but Cooper emerged from the 1981 Finals with an almost maniacal desire to out-rodeo everyone else.

In the days of unrestricted rodeo entries, Roy was hitting up to 150 rodeos a year and was on the road incessantly. When he was home, he was practicing. The price was high, but the dividends were great—Cooper managed to hold onto the calf roping world championship for five consecutive years beginning in 1980.

In 1983 Roy had the biggest season of his career. He was living in Durant, Okla., and

as the leading money-winner going into the NFR, he proudly carried the state flag into the Myriad Arena at the finals in Oklahoma City. He'd already won the world title at the National Finals Steer Roping, which was held separately to accommodate the space requirements necessary for the event. Cooper also led in the calf roping and seem-

Roy's triple crown put him into an elite class of competitors who claimed three titles in a single year ... .

ingly had a lock on that title. But he'd yet to win the all-around, and he craved that title above all others.

"In the past, I hadn't really thought about the all-around title much, but after losing to my cousin Jimmie by $47 in 1981 and finishing second to Paul (Tierney) in 1980, it was on my mind," he said.

More than simply on his mind—it was nearly an obsession. Roy became a stealth competitor, traveling in his airplane to an estimated 60 rodeos that season and logging more than 300 flight hours. But with the NFR in his own backyard, in an arena he was well familiar with, Cooper came into the National Finals rested and ready, with a hometown edge that could not be calculated but that was tangible and real nonetheless.

Roy flat smoked his fellow calf roping competitors. After a slow start in rounds one and two, Cooper clicked with a 9.0-second win in round three, then went on to place in five of the remaining seven rounds. Again, he captured the calf roping average (his third) and led all contestants in single-event earnings for the year with a record $122,455. Although his cousin was again his closest rival, this time the contest wasn't even close. Roy topped Jimmie by a margin of $38,413. Roy's triple crown put him into an elite class of competitors who claimed three titles in a single year: Bill Linderman, Casey Tibbs,

Harry Tompkins, and fellow Oklahoman Jim Shoulders.

Texas singer and cowboy bard Red Steagall had a brief moment to congratulate the Sooner state hero, and he sagely told Roy to savor the moment.

"(He) told me after I won the triple crown that I'd see it good again, but I'd probably never see it this good again," said Cooper.

And indeed, that would prove true. In 1984, Roy claimed the calf roping world title but ceded the all-around crown to Dee Pickett. After Pickett, emphasis in the all-around race would shift to the rough-stock end of the arena, first with Lewis Feild and then with the phenomenal Ty Murray. It would be more than a decade before a "timey" wore the all-around buckle again.

The price for Cooper's successes was high. Roy had married his college sweetheart, Lisa Mann, but the constant travel made domestic life nearly impossible. Cooper says he "wasn't around much" for his son, Clint, born in 1982 in the midst of Cooper's barnstorming days. Finally, the ribbon that tied Roy to Lisa snapped, and the two divorced in 1985.

Roy's breakup served to help him reprioritize his life and his career. Already a legend, Cooper had little left to prove. In 1987 he married Shari Smith, the daughter of two-time NFR calf roping qualifier Clifton Smith. The two settled in Childress, Tex., not far from her childhood home.

Coming from a rodeo family, Shari was understanding of Roy's competitive demands. But Roy was also more committed to a successful home life, and he adjusted his schedule to spend time with his growing family, which now included sons Clif and Tuf, both born to Shari and Roy, as well as Clint and Shada, Shari's daughter from a previous marriage.

Roy's competitive fire may have dimmed somewhat — he would not capture another world title as the 20th century came to a close. But he continued to be a winner well into his 40s.

In 1995 Cooper proved that age hadn't dulled his competitive edge when he won the National Finals Rodeo for the fourth time in his career, matching the record for NFR calf roping average victories set by Olin Young, one of the men Cooper had modeled his roping after.

In 1996 Cooper celebrated his 40th birthday and gave himself a belated present: his fourth National Finals Steer Roping average with a time of 131.5 seconds—the fastest time in the event's history (as of 2000). With eight average titles in two events, Roy

DAN HUBBELL

Two decades after exploding onto the pro rodeo scene, Cooper still sets the standard by which calf ropers are measured. 1995 Pikes Peak or Bust Rodeo, Colorado Springs.

holds the record for the most National Finals average wins.

Time, however, has exacted a toll on the master. Two years before his final average victory, he'd undergone reconstructive surgeries on both his shoulders. A fall with a horse forced him into the hospital with a damaged rotator cuff in his roping arm, and when that was repaired, he felt so good he had the other one repaired too. To hear Roy tell the story, the joints had simply worn down from years of use, like the tires on an old truck. Ever since the surgeries, he says he has felt like — and roped like — a man half his age.

In 2000 Cooper returned to the NFR to celebrate his 32nd qualification (13 in steer roping and 19 in calf roping), second only to Tee Woolman in all events combined. He holds the current record for the most trips to the NFR in calf roping, with 19 qualifications over the 25-year span of his career.

But Cooper achieved another milestone in 2000. He became the first rodeo cowboy to surpass $2 million in career earnings. It's a distinction he's paid for in an equal number of miles traveled, two shoulder surgeries, a reconstructed wrist, and the deep laugh wrinkles around his eyes from recalling the predicaments he's gotten into over the years.

Roy Cooper passed the $2 million mark not far from the town where it all started, Hobbs, New Mexico. The Lea County native was just $168 shy of the mark when he arrived for the Lea County Fair & Rodeo, held August 9-12 in Lovington. A fourth-place check in the first round's calf roping put him over the top; then Cooper went on to cap the feat with a second-place finish in the calf roping average. His total take for the rodeo was $2,342.

Cooper has earned permanent displays in the Cowboy Hall of Fame in Oklahoma City and the ProRodeo Hall of Fame in Colorado Springs. Roy's achievements will undoubtedly be a highlight of his own tribute project, Roy Cooper's Museum of Champion Ropers, which he plans to open in his hometown.

Looking back at his career, though, Roy says it's not the titles and records that he

DAVID JENNINGS

The man they call the "Super Looper."

cherishes most, but rather the memories of the friends he's made and the good times they've shared. When he came into the game, he got the chance to compete alongside men who had roped with his father and who were legends in their own rights. In the twilight of his career, Cooper has roped with legends-in-the-making who, as children, grew up with the dream of winning world titles — just like Roy Cooper.

Among the many celebrities who have ridden the trail with Roy over the years are Charlie Daniels and George Strait, both avid team ropers. Cooper and Strait have often gotten together to team rope, and Cooper has spent hours in the studio with Strait.

"He's my man. I respect him more than any living person I know of. We met in 1983 at Oklahoma City, where he was playing at the state fair," said Cooper. "We've become friends. He's my hero. The time we spend together is very valuable."

It's fair to say that Strait feels the same way, and that he admires Cooper's records as much as Roy admires the singer's.

"If I could sing, that's what I'd do. But I can't, so I guess I'll just have to keep roping," Cooper once remarked. Over a career that spans four decades, that is exactly what he has done.

JAMES FAIN

TOM FERGUSON

TOM FERGUSON was born in the same eastern Oklahoma farming country where baseball hall of famer Mickey Mantle was raised. Even today, Tom lives in Miami, just a few miles down old Route 66 from Mantle's boyhood home in Commerce.

As a kid growing up in the 1950s, Ferguson was as caught up in the excitement that Mantle generated with his mighty hits as any child who dreamed of playing in the big leagues. But when it came time for Ferguson to take his at-bats, he was shut out.

"I liked to play baseball in grade school. I got to where I worked really hard at it, but when it came time to play, I had to sit on the bench. So, that forced me into the rodeo end — I felt that I could be out there; I could be as competitive as anybody. And if you had $20 for the entry (fee), you got to play."

Years later, cowboys would wish Ferguson's coach had just let the kid play ball.

Ferguson's career in rodeo was nearly as magnificent as Mantle's in baseball. His most significant accomplishment was winning six consecutive world champion all-around cowboy titles between 1974 and 1979. Those six world championships matched rough-stock rider Larry Mahan's career record for all-around awards, a quantity that was not exceeded until 1998, when Ty Murray claimed a seventh.

Ferguson and his horse Catfish were regarded as among the greatest teams in the rodeo game.

Tom Ferguson was born in Tahlequah, Okla., December 20, 1950, the second son of Ira and Maxine Ferguson. The Ferguson family moved to San Jose, Calif., in 1952, finally settling in nearby San Martin. Ira, who had competed in Oklahoma and Texas in the 1930s and '40s, was quick to build a practice arena on the family's acreage.

Over the years the Ferguson place attracted some of the best timed-event riders in the central California region. Soon-to-be steer wrestling champs Jack Roddy and Bob Marshall, as well as NFR qualifiers Mark Shricker and Joe Watkins, were among the cowboys who practiced under Ira's watch.

Ira's boys, Tom and his older brother, Larry, looked up to and tried to emulate the older cowboys. Tom, especially, was seldom without a small rope in his hand, which he used to terrorize any stray animals that happened to be available.

It's said that the boys would hold an animal between their knees, forming an impromptu chute, then release it and rope it as it ran away. The boys had a small pet goat, and they roped, tied, and bulldogged it so often that the goat would climb up on the hood of the Ferguson's panel wagon to get some peace. But even there, the goat wasn't safe from Tom's loop.

"You'd see that little rope go around the top of the truck, and there would be Tom," Ira remembers. "He'd heel that goat nine times out of ten."

When Tom was about 5 and his brother 6, Ira bought them a Welsh pony. From that

the burro, telling the boys they couldn't bulldog until they were 16.

But that didn't stop the boys from competing, first between themselves, and later at junior rodeos throughout central California. Maxine loaded up the family station wagon and took the boys to their first rodeo, a kid's contest in Livermore, when Tom was 11. Tom and Larry paired up in the team roping, but Tom, who never did particularly well in that event, missed his first catch and had to settle for a second throw and a long, losing time. But he took first place in the calf roping, claiming a buckle.

"I remember that I felt like, 'Gee, there will never be a poor day,'" Tom recalls. "Winning that buckle was the supreme reward. I've got that buckle still."

As the boys reached their teens, their practice sessions grew lengthier and more serious. When the school bus was still a mile from home, Tom would get off and walk to his house, gaining some extra time as the bus continued dropping off the other kids. After a snack, he'd head out to do chores. Then, it was off to the practice pen.

He and Larry practiced until their father, who worked in construction, got home. Then, they soaked in their dad's advice on how to improve their technique. Then, it was back out to practice until the sun had set and it was too dark to see.

"They'd tie calves for two or three hours at a time, one right after the other. You don't see too many kids who do that. And that's what made them so good—practice, practice, practice," said Ira.

As a high-schooler, Tom Ferguson tried to catch eight calves and jump ten to fifteen steers each night in his father's backlot. That almost monastic devotion to practice would characterize Tom Ferguson's pro career. He often said that he wasn't a natural athlete. In high school the other kids in gym class could always run faster and jump higher. So Ferguson made up for his lack of athleticism with hard work and determination.

"When I was small, I wasn't fast. But I

day on, it was a race to see which boy got to the barn first each day. Ira remembers that when the pony first arrived, he would barely walk 10 feet before refusing to go any farther. Ira trained the pony a little, and soon the boys were putting more miles on him than a teenager puts on a new car.

"One of them would ride him for two or three hours, then the other would get on. When Tom got on, you wouldn't see him 'til dark. They'd wear the shoes off that

"Many people asked if I went to college to rodeo. It was just the opposite— rodeo was a way for me to get a college degree."

pony; we had to shoe him every four weeks," says Ira.

Soon the kids were roping off the pony and trying to bulldog a burro they owned. But the burro grew weary of the boys' games, and he would set up on the boys as they dropped onto his head. The wannabe bulldoggers would tumble to the ground. Ira soon put a stop to their harassment of

learned my trade by trying to make no mistakes. Every time I made a run, the speed came with the technique. My whole deal was to be consistent, and I refined my trade to make it easy and comfortable," he said.

Tom was a keen student of the game, and he had at his disposal some of the best cowboys of the era to teach him not only how to throw a steer or rope a calf, but how to win.

"Jack Roddy would come down and we'd practice with him. He was a two-time world champion who had a big ranch in San Jose. He had a good energy level, he was positive, he knew how to win. Jack's friends would stop by, so that exposed me to lots of world champions. It made me nervous, but I learned to control that. We got to be good friends," said Ferguson.

In addition to Roddy, Tom credits a little-known roper named Guy Pickner with his development as a rodeo cowboy. "Guy was in the service in Salinas, and he came up and roped with us a couple of times a week. I was only 12 or 13, and Guy showed me the fundamentals. He stuck with the basics, and I still work on those today," said Tom.

When the Fergusons found that junior rodeos didn't offer them the level of competition they desired, they graduated to the California Cowboys Association, an amateur association only in name, since the contests brought out the West Coast's best competitors, all of them hungry to take one another's money. It wasn't long before the Fergusons proved adept at leaving grown men penniless.

At one point, Ira recalls one cowboy who was in his mid-30s watching Tom rope calves at a rodeo. The cowboy said to Ira, "Any kid that can beat me like that, I quit." The cowboy took out his ropes, cut them up, and was never seen at CCA rodeos again.

Tom quickly climbed up the association's championship ladder. In 1969 the high school senior won the CCA's calf roping championship. In 1972, while in college at California Polytechnic Institute, he captured the association's steer wrestling title. But there was more to competition than winning titles; Tom Ferguson was serious

about his education, and rodeo enabled him to pursue a degree.

"Once I started winning, my plan was to use the money to supplement my college expenses. I believed in getting an edu-

CAREER MILESTONES

Tom Ferguson

born: December 20, 1950
Tahlequah, Oklahoma

Six-Time World Champion All-Around Cowboy (1974-79); World Champion Calf Roper (1974); World Champion Steer Wrestler (1977-78); PRCA Champion Steer Wrestler (1976-77).

1986 In March becomes the first cowboy in pro rodeo history to surpass $1 million arena earnings mark.

1983 Competes in his 11th consecutive National Finals Rodeo.

1982 Ferguson stretches the PRCA regular-season, single-rodeo earnings record to $17,225 at the Houston Livestock Show Rodeo.

1979 Ties Larry Mahan for the most all-around titles won (6), and becomes the first cowboy to win six consecutive all-around titles.

1978 Ferguson becomes the first cowboy to surpass $100,000 in season earnings ($103,734).

1977 At a rodeo school he was teaching, Ferguson gets his leg crushed by a hydraulic gate, but recovers sufficiently to qualify for the National Finals Rodeo that season. There, Ferguson claims both the PRCA and world titles in steer wrestling, as well as the PRCA and world all-around cowboy titles. Ferguson also claims the record for the fastest 10-round "average" time at the NFR, with a cumulative time of 65.8 seconds.

1976 Ferguson wins the PRCA title in steer wrestling for the most money won in the event; that year, a system was in place that awarded world titles to the National Finals Rodeo champions. In the all-around title race, a tie leads to a sudden-death decision that gives Ferguson the all-around crown over bareback ace Joe Alexander.

1975 Ferguson shares the world all-around title with Leo Camarillo in a controversial decision that embitters the Oklahoma cowboy. At the NFR Ferguson throws a steer in 3.5 seconds to set a new NFR arena record.

1974 At the National Finals Rodeo in Oklahoma City, clinches his first world champion all-around cowboy title in a string of six consecutive all-around championships. He is 23 years old, just a few days shy of 24. He also wins the calf roping world title, his only world title in that event, and finishes as the runner-up in the steer wrestling title race, just $360 behind that year's winner.

1973 After qualifying for the first time for the National Finals Rodeo in both calf roping and steer wrestling, finishes as runner-up to world champion all-around cowboy Larry Mahan.

1971 Joins PRCA as a permit holder.

1970 Men's all-around champion at the Collegiate National Finals Rodeo.

1969 1969 California Cowboys Association ribbon (calf) roping champion.

cation," he said. "Many people asked if I went to college to rodeo. It was just the opposite—rodeo was a way for me to get a college degree."

Ferguson, however, was anything but your typical college freshman. The university's animal husbandry department agreed to lend him stock pens, and he showed up for school with six steers, ten calves, and a roping horse so that he could maintain his brutal practice routine. Ferguson also showed up with the discipline of a mature adult, maintaining a grade point average above 3.0 while majoring in agricultural business management.

At Cal Poly, Tom Ferguson helped his team to three national championships while winning individual titles in ribbon roping (1970) and calf roping (1973). During his last semester of eligibility, he began to be a little restless. There were no college rodeos to speak of in the winter, so Tom struck out for Odessa, Tex., to try his luck among the pros.

"At Odessa, I made a good run. Everybody was there, all the top riders, and it was a big thrill for me to win the first round," he said. "That was an accomplishment." To this day,

Ferguson trippin' a steer at the 1979 National Finals Steer Roping in Laramie, Wyoming.

Ferguson counts the go-round win among his most cherished memories.

Emboldened by his success, Ferguson went to Denver in January for the National Western Stock Show, where he placed third overall in the steer wrestling. He decided to lay off the semester and keep going. He managed to place in 25 of the 30 rodeos he entered. He returned to California to finish out the quarter at college, and that summer he accompanied the Cal Poly team to the College National Finals Rodeo. There, his team claimed the championship, buoyed by Tom's individual titles in the calf roping and steer wrestling.

In the pros, Tom hadn't set out to qualify for the '73 National Finals, but momentum carried him through the season, and he wound up a qualifier in both the calf roping and steer wrestling events. Despite his youth (he was 22), Ferguson placed in two rounds of calf roping and stayed consistent enough over ten rounds to place second in the ten-round average competition behind Barry Burk.

In the steer wrestling Ferguson won a round with the second-fastest time of the finals (3.9 seconds), placed four times, and finished fourth overall in the 10-round average.

Most telling, however, was his second-place finish in the world champion all-around title race. Although Larry Mahan handily won the title, Ferguson made it clear that he might be the heir to Mahan's throne.

And so he was the following year when he ascended to his first all-around world championship in grand style. Ferguson, who was by now living in Miami, Okla., gave the Oklahoma City crowd reason to cheer for their native son when he grabbed the win in the first round of calf roping. He went on to place in four more rounds and finish third in the ten-round calf roping average.

Ferguson's 1974 calf roping world title, however, had never been in jeopardy. Even if Tom had not earned a dime in Oklahoma City, the young gun would still have handily defeated Dean Oliver, the legendary roper who had won eight world championships.

Ferguson's year-end total of $40,839 was nearly twice as great as Oliver's.

Things were much tighter in the steer wrestling competition. Ferguson entered the 1974 NFR ranked second in the world, just $659 behind Tommy Puryear of Norman, Oklahoma. He'd narrowed the money gap during the competition, and the championship literally came down to the final steer.

The 24-year-old Puryear turfed his final steer in 4.91 seconds to place third in the round, picking up $375. Ferguson finished just out of the money. Puryear's go-round check put him $360 ahead of Ferguson in the title race.

Despite winning his first all-around title and the calf roping championship, Ferguson was miffed that he missed claiming the steer wrestling buckle. It was always his goal to match Everett Bowman's 1935 record sweep of the calf roping, steer wrestling, and all-around titles.

"I am a competitor who hates to leave something on the table," Ferguson said. "On the final day, I had to beat (Tommy), and he was simply faster than I was. They were timing by hundreths of a second, and he beat me by 13/100ths of a second. It might as well have been two hours. I was way above my head on that last run. I performed well, and that was all I could do."

Ferguson was quite a contrast to the previous year's all-around champ, Larry Mahan.

Mahan was always smiling, always willing to grant an interview or sign an autograph. His short, muscular physique and bow-legged swagger earned him the nickname "Bull."

Ferguson, on the other hand, was dark, serious, and aloof. He'd grown to be quite a handsome man, with a jutting jaw and cleft chin seemingly carved from granite, and heavy eyebrows that framed deep-set blue eyes. At 6 feet and 185 pounds, he was smaller than most bulldoggers.

And he seldom gave interviews. At one point in his career, he turned down an appearance on *The Tonight Show*, a star-making engagement if ever there was one, citing as his reason the possibility that he might miss a rodeo.

The media came to interpret Ferguson's reclusiveness as a sign that he didn't like to be troubled by the press. In fact, the cowboy was painfully modest and usually too busy with his horses or traveling to concern himself with press deadlines.

"I was never much good at braggin' on

"I wasn't flamboyant like Mahan. Not everyone is made like him. He had a certain charisma that not many people have."

myself. I wasn't raised that way," he would say. "I wasn't flamboyant like Mahan. Not everyone is made like him. He had a certain charisma that not many people have."

Roy Cooper, himself an upcoming superstar in rodeo and an immediate calf roping sensation when Ferguson was knocking off world championships, often traveled with Ferguson in those early years. He characterized Ferguson as a man of great seriousness and purpose.

"Tom wasn't outspoken. He didn't come to shake hands and visit. He roped and bulldogged and got his check and went on. A vacation for him was to go home and have 30 fresh calves to rope," said Cooper.

According to Cooper, Ferguson bucked the myth of the hell-raising cowboy. He didn't smoke, didn't drink, didn't party. At one point in his stellar career, Ferguson even turned down offers from tobacco and liquor sponsors because he didn't feel right about endorsing their products. Ferguson's ascetic lifestyle, combined with his unwillingness to bare his soul to reporters, didn't make for the most lively copy. And Cooper thinks that hurt Ferguson.

"I don't think people realized how tough he was, and he never got the recognition he deserved," said Cooper. Others concurred.

HUFFMAN

Ferguson goes after his final calf to claim his fifth consecutive all-around title at the 1978 NFR.

"Because of his terse public temperament, Ferguson has not been accorded a hero's status among observers and fans of the sport," wrote Bill Armour in 1984, when he was with the PRCA publicity department. "Detractors who dislike Ferguson's disposition have anxiously awaited his decline and demise."

But among the rodeo cowboys themselves, Ferguson was highly regarded. In some ways, he and Cooper carved the way for a new generation of college-educated cowboys who trained as athletes in other sports trained: through endless practice and a single-minded devotion to their crafts.

"Tom and Roy (Cooper) make just about as perfect runs as can be made," said Olin Young, a champion roper who was in the twilight of his career when the young guns came on the scene. "Both of the men's work with the tie string is a series of calculated moves they've practiced so it's automatic."

Before long, Ferguson's metronomic consistency, his perfectionist personality, and his grueling rodeo schedule (he typically competed at over 120 rodeos a year, logging more than 170,000 miles on the road) earned him the nickname "the Bionic Cowboy." Whether he was roping for $5 or $5,000, Ferguson always roped with the same intensity, focus, and style.

It should be said that many of the controversies that swirled around the cowboy weren't always of Tom's own making. Tom's second world all-around championship came

amid such a controversy. And it was won as much in the courts as it was in the arena. At the NFR, the great PRCA team roper Leo Camarillo had been named as the world all-around champ. But Ferguson, who had seen his wins credited to his own brother in the past, was confident he'd won more money. So he dug a little deeper into the tally books.

In those days, the PRCA kept most of its records by hand. Although PRCA officials said they'd had an independent audit of the books, Ferguson went to their offices in Denver and discovered that some of Leo Camarillo's earnings had actually been won by his cousin, Reg.

Attorneys were hired by both competitors, and the PRCA held a series of meetings. Ferguson's attorney felt that if a lawsuit was brought, a victory by Ferguson might bankrupt the rodeo association. If that were the case, Ferguson's win would have been a hollow victory — he'd have his championship, but nowhere to compete. So, according to Ferguson, the attorney, Don Harris, proposed a co-championship. In the record books, the earnings are shown as being equal — each cowboy is recorded as having earned exactly $50,300. It is the only co-championship recorded in the PRCA history books.

Needless to say, the legal controversy didn't endear Ferguson to the PRCA. "When it was over, it was kicked around that I'd cost the association a lot of money — about $50,000," notes Ferguson. "But it wasn't me who made the mistake."

Later, the association singled him out for participating in a fledgling professional tour, and Ferguson was fined. Though he never went so far as to say that the action was retaliatory, Ferguson did note that other cowboys who'd participated in the tour hadn't been punished in the same way he had.

Ferguson, however, never lost his stride as a competitor. He continued to knock off all-around championships, and in 1978 he became the first cowboy in history to secure more than $100,000 in arena earnings, including bonuses.

In 1976 the PRCA changed its system for determining world champions. Prior to 1976 championships were based on money earned throughout the regular season plus money made at the National Finals Rodeo. From 1976 to 1978, each cowboy's slate was wiped clean, and the biggest winner at the NFR was also the world champion. Separate championships (called PRCA championships) were awarded to the highest regular-season money-winners.

Ferguson didn't like the system, but neither did a lot of the top-drawer cowboys including Don Gay and bareback champ Joe Alexander. Why, they reasoned, should someone who earned half what they did over the course of the year get to compete on an equal level at the National Finals? With the new system, every cowboy had an equal chance at the world title—and yet, Ferguson still continued to win.

"At the National Finals, everyone thought they could beat me. But I would win. I had good technique, good horses, and I scored (got out of the roping box quickly and penalty-free) great. Those were the key things that made me a world champion," said Tom.

Ferguson was regarded as a big-event competitor, able to endure and thrive under pressure. "Tom was tough at the big rodeos, and he got ready for the big money," said Roy Cooper.

In 1976 Ferguson won the PRCA championship in steer wrestling, and in calf roping he finished second to Cooper in both the year-end PRCA title race and the world championship. But the new rule robbed him of the steer wrestling world title. His year-end earnings were nearly $8,000 greater than the second-ranked competitor, his old friend Bob Marshall of Chowchilla, California.

But at the National Finals, Ferguson had an up-and-down experience, placing in five rounds but taking a nearly 60-second time in round five. In the world title contest, he finished fifth, well behind Rick Bradley of Burkburnett, Texas.

It would be the last championship that the Sooner cowboy would leave on the table.

He rebounded in 1977 to defeat Paul Tierney for the NFR all-around, earning $10,749 to Tierney's $7,888. Tom also defeated old rival Tommy Puryear in the steer wrestling with a blistering 65.8-second time, the fastest 10-head time in NFR history up to that point.

Ferguson was not a factor in the calf roping race: A red-hot Roy Cooper handily won that event.

But Ferguson's NFR earnings, combined with his year-end totals, approached the $100,000 mark. In 1978 he repeated as the steer wrestling and all-around champ, and

From 1976 to 1978, world titles went to the biggest money earners at the National Finals, with PRCA championships awarded to the regular-season top money-earners. Ferguson claimed both titles in the all-around during that three-year period.

Ferguson relied on perfect technique rather than brute strength to win at bulldogging.

he garnered in excess of $100,000 in arena earnings and bonuses.

By 1979 the PRCA had reverted to its old system of determining champions. Years before, Ferguson had been at a rodeo where Larry Mahan was introduced as having "a record never to be equaled, with more all-around titles than any cowboy in history."

Tom Ferguson, who was the reigning all-around champion at the time, had sat on a horse beside Mahan. According to one reporter, Ferguson picked at his saddle horn, studied the toe of his boot, and gave no sign that he'd heard the announcer. But after the ceremony, Ferguson's chin jutted forward and his body language seemed to say, "Well, let's just see about that." Less than three years later, he'd matched Mahan's record.

Today Mahan is still a celebrity in the rodeo world. But when Ferguson shows up at a rodeo, he seldom is recognized by any but the oldest hands, many of whom came along in the later days of his career. After

winning his sixth world title, Ferguson had a string of bad luck with his horses.

He'd always had exceptional mounts. His first horse, Kodiak Bar, C.R. Jones' horse Peanuts, Turkey, and Wonder Troubles were among the great horses in rodeo. After those, though, Ferguson admits that finding a quality horse grew difficult.

"Sellers would see us coming, and immediately double the price," said Ira Ferguson.

"I got to where I was training green horses, and I wasn't experienced enough," admits Tom. "I am not a horseman. I could get them to win, get them to the winning position. I would upgrade them, like an employee."

Time also took its toll. Ferguson began to lose a step to the younger cowboys who'd worked at and perfected their craft by observing men like himself and Roy Cooper.

Tom Ferguson played a big role in some of those cowboys' careers. And in some ways, he got as much of a kick helping them to win as he himself had enjoyed earlier in his career.

"Dave Brock, Jimmy Cooper, Chris Lybbert, D.R. Daniel—they were some of the guys I traveled with. They respected my judgment; they listened to me. I stepped up their abilities without changing their styles," he said. "I improved their thinking." Notably, both Jimmie Cooper, who is Roy Cooper's cousin, and Chris Lybbert claimed all-around titles in the 1980s.

Ferguson continued to qualify for the NFR through the mid-1980s, and in 1986 he became the first cowboy in PRCA history to cross the $1 million mark in career earnings. But the fire that had characterized his early years seemed to have left him. Ferguson had moved to Florida and was working in construction, and the grueling hours cut into his practice time.

"I'd work 72 hours a week and didn't want to go out and practice. I lost the desire to do it. I knew the preparation it took to win. When I went all the time, I was prepared," he said. "A couple of years ago, I went to Springdale (Arkansas). I was trying to get a business going, and I'd quit practicing, quit working at it. I had two good steers at Springdale, a good horse, and I didn't win. I was tired of going to rodeos, of hearing my name called, and that was it. I quit," he said.

Well, not entirely. Ferguson says he still gets out and team ropes. At the rodeos he likes to visit with old friends, but says he doesn't spend much time watching the young calf ropers and steer wrestlers who have taken his place among the contenders. "You reach a point where it's time to move on," he says.

Ferguson has two children, Matt and Marsee, the son and daughter of his marriage to his college sweetheart, Debra. Ferguson and Debra divorced, and Ferguson has been twice married—and twice divorced—since then. Today, he lives a bachelor's life in Miami, Okla., where he owns a landscaping company. "It's physical work, and I like it. My employees— me, myself and I—work pretty hard at it."

In 1999 the selection committee for the ProRodeo Hall of Fame in Colorado Springs chose Ferguson as an inductee. In the past,

Ferguson had declined the honor, an indication of the deep-felt rancor between himself and the rodeo association. Still, it would be a great oversight not to include Ferguson among this collection of rodeo's greatest champions, and the selection committee went ahead with the induction despite Ferguson's wishes.

But even in spite of the bitterness he feels about certain aspects of his former career, Ferguson recalls his competitive days, and the friends he made while competing, with fondness.

"I enjoyed the times I traveled, enjoyed staying at people's homes all across the country. I helped a lot of other cowboys. I worked hard at it," he said.

During his tenure as the sport's top hand, he held records for most money won at a single rodeo (Houston, 1979, '82), the fastest steer wrestling time at the National Finals Rodeo (3.5 seconds in 1975), and the most money won in a single season ($103,743 in 1978). Ferguson also won the National Finals Rodeo steer wrestling average award three times.

Although the earnings records have long since been surpassed, and the times whittled even lower, Ferguson will long be remembered as the most dominant figure of his era.

"It's always good to be important. And I was that," said Ferguson as he reflected on his long and celebrated career.

GAVIN EHRINGER

In 1999 Ferguson's son Matt got to see his dad finally take his rightful place in the ProRodeo Hall of Fame.

BRUCE FORD

BRUCE FORD is a cowboy's cowboy. Tough as the rawhide on his custom-built bareback rigging, as enduring as a pair of bullhide boots, he could have walked right on to the set of a John Wayne-era western. He was as thin as a straw of wheat, with long muscles stretched over a bony frame. His walrus mustache hid thin, tight lips, and when he smiled, his eyes crinkled into deep crow's feet, the result of squinting into a thousand western sunsets.

He was the real deal, a genuine dime-novel hero, the cowboy you counted on when the chips were down, who strummed a guitar and sang corny songs by the campfire, and who dealt with defeat as gracefully as victory.

But looks could deceive. Bruce may have had one boot planted firmly in the 19th century, but when it came to bareback riding, he was the future. His fully laid out, eyes-to-the-sky style had only recently come into vogue when he joined the professional rodeo scene in 1972. He called it "controlled exposure," likening a ride on a bareback horse to a boxing match.

"That first buck, you have to take it like a punch. Then the second, you duck and then real fast—pop, pop, pop—you hit back and take control," he said.

Although there were other riders who shared Ford's pugilistic style—the Mayo brothers, Paul and Bob, were among the earliest—it was Bruce who did the most to popularize it. Although his predecessor, Joe Alexander, earned five world titles with a riding style that resembled a man in an easy chair, Bruce set his legs higher up on the neck than anyone before, the better to grip the horse. In doing so, he claimed to get extra leverage, undoubtedly at the expense of being able to see much except open sky or the roof of a coliseum.

Bruce claimed victories and seemed attached to the spines of the bareback horses he rode. Although the older riders may not have favored Ford's radical new style of riding, the kids who came to pattern their riding after Bruce's loved it. Two decades later when Ford was still going as strong as the Energizer® bunny, there wasn't one bareback rider who didn't copy him.

"There isn't anyone out there who changed the event as much as Bruce," said 1996 World Champion Bareback Rider Mark Garrett. "He was darn sure aggressive, and he gave a horse every opportunity to throw him."

"He (was) an all-out rider," agreed Steve Fleming, director of media for the Professional Rodeo Cowboys Association. "Bruce is recognized as one of the best ever at bareback riding because he (was) so wild about it." So wild, in fact, that his peers saddled him with a nickname of honor: They called him "Wild Horse."

Bruce Ford was born and reared on the Colorado plains east of the Rockies, near the agricultural town of Greeley. Growing up, he didn't have to look hard for a role model and hero. That was his dad, Jim

At the 1987 NFR, Ford clinched his fifth bareback world title, tying Joe Alexander for the most titles in the event.

first to come up on the bus and, seeing kids scattered everywhere, they went right to picking everybody up and putting them in other farmers' cars. Going to work, getting us to town. That was what it was all about.

"A kind of calm came over them. They didn't panic," he said. Grace under extreme pressure was passed along to the surviving Ford boys that sad day. Jim and his wife had many other important life lessons to pass along to the boys: love of family, concern for the well-being of animals, and a deep sense of religious spirituality chief among them.

"The most important thing Dad taught me was love for family and the inspiration I had to seek Jesus as my savior," Bruce said some years after his father passed away on December 31, 1983. "You know, I think that is a very important thing in my life. We've had a good walk with Jesus. We're here only for a short while, and I am lucky to have (had) a mother and father who showed me that."

Jim also taught his boys about horses and about rodeo. In his capacity as a horse trader, Jim Ford acquired bucking stock that he would then sell to a local stock contractor. The Ford boys were keen to learn, and they were willing to try anything that came through their father's stock pens.

Colts, saddle horses, calves, cows, steers—nothing was safe from the boys' enthusiasm to ride. Jim was usually there to give them pointers. When they fell, he'd pick them up, dust them off, and admonish them to get back on and try again. Both Bruce and Glen, who would also make it to the pro ranks, gave their father all the credit for teaching them how to be cowboys.

Ford, a brick mason, horse trainer, and former rodeo cowboy. Although Jim didn't exactly dote on his three boys, he gave them love and attention in abundance. Home movies of the Ford boys at play show a father loading them on Shetland ponies, helping them build snowmen in the winter, and riding them around in the saddle of his horse. In some ways, the dad resembled a big, fun-loving kid himself.

But there was a very adult side to Jim and

"They were men, and we were boys, 16 or 17, and we won the money. So we said, 'We'd better go do this.'"

to his wife, Loretta, one that came to the fore in one particularly tragic incident that might have easily destroyed many families. On a misty morning in 1961, all three of the Fords' sons were on their way to school when the bus they were riding stopped on the tracks with a train approaching.

"The train cut the bus in two," Bruce remembers. "My older brother, Jimmy, was killed right along with 13 other children. The thing about it was, my parents were the

Bruce entered his first contest in 1962, a kid competition at the Brighton (Colo.) County Fair. Both he and Glen competed in the ranks of the National Little Britches Rodeo Association, which was and still is very active in the Centennial State. But as the two boys reached their teens, rodeo took a back seat to fast cars, fishing, and friends. It wasn't until they were nearly out of high school that the two returned to rodeo.

The Ford family was living temporarily in Oregon, and Bruce and his brother decided to compete in an amateur rodeo. Both won. "They were men, and we were boys, 16 or 17, and we won the money. So we said, 'We'd better go do this,'" said Bruce.

The two Ford brothers began contesting in small rodeo competitions with the goal of getting their PRCA cards. Bruce filled his permit in 1972 at the age of 19. He was encouraged to campaign hard by an accomplished local bull rider named Jerome Robinson. Ford borrowed a small sum from his parents and hit the road, eventually building to 100 or more rodeos a season. In his second full year of competing, Ford climbed into contention for an NFR berth, earning a top-15 ranking by mid-July, only to fall short of the goal by season's end.

But in his third full season as a pro, he made the cut and was put on the roster for the big show in Oklahoma City. At the time Ford was competing right alongside Joe Alexander, or "Alexander the Great," as he was known in the rodeo game.

Alexander was in the prime of his career, and he'd built such a comfortable lead in the 1974 bareback title chase that nobody could possibly have overtaken him. It was Alexander's fourth of what would be five consecutive bareback world championships, a benchmark that Ford scarcely felt he could hope to match at the time.

And yet, Ford outrode Alexander and a number of the other top riders that year, finishing the rodeo as the fifth-highest money-earner among the 15 bareback qualifiers.

It was a strong, if not stellar, debut. At that time the bareback event was crowded with talent. In addition to Alexander, Larry Mahan was still going strong. Mahan finished second in the bareback riding at the NFR, having garnered his sixth world all-around title only one year previously.

But it was a new generation of riders, most of them well-versed in the riding style pioneered by the Mayo brothers, who really shone in '74. Among Ford's peers was Coloradan J.C. Trujillo, who would

CAREER MILESTONES

Bruce Ford

born: October 7, 1952
Greeley, Colorado

Five-time World Champion Bareback rider (1979-80, '82-83, '87); PRCA Bareback Champion (1988).

1998 Coming out of semiretirement, Ford competes at the NFR for the 19th time, a record.

1991 Ford competes in his 18th straight NFR— five more than Alexander— and surpasses the $1 million career-earnings mark, the first PRCA cowboy to do that while competing in only one event.

1987 Ford wins his fourth NFR average and his fifth world title, tying Joe Alexander as the most successful bareback rider in history. His four average titles set a record. Alexander, a 13-time NFR competitor, never won the average there.

1985 Ford bucks off his second horse at the National Finals, ending a streak of consecutive rides there dating back to 1978—a run of 63 straight qualified rides.

1983 Ford wins his fourth world title, drawing even with Jim Shoulders and Eddy Akridge, but remains one world title short of the record set by Joe Alexander.

1982 En route to a third world title, Ford surpasses the $100,000 earnings mark, the first cowboy to do so in a single event. In addition, Ford claims a third NFR bareback riding average to bring his total earnings for the year to $113,664. Competing in regular-season bull riding, Ford qualifies for the all-around title race, finishing second at year's end. It is his only career showing in the all-around.

1981 Ford relinquishes the bareback crown to J.C. Trujillo and ends speculation that he might top Joe Alexander's record five consecutive bareback titles. Trujillo earns $11,000 at the NFR (to Ford's $8,000) and wins by $3,000.

1980 After falling behind Mickey Young in the regular-season standings, Ford rallies to win the final rodeo of the year, the Grand National at San Francisco. Closing the gap to less than $5,000, Ford places in four NFR rounds, wins the average for the second time, and by a margin of nearly $3,000 claims his second world title.

1979 When the PRCA reverts to the old system, awarding championships to whoever wins the most money for the year, Ford handily wins with a record $80,260. He also claims the bareback riding average at the NFR, scoring 719 points on 10 head.

1978 Ford jumps to an early lead with five consecutive first-place wins, a third-place finish at Houston and holds the No. 1 ranking through the year and into the National Finals. Ford wins the PRCA championship for the most money won, but loses the world title to Jack Ward.

1977 Under a new system for determining world champions, Ford finishes as runner-up to Jack Ward on the strength of his success at the National Finals Rodeo.

1974 Ford earns his first trip to the National Finals Rodeo, finishing 10th for the year in the world standings.

1972 Ford fills his permit, becoming a full-fledged member of the Professional Rodeo Cowboys Association.

Ford's wild style is evident in this winning ride at the Pendleton Round-Up.

DAN HUBBELL

soon mount the podium to claim a world title. Likewise, a young singing cowboy from Wyoming named Chris LeDoux. Also in the mix was Jack Ward, winner of the NFR average that year and a future ProRodeo Hall of Famer, and T.J. Walter, a Midwesterner whose career would include a dozen NFRs.

Other than his hard-charging style and a propensity to spur a horse with a degree of abandon that few others dared to match, there was little to suggest that Ford might emerge from this group to become Alexander's successor. But it didn't take long for the 22-year-old to begin establishing his dominance in the talent-rich field of bareback riders.

What made Ford different was his flashiness — if the other cowboys didn't think the horse he'd drawn was a winner, Bruce simply willed the horse to be better. Because of the wild way he flailed his legs, popping his chaps with each whipsaw motion of legs and spurs, he tended to make even a bad horse look as though he was a three-legged washing machine being shoved down a flight of stairs.

"His attitude is to 'try every horse and believe that you can win on every horse

you draw,'" quoted Randy Witte, then the news bureau director for the Pro Rodeo Cowboys Association.

Early in the 1975 season Ford went on a roll at the big indoor events, gathering $2,500 at San Antonio and $2,600 at Fort Worth, as well as lesser checks at Denver and Houston. For a while it looked almost certain that he would topple Alexander, but the more experienced rider prevailed by season's end, setting an earnings mark of $41,184 en route to claiming his fifth world title.

In 1976 the PRCA switched its system of deciding world championships. That year, and for the next two years as well, the winner of the most money at the National Finals Rodeo would also be the world champion, and a separate PRCA championship would be awarded to the rider who earned the most money over the season. The reason for the new system was that many of the world titles were decided long before the contestants got to the NFR — a problem that was resolved when the NFR moved to Las Vegas in 1985, and prize money was upped considerably.

However, at the time, the system quickly came to be criticized by top cowboys who competed hard all season, only to lose to a much lower-ranked rider when the top hands drew a bad horse or missed a calf at the NFR. Before the system was changed back to the old format, Alexander would be twice victimized, and Ford would replace him as the dominant bareback rider of the era.

In 1976 Alexander continued on his big roll, which stretched back to 1970. But despite winning $48,000 for the season, he watched as the world championship buckle was handed to Chris LeDoux, who had earned less than one-third as much as he that year. At the NFR, where the sudden-death world-title race took place, Ford opened the rodeo with a victory, and Alexander closed the rodeo with one. But neither had the juice to claim the world title, which went to Chris LeDoux, the big money-winner with $4,912.

In 1977 nearly the same thing happened again. Although Alexander won nearly twice as much as his nearest opponent, he lost the world title to Jack Ward Jr., an Arkansas cowboy who got very hot when the lights came on in Oklahoma City. Still, Ford was within shooting distance of Ward going into the final round. When both riders bucked off their final horses, the title went to Ward. Still, Bruce had his best NFR to date, placing in five rounds (including a 74-point win in round three) to qualify as the reserve world champ.

In 1978 it was Ford's turn to take the hit.

If there was any question as to who would succeed Alexander, Bruce answered it that season. He began in the dead of winter by taking the lead in the world standings, scoring five victories in a row at rodeos in Sioux Falls, S.D.; Odessa, Tex.; Denver; Rapid City, S.D.; and Jackson, Mississippi.

Things slowed briefly in March, and then Ford roared back into the lead with a third-place finish at the huge Houston Livestock Show. After that the 26-year-old rider piled on one victory after another.

At rodeos from Phoenix, Ariz., to Montgomery, Ala., Bruce dominated the bareback riding. During the hectic Fourth of July run, he captured back-to-back wins at Reno, Nev., and North Platte, Neb., two of the biggest rodeos of the summer. By the end of July, he'd won twice as much as Alexander, who trailed by more than $12,000.

It was almost a complete reverse of the previous season, when Alexander had a $12,800 lead over his next closest competitor. By October Ford was knocking up against Alexander's record for the most money won in a single season.

At the NFR it seemed at first that Bruce's incredible year would have a storybook ending. He won the first round, split second

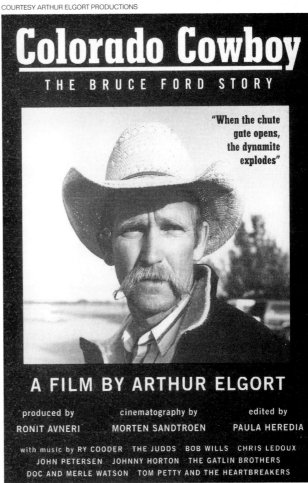

COURTESY ARTHUR ELGORT PRODUCTIONS

Fashion photographer Arthur Elgort was so intrigued by Ford's authentic cowboy look, he built a documentary around the cowboy's life.

place with Alexander in round two, and then won the third round. But then, in round four he scored a miserable 54, and in rounds eight and nine, he bucked off.

Ward, again the model of consistency at the NFR, surged ahead of Ford to win the world title with $15,000 in NFR earnings. As a consolation, Bruce had won the PRCA championship which, when combined with his NFR earnings, put him ahead of the all-time earnings record set two years previously by Alexander.

It was definitely a disappointment not to get the world championship, but Ford accepted it with equanimity. After all, Alexander had lost two world titles to the same system. But Bruce was glad the following year when the old system of deciding world titles was reinstated.

In any case, it would not have mattered which system was being used in 1979 — Ford dominated not only the entire regular season, but the National Finals too. He came into the NFR with an insurmountable lead in the world standings. Thanks to the bonus money that kicked in from Winston, he had already far surpassed his own record earnings of the previous year, racking up $60,000 by October.

But perhaps to vindicate himself after the previous year's loss, he set out to dominate the NFR too. "The finals was almost a letdown with no goal to shoot at," he said. "There was a slim chance Sam Perkins could beat me, and I didn't want to lose it

Following the example of Larry Mahan, Ford was thinking about his future beyond rodeo.

after working that hard all year. I began preparing myself after the Cow Palace, because I wanted to prove at the finals that I was the best in the world."

After a fairly slow start in the first four rounds, Bruce got tapped off in the fifth and won the round with 76 points. Then he placed in the final four rounds to seal the deal, winning the average competition with a score of 719 on ten head.

When the $15,000 in NFR winnings had been added to his regular-season total, Ford had an amazing $80,260 to his credit — by far the biggest sum of any single-event rodeo competitor in history up to that time.

By comparison, bull rider Don Gay, the second closest money-winner among that year's crop of single-event world champs, earned just a buck less than $60,000.

Bruce had always been a goal-setter, and now he'd finally realized his goal of winning the world title. Like many cowboys who achieve that goal, he seemed to forget that it was time to set new goals. In the fall of 1980 he had fallen well behind his friend Mickey Young in the world-title race.

Perhaps this laxness was excusable — after all, Ford was distracted by Susan Palmer, whom he was to marry that October. But the situation became dire when he realized that he was nearly $12,000 behind Young with scarcely a month remaining before the books closed on the year.

"All of a sudden, it was like, 'Okay, so what are you gonna do now?'"

Bruce remembers that he felt that if he could close to within $10,000 of Young by winning the Grand National Rodeo in San Francisco, he had a credible chance of defending his world title. He let his plan slip to the Bay Area press, and when word got around that Ford was predicting victory come December, that piled yet more pressure on the cowboy to perform. Bruce did, in fact, win at the Cow Palace, narrowing the gap between himself and Young to $4,725 when the Fords rolled into Oklahoma City for the NFR.

After mouthing off in San Francisco, Bruce felt that he not only had to prove that the last two years hadn't been a fluke, but that he had to back up his bold words with a title win. Adding to the challenge was fellow Coloradan J.C. Trujillo, who occupied the third spot in the world standings, just $635 behind Ford.

What ensued was one of the more exciting title bouts in NFR history.

After winning the first round on a horse called, fittingly, Easy Money, Ford continued making ride after ride. Meanwhile, Mickey Young missed spurring his horse out in the second round, then bucked off a horse called Rodeo Rose in the fifth. Trujillo, meanwhile, was hot and cold. After bucking off a horse early in the rodeo, he charged in the closing rounds, winning the ninth and tenth round. Bruce knew his best hope of winning was to ride every horse and hang tough in the 10-round rodeo average.

"I knew that I had a chance if I could stay with it in every round." Ford mastered his next four horses, then ironically drew Rodeo Rose as his final ride.

"I was trying to talk myself into taking it easy on that ride, but I also knew that I had to ride, and I couldn't just go out and do nothing," he said.

With the world title on the line, Bruce eased down onto the bronc and nodded for the gate. He rode as though the world title was at stake, as indeed it was, rather than playing it safe to make the whistle. Although Trujillo won the round and Ford failed to get a go-round check, he did win the 10-round average, which gave him the margin of bankable assets needed to steal the lead from Mickey Young.

After his 1979 world title Bruce had said that his goal was to "do this again and then announce that I am not going to try again."

Following the example of Larry Mahan, Ford was thinking about his future beyond rodeo. He was holding regular rodeo clinics and acquiring livestock to form a stock contracting business with his father. He and Susie had a new child, and Bruce made it a priority to spend more time with his family.

But midway through the 1981 season, Ford was having another brilliant year and the goal of snaring a third world title burned in his gut. Moreover, he'd decided that it would not be enough to merely be a two- or a three-time world champ. He wanted to go after Alexander's record of five world titles.

"Joe is every bareback rider's hero, and his record provides the motivation I need," he told a reporter for the *ProRodeo Sports News* in 1980.

Bruce arrived at the 1981 Finals with the lead in the world standings once again, but he was outdone by J.C. Trujillo. Ford failed to win the NFR average and was edged by Trujillo in the world-title race by just under $3,000. Frustrated by his lack of

SUE ROSOFF

The family that plays together: Bruce with wife Susie, daughter Courtney, and son Royce.

focus, Bruce resolved to make a more determined effort in 1982.

What followed was perhaps the most perfect season ever by a single-event rodeo contestant. For the first several months of the season, Ford went on an unbelievable run, placing at or winning nearly every winter rodeo.

By July he was far in the lead in the world standings when he tore off a 90-point ride on the horse Slim Jim Velvet at Nampa, Idaho. It was the second-highest bareback score in rodeo history at the time. At Cheyenne Frontier Days, the biggest summer rodeo, Bruce won a round and captured the average competition, boosting his season earnings by a whopping $6,600.

Realizing that he had a shot at the all-around title as well as the bareback championship, Ford shook out his bull riding rope and entered a few bull riding events in August. After placing in that event at a rodeo in Gordon, Neb., he became a contender for the all-around crown too.

Ford's dream season continued at the NFR. After placing second in the first two rounds, he took top honors in round four. He then placed in three of the remaining rounds to handily win the ten-round bareback riding average, the third of his career.

His total earnings that year were $113,644, making him the first cowboy ever to surpass the $100,000 season-earnings mark in a single event. He fell just $10,000 shy of beating talented timed-event hand Chris Lybbert out of the all-around title too.

Ford maintained that same frantic pace throughout 1983. Considering how many irons he had in his branding fire, it is astounding what he was able to accomplish. By one report Ford competed at 110 rodeos, produced 10 rodeos as owner of the Ford Rodeo Co., and conducted 6 bareback bronc riding schools during the year.

According to one source, Bruce got on 150 bucking horses that year—and didn't buck off a single one of them.

Again Ford went to the finals with an

Ford is one of a handful of cowboys who have been inducted into the Colorado Sports Hall of Fame.

COURTESY PRCA

insurmountable lead in the world title race. Clearly his goal was to win another NFR average. This didn't happen, but he did manage to place in six rounds and continue his amazing streak of consecutive NFR

bareback rides dating all the way back to 1978. Ford iced the 1983 world title with $84,126, trailing only all-around winner and calf roping champ Roy Cooper and saddle bronc rider Brad Gjermundson for the most money earned in a single event that year.

Ford's year, however, ended on a dark note. His father died on the final day of the year, leaving Bruce heartbroken. Managing the stock contracting firm had been a full-out family effort, and without his father Bruce wasn't sure that he could carry on and remain a top contender in the bareback riding.

With several months to grieve, Bruce reflected on whether he was living out his dream of being a rodeo producer, or his father's. He struggled through another couple of years wearing three hats: competitor, riding instructor, and stock contractor.

When he failed to repeat as world champion in 1984, he decided that what he really wanted to do, what he was really good at, was riding bucking horses. He began casting about for someone to buy his rodeo company, eventually selling it to his old adversary Mickey Young.

And Ford went back to riding bucking horses in earnest. He said that his dad would have supported his decision.

"Riding bucking horses was his dream, too, so I guess I am living out that dream too," he said.

By 1987 Bruce had reduced his distractions to a minimum. He was ready to complete his assault on Joe Alexander's record of five world titles. Now that the stock business was behind him, he found it more comfortable to stay on the road. Unlike many of the married cowboys, though, he did his best to include his family in his extensive travels, and he returned home each week when his family was unable to come along with him.

"My father spent important time with me when I was growing up, and I was determined not to shortchange my kids when it was my time to give," said Ford, whose brood eventually grew to include a second son and a daughter.

By now Bruce was no longer the new kid on the block. In fact, he was at an age, 35, when most bareback riders are retired or at least eyeing retirement. As he looked around the dressing room at the NFR, which had found a new home in Las Vegas, Ford realized that seven of the fourteen competitors had gone through his riding school as kids or teens. It was his 14th consecutive trip to the NFR, one more than Alexander. Another record. He'd already far surpassed Alexander in career earnings, and Ford was inching toward becoming the first cowboy ever to win more than $1 million in a single event. But it was the prospect of tying Alexander's five world titles that put a fire back in Bruce's belly.

"I started the year to win the world, and I wanted everyone to feel the heat at the NFR," he said.

The heat was that of a blowtorch. Having his typically consistent run, Ford began slowly, placing in two of the first six rounds. But in the remaining four rounds, he showed that he was still at the peak of his game.

He tied for third place in round seven, tied for second place in round eight, and closed out the rodeo with back-to-back wins. With just over $100,000 in earnings he had tied Alexander. But that wasn't all: As a four-time NFR average winner, he had exactly four more than Alexander.

Bruce Ford's incredible run of consecutive National Finals qualifications finally came to an end in 1992. It was his 18th straight trip. Afterward he continued to compete, but his attention turned increasingly to horse trading and the rodeo careers of his three kids.

This latter phase of his career was aptly captured in the documentary film *Colorado Cowboy*, produced by famed *Vogue* photographer Arthur Elgort. Ford had come to Elgort's attention while the photographer was doing a photo shoot with supermodel Cynthia Crawford in Cheyenne. During the day he would go back behind the chutes and photograph the cowboys, and he found his lens gravitating naturally to Ford, whose face told the story of a lifetime spent living the rodeo life.

"I'd been told about younger stars like Lane Frost and Tuff Hedeman, but I liked

Ford's career spanned three decades, earning him the nickname "Rodeo's Ironman."

this guy's look. You could see the years in his face and, to look at him, you just thought, 'That's a cowboy.'"

A cowboy indeed. In 1997 a fire broke out at the Ford family's ranch in Kersey, Colorado. A spark from a welding machine was believed to have been the cause. In any case, the indoor riding arena where Bruce had taught riding classes for decades burned to the ground, and with it a lifetime of mementos gathered on the rodeo trail.

In 1998 Bruce went back on the road. He claimed that it was just a whim, that he'd gotten a call from former student and four-time world title-holder Marvin Garrett asking if he'd like to join him on the trail. Maybe Bruce wanted to scare up a little scratch to replace the poorly insured barn.

Bruce was now 45 years old. Other than a separated shoulder in 1979, he had suffered no real major injuries as a rodeo competitor—one reason for his amazing longevity. But few thought that he could make it back to the NFR at such an advanced age.

"Society says you are old at 40. Well, lots of friends I know say you only get stronger at 40," said Ford, who ended up qualifying for his 19th NFR that year.

"Of course, they are all over 40."

DAN HUBBELL

MARVIN GARRETT

BRUCE FORD once said that, in bareback riding, the cowboy lights a fuse on a stick of dynamite, then he tries to control the explosion. Nobody — not even Ford himself — got as much bang out of a bucking horse as his protegè Marvin Garrett.

Garrett came along at the perfect time to apply his short, powerful physique to the discipline of bareback riding. In the late 1960s, bareback riding went through a radical transformation in style.

Although the great bareback riders of the 1940s and 1950s rode upright, their legs splayed out before them in a wide, stiff, "V"-shaped fork, a group of young upstarts led by Paul Mayo in the 1960s began experimenting with an entirely new form of riding.

Mayo laid back along the spine of the horse, eyes pointed skyward. By lying back, the rider could raise his spurs high on a horse's neck. With each jump, Mayo would draw his spurs toward the body, firing his legs like pistons in time with the horse's leaps.

What made this new approach possible was a stiff-handled riggin', first made of pipe or fiberglass, later of laminated rawhide.

Judges, at first, weren't sure what to make of the new horizontal style. Some rewarded the riders with top scores, while others disdained the new riding form and penalized riders.

Marvin and the All-Star Rodeo bronc Superstar collide at the '95 NFR.

One judge and well-known wit, Leonard Lancaster, went so far as to tell Paul Mayo, "If you had a spur on the back of your head, you'd win every time."

But young cowboys liked the wildness they saw in pioneering riders like the Mayo brothers. Bruce Ford, who rode upright before adopting the laid-back style, probably did the most to popularize the aggressive approach as he flopped and popped his way to five world championships.

But Garrett, who counted Ford among his heroes and later as a close friend and mentor, took the new style to its most ridiculous, artistic, and wonderful extreme.

A typical Garrett ride begins with the rider hunched up over his horse in the chute. A clenching of the teeth and a vigorous head nod, and Garrett lies back, his legs shooting forward to embrace the horse's neck as the animal rears out of the chute and makes his first move into the arena.

After a jump or two, Garrett finds his rhythm and then the fireworks truly begin. Although other riders try to stay centered over the horse's spinal column, Garrett tilts and tips, letting the horse whipsaw him along his rear flank before righting himself with an aggressive spur lick that squares him up for the next giant leap. Catastrophe seems imminent with each heartbeat, and yet Marvin almost always manages to stay in time with his mount and make the whistle.

"I don't think there is a bareback rider today who doesn't admire Marvin's style. And there isn't a one who can ride like

Marvin, myself included," says his younger brother, Mark. "He pushes control to the limit."

If there is one axiom that guided Garrett through his childhood days riding steers out on the plains of western South Dakota, it was that he could improve with each ride.

Marvin Garrett was born July 28, 1963, in the Black Hills town of Belle Fourche. His parents split up when Marvin and Mark were still in grade school, but his

"Phil was my hero because he did every event. Something about him just stood out in my mind."

mother remarried to rancher Dick Deyoe. The family settled on an acreage just the other side of the Wyoming border, near the town of Aladdin.

"It was a great upbringing," recalls Marvin. "We hunted every year and were horseback the year around. Dad ran some cows, so we were busy with calving, moving bulls in and out. When we weren't busy with something like

digging fence post holes, we were out playing cowboys."

The boys attended a country school with a dozen other students, all ranch kids like them. After school, the boys would saddle up and go riding, playing hide-and-seek on horseback (not as hard as it may sound given the rolling meadows, small canyons, and timber that characterized the family's ranch). Sometimes, they had BB gun fights in which they acted out some Old West saga. But their favorite pastime was imitating the rodeo stars they saw each year on the National Finals Rodeo telecasts.

"I can't remember a time when we didn't watch the National Finals," recalls Mark of his childhood. "We had a bucking barrel down in the barn, and we'd go down there and play at riding bulls and broncs. We would be Jim Shoulders or Phil Lyne or Larry Mahan, riding for the world championship."

"We would have an entire NFR there in the barn—10 bulls and 10 broncs apiece," Marvin adds. "And it was cold. The barn was a century old and built of logs with really tall rafters and stalls on both sides. But it didn't matter how cold it was outside, you were gonna buck that thing and work up a sweat."

Marvin's gold buckle dreams were also stoked by a documentary film he watched called *The Great American Cowboy*. The film focused on Larry Mahan and Phil Lyne, two exceptionally talented all-around hands with very different personalities.

"Phil was my hero because he did every event. Something about him just stood out in my mind. He was the quiet type while Larry was much more of a self-publicist. I guess I could relate better to Phil myself." Later in his career, Garrett would meet both legendary riders, describing Lyne as "a nice, humble man," and gaining Mahan's praise when the then little-known rider made a show-stopping effort at a rodeo in Pueblo, Colorado.

As a boy, Marvin set his heart on riding bulls. His first foray into rodeo competition was as a junior steer rider. When the family moved to Aladdin, the two boys would go to the local roping club arena and ride the roping steers for practice. That led to youth rodeo events, in which both boys were quite successful. By the age of 15, however, Marvin was due to graduate to full-size bulls, and his mother wouldn't let him.

"She told me that I couldn't ride bulls until I could sign my own (liability) release," said Marvin. Stifled but not deterred, Marvin simply shifted his interest to bareback riding, an event he found equally thrilling and challenging. His stepfather loaned Marvin an old two-handed leather bareback rigging, and Marvin entered his first rodeo in Hulett, the nearby town where he would soon attend high school.

"It was exciting, but the ride didn't last long," he says now with a laugh. "I was about 15, and had no fear at all. As soon as the ride was over, I wanted them to run him back into the chute again 'cause I was pretty sure I could ride him."

Now that the hook was set, Marvin began riding bareback horses with abandon. A well-known and well-liked local cowboy named Gene Griffith wanted to give the young kids in his area a chance to practice and improve their skills, so he convinced some of the parents to chip in on a herd of bucking horses.

A gather was organized on the Red Desert Wildlife Refuge in Wyoming, and the kids netted 30 head of practice stock. Marvin was among the first to try the new broncs, and he went to the arena twice a week to get aboard as many head as he was allowed. Mark began to join in on the action, and soon the two brothers became formidable challengers in Wyoming high school rodeo.

"At the time, high school rodeos in Wyoming paid cash prizes," recalls Mark. "It didn't take long for us to figure out we could make a little money at this."

As the boys progressed, they began to mimic the riders they'd watched competing at the NFR in Oklahoma City. And that didn't set well with Gene Griffith.

"Gene had that old style of riding, and he made sure his boys set their spurs before the gate opened. But I would leave my legs up, in a bent position because that's what the guys did who were competing at the NFR," says Marvin.

"Gene didn't agree with what he called 'the pro style.' I got a kick out of it. I remem-

CAREER MILESTONES

Marvin Garrett

born: July 28, 1963
Belle Fourche, South Dakota

Four-Time World Champion Bareback Rider (1988-89, 1994-95). Three-Time South Dakota High School Champion Wrestler.

2000 Coming back from injuries sustained in a near-fatal plane accident, Garrett wins the New Mexico State Fair Rodeo in Albuquerque & the Calgary Stampede en route to earning his 12th trip to the National Finals.

1998 Marvin Garrett is inducted into the ProRodeo Hall of Fame in Colorado Springs.

1996 After winning major victories at the San Antonio Stock Show and the Houston Livestock Show Rodeo, he goes on to claim victories in Pecos, Tex., and Dodge City, Kansas. At the NFR, Marvin looks on as his NFR average record is surpassed by his younger brother, Mark. He narrowly loses the world title to his brother at the National Finals. However, Garrett walks away a millionaire, having surpassed the $1 million in career earnings mark at the NFR.

1995 Claims his fourth PRCA world title by winning the NFR average with a score of 775 points -- precisely the score he'd earned when he won the average for the first time, in 1989.

1994 He has one of the best seasons of his career, winning his third world title at the NFR, winning the Coors Chute Out Series championship and the Wrangler® World of Rodeo Series championship.

1993 Garrett wins the $50,000 bonus at the Calgary Stampede and also claims victories at the Cow Palace in San Francisco and at the Dodge City (Kan.) Roundup.

1989 In addition to defending his bareback riding championship, Garrett wins the National Finals Rodeo average for the first time with a then-record score of 775 points on 10 head.

1988 Competing in his third NFR, Garrett wins his first world championship in bareback riding, defeating his mentor, Bruce Ford.

1987 Wins the bareback riding at Cheyenne Frontier Days Rodeo and the PRCA bareback riding circuit title in the Mountain States Region.

1986 Earns his first trip to the National Finals Rodeo.

1984 Garrett joins the PRCA and wins the bareback rookie of the year award.

Garrett on the sunfishing bronc Khadafy at Cheyenne, 1993.

DAVID JENNINGS

ber at that age, he wanted us to do it the way he did it, and we wanted to do it like we'd seen it done on TV."

Still, the Garretts were attentive students and gleaned from Griffith the techniques for properly and safely going about their chute routines and getting out of the gate without fouling. "We both owe Gene a lot," said Marvin.

In 1979, Marvin attended a summer Bible camp for cowboys to get some additional riding instruction. Now, he had some theory to go along with his practice. The following year, he once again returned to Belvedere, S.D., to take part in the camp. He

was anxious to meet Bruce Ford, who had committed to teaching the camp.

However, Ford was unable to make the trip, and bull rider Melvin Eaton substituted. Marvin was still using an old leather-handled riggin', and every time he tried to lie back on it, as he had seen Ford and others do, his hand would get yanked out. Still, things clicked for him at camp, and he began paying greater attention to riding form. By the end of the camp, he was voted "most likely to succeed," and awarded a trip to Bruce Ford's practice arena for a clinic, which had been promised by Ford to the rider who showed the most promise.

Before leaving for Ford's Colorado ranch, Marvin bought a used riggin', a Bob Blackwood number with a half-leather, half-rawhide handle that was much closer to the type used by the top professionals of the day. With the stiffer handle, he felt confident he could ride more aggressively.

His theory proved right — at Ford's school, Marvin was a standout student. On the final day, Ford even went so far as to ask Marvin to try out a new horse that he'd just bought. Marvin lasted a half dozen bucks as the horse jumped, kicked, and dove to the right. Although he didn't make an 8-second ride, Garrett earned Ford's praise for his "try."

It was that last quality—the willingness—that would prove crucial to his later success. As Garrett himself said, "Every time I see a kid with ability, I am really happy for him. But even if they have all the ability, they have to have the necessary mental attitude. The desire to get to the rodeos, to avoid the wrecks you can get into, and to get past the ones you can't avoid. I say a prayer and hope they have that mental strength," he said.

Garrett developed his own mental fortitude and competitiveness both as a rodeo contestant and a high school wrestler. When it came time for him to choose a high school (as a rural student, he had two choices), he picked Hulet High because the principal there, Dick Claycomb, was also the wrestling coach. Claycomb had seen the young man at a tournament, the first Marvin ever wrestled in and which he'd won.

Wrestling appealed to Marvin for the same reason he liked rodeo. If he failed, he had only himself to blame. But he seldom failed. For three successive years, Garrett was the Wyoming high school wrestling champ in his weight class. In 1982 he won the All-America Award in wrestling and was recruited by famed coach Dan Gables to attend Iowa State — an invitation he turned down when he found out the school lacked a rodeo program.

He did, however, suffer one defeat that would serve as a lesson throughout his athletic career. "Wrestling had gotten so easy for me, I would make games to challenge myself in the matches. My junior year, I was competing at regionals against a kid I'd wrestled several times. Everyone came to watch; they wanted to see a good match. I decided to try every move I knew on the kid," he says.

Having exhausted his repertoire of well-practiced moves, Marvin decided to try something his coach had shown him in practice, but that he'd never actually performed. He shot underneath his opponent to execute a move known as a roll-over cradle, but instead found himself flipped over onto his back and pinned.

"That was terrible for me ... I was really hot at myself. But I learned a lesson: Don't take anything for granted, stick to business, and don't showboat."

Garrett enjoyed ups and downs in the rodeo arena too. In his junior year, he set his heart on competing at the National

SUE ROSOFF

Calm before the hurricane. Garrett on deck, Dodge City, 1986.

High School Rodeo Association's finals but failed to spur his horse out of the chute at the state championship and missed his opportunity. The following year, he won the state championship and competed side-by-side with brother Mark for the National High School Finals Rodeo year-end championship. Mark had a broken foot, which was bound up in a cast, but he made a brilliant ride to win the 1982 national title. Marvin had a poor ride and dropped to ninth place.

All Marvin could say was, "Doggone it!" He went home in a blue funk that lasted for nearly a week. To this day he admires the tidiness of Mark's trophy case, which includes the National High School Finals buckle, a North American Rodeo Congress (amateur) national championship buckle, and a PRCA world champion's buckle.

His high school career behind him, Marvin briefly entertained the idea of college. He had numerous scholarship offers for wrestling, rodeo, and art. He decided on tiny Powell (Wyo.) Community College. After only a few weeks, though, he decided college wasn't his game, and he left to pursue a pro rodeo career. His coach and principal (whose daughter Garrett had dated for some time) counseled him that "only one in a hundred cowboys succeeds in rodeo."

Garrett, though, would not be discouraged: "I never doubted that I was gonna do it," he said. In the ensuing years, Garrett would run into his old coach, who had to concede that Garrett had made a good choice.

"He liked my attitude, my willingness to stick it out and make it work. I am sure that he is proud of me—now," Marvin says.

Although Garrett's future may have seemed too uncertain for the daughter of his high school coach, he'd met another girl who was willing to take her chances on the blond-haired Irishman. The girl, Lisa Vikula, attended school in Gillette, Wyo., and had met Marvin through an acquaintance. For both, it was love at first sight.

"She was from Minnesota and didn't know what she was in for," remembers Marvin. "We dated for four years and married in 1985."

By then, Lisa knew that rodeo was as much about thorns as it was about roses. Mark had filled his rookie permit in 1983 and thrown himself heartily into his rookie season. After exhausting his rookie partner Jim Reeves (the brother of many-time NFR saddle bronc riding contestant Tom Reeves) and rider Lonnie Hall, Hall suggested that if Garrett wanted to get to the

Hung-up and in trouble, Garrett looks for a way out at Pendleton, 1996.

NFR, he needed to find someone with equal ambitions. He suggested Mickey Young, a seasoned NFR competitor and world-title contender. Marvin met the rider at Longmont, Colorado. He called Young that spring to ask if they could rodeo together. Their partnership would last for four years.

"Mickey was a hard-core rider, always trying to improve. That was the way I thought, too, so we really clicked," says Marvin. "We were good for each other. My enthusiasm gave Mickey some new life, while his experience really helped me. To see what he did, how he did things, to be with someone who'd been to the National Finals … I was very appreciative."

But to travel with Mickey meant having to cash lots of checks. When the two started out, Mickey had an unlimited free airline ticket from then-rodeo sponsor Continental Airlines. Garrett had to pay for his tickets. "When I didn't make the National Finals that first year, I could see that my future in rodeo depended on qualifying."

Though he missed making the '84 National Finals, Garrett did win the '84 Bareback Rookie of the Year Award amid a class of young riders that included Clint Corey and Wayne Herman, both of whom would go on to win world championships later in their careers. And Garrett resolved to do better the next year.

"I wanted to make the NFR so badly. Coming from where I came from and knowing how hard I'd worked for it, I realized that I would just have to work harder. And that I would make it. The next season, every time I rode, I told myself, 'Faster feet! faster feet!'"

As his rookie season wound down, Marvin and Lisa wed. At the first major rodeo of the year, the National Western Stock Show in Denver, Marvin caught fire and won a check for $2,400. He could scarcely wait to get home so that he could show the check to Lisa. It was the most money he'd ever won. The next month, he won another big check at the Fort Worth

Stock Show. Word was spreading about the wild-riding young kid traveling with Mickey Young.

"After my rides, the judges were coming up to me to congratulate me. They would say, 'Man, that was some ride!' It reminded some of the Mayo brothers, which to me

"… I thought about how much I would give it when I got back to riding again, and I put that away and stored it up."

was a great compliment because they rode really wild but in control," he said.

But before he really got rolling for the summer season, Garrett had a disastrous setback. Traveling with Bob Logue, Garrett flew to a rodeo in Hugo, Oklahoma. The two were cutting a tight schedule, and when they arrived, their horses were already loaded and waiting. Garrett had a big buckskin who was unfamiliar to the rest of the riders. The horse circled to the right, and Garrett made a spectacular ride. But as he made ready to dismount, one of the pickup men's horses bumped his bronc and Garrett caught a foot in the arena rail.

Marvin's foot went numb and he recalls bailing off into a big mud puddle, raising a belly roar from his friend Bob Logue. But the laughing didn't last long when he saw that Marvin was seriously injured. Garrett had suffered a spiral fracture of the ankle, a bad break that would take him out of action for the rest of the year.

Lisa's job kept the couple going, but Marvin's spirits plummeted. "I spent a lot of time fishing and thinking. More thinking than fishing. I was out there sitting on the bank with this cast up to my waist, thinking about my family and my responsibility to them. I thought about how much I would give it when I got back to riding again, and I put that away and stored it up."

Rusty and still weak, Garrett mounted his comeback at the Denver National

Western. But the checks didn't come, and he wrote out a bad check to cover his entry fees at Fort Worth. When he most needed it, Marvin won the rodeo. "I've told a lot of kids that story when they were complaining," he said.

After the bad break, the good breaks returned to the rider. Bumped off the Pro Tour due to his broken leg and unable to qualify for 1986 due to the injury, Garrett earned a spot when two riders — J.C. Trujillo and Jo Jo Talbott—were forced out of the tour by injuries. Riding in the Pro

"I had a huge smile on my face. I was there to give the people in the stands a smile and show them something they'd never seen before."

Tour was a big boost for Marvin — he cashed in the final two rodeos of the tour and earned enough to assure him of a ride at the 1986 NFR.

By that time, Garrett was traveling occasionally with Wayne Herman, who'd already been to the National Finals twice. Marvin wanted to know what the experience was like, and Herman replied that it was overwhelming, that he had felt intimidated just being there competing against guys he'd looked up to coming up. But when Garrett pulled into Las Vegas (he was dismayed to have lost the opportunity to compete at Oklahoma City, having watched the NFR there throughout his life), he didn't feel the least bit daunted.

"I had a huge smile on my face. I was there to give the people in the stands a smile and show them something they'd never seen before," he said.

Marvin did just that. In the first round, he jumped out on the horse Butterbar of the Ivy rodeo string. The horse made a circle to the right, kicking, bucking, and snorting the whole way. Garrett ended up in a tie for first place with Clint Corey, the season leader going into the NFR.

Making the maiden trip even more special was competing alongside Bruce Ford, who had been Marvin's idol for as long as he could recall.

Garrett's chances for a world title would be stifled by a red-hot Lewis Feild, who cashed checks in seven rounds to handily win the ten-round average and overtake Corey down the stretch. But Marvin closed the rodeo as he'd begun it, scoring a knockout punch on the horse Blackburn of the Aber Rodeo string.

"That horse was cool," said Garrett, reflecting on the ride. "He would scoot out there, and it was like a stick of dynamite went off. He blew out strong, then jumped and kicked rapid fire. Real quick. On his first jump, he went way up in the air and I heard a 'pop!' I'd separated a rib, torn it away from the cartilage. It was a good thing it was the final round, 'cause I was sure sore."

Marvin won the round with 84 points, which helped assuage most of the pain he felt.

By 1987 Mickey Young was moving toward retirement and had bought a stock contracting business. Garrett was living out his dream, traveling part-time with Bruce Ford and Bob Logue. His brother had also joined him on the road along with Kenny Lensegrav, a young rookie who'd grown up competing with the Garrett boys. It was the beginning of a nucleus of young riders who would dominate their event throughout the 1990s.

Garrett was pretty high on his chances of winning a world title that year. It was his hope to catch gold while his mentor, Bruce Ford, was still actively competing. But it was the ol' Iron Man himself who dominated the action at the '87 Finals. Ford was on fire, cashing checks in six rounds and winning the average title. Ford won the grand sum of $53,353, clinching his fifth world championship to tie the great Joe Alexander for bareback world titles. Marvin acknowledged that short of winning the buckle himself, it was the best possible outcome.

"Bruce won his fifth world title that year, and I was runner-up. And I felt good about that. I thought, 'He deserves to win five.' He belongs up there beside Joe Alexander."

And it certainly wouldn't be Ford's swan song, of that Garrett was sure. The next year, it was Ford's turn to watch and admire. Now all of 25, Marvin came into the 1988 National Finals ready to shine. He'd taken the world standings lead during the regular season and felt confident that, if he rode to his potential, he could capture the gold buckle. He'd already proven himself a strong starter at the NFR, having cashed big checks in round one on both of his previous trips.

This time, he jump-started the rodeo with a 79-point opening ride to tie Lewis Feild for the victory. In the second round, he deflated the hopes of nearly every rider when he tied for second with Feild and Ford. Statistically, the world title race was nearly over. But Garrett never backed off the throttle. He iced the cake with back-to-back wins in rounds seven and eight, and surely would have won the average, too, were it not for a buck-off in round five that marred an otherwise flawless ten days in Vegas.

He mounted the stage to accept his buckle, a clothing accessory he'd dreamed of owning all his life. Years later, he would look back with humor to think that his feelings at the time were, "Why did it take so long?" For, as he added more buckles to his collection and wrinkles around his eyes, he would come to realize that at 25, he was still a wet-eared pup among the big dogs of bareback riding.

Dubbed "Marvelous Marvin" at the '88 Finals, Garrett returned to the '89 NFR as a definite crowd favorite. This year, however, he would find defending his world title more difficult than winning the first one.

Ranked third in the world standings going into the event, he was still trailing Clint Corey and Canadian champ Robin Burwash after nine intense rounds of action. He needed to close a gap of more than $8,000 that separated him from Burwash, who not only led the world standings but also had a legitimate shot at the $21,080 average prize awarded to the rider with the highest cumulative score.

But Garrett wasn't doing the math. He was figuring the man to beat was himself.

"I knew I had only one person to worry about, and that was me. If I won it or didn't, it was going to be good enough for me, because anytime I devote myself 110 percent, that's good enough for me."

Okay, so his understanding of percent-

DAN HUBBELL

Flyin' cowpokes: Marvin, Ken Lensegrav, Mark Garrett, and Larry Sandvick flank pilot Johnny Morris (center) at the '95 NFR.

DAN HUBBELL

Rides like this one, at the '94 NFR, earned Garrett the admiration of his peers. And, of course, four world championships.

ages was a little shaky, but his riding proved rock-solid. Garrett had drawn the horse Wiggles of the Flying Five Rodeo Company, on whom he scored 79 points to tie for third place in the round and lock up the rodeo's average title with 775 points. The average bonus was the boost he needed to pull ahead of Corey and Burwash, winning his second world title with $105,931.

No longer the youthful challenger but the man to beat, Garrett seemingly gave in to the complacency of a man who had fulfilled his goal. In 1990 the cowboy made the National Finals, but finished only eighth in the world standings. The following year, he failed to qualify.

"It was awful tough and probably that first week after San Francisco, knowing I didn't make it—it was tough," he said. "A guy has got to do a lot of mental work after a deal like that. It's a letdown. You've got to work on your mental attitude and get it back up."

Reality, he said, hit him square in the face as he watched yet another NFR on television, just as he'd done as a kid. "Watching that gave me a you're-late-and-you-better-get-started-getting-ready feeling," he said. It was exactly the motivation he needed to jump-start his career ambitions.

"It made me stronger, and I had to rodeo all year long and go to those fall rodeos that I didn't want to go to."

Re-energized, Marvin returned to the NFR in 1992, this time finishing sixth in the world. This was the year that Garrett's sometime traveling partner Wayne Herman made a valiant run at the world championship, getting battered, beaten, and bruised but enduring through 10 rounds to win the title. Marvin and his cohorts acknowledged that just watching Herman's trials fired them up and reminded them that the gold goes to the man who wants it the most and digs down the deepest.

Two years later Garrett was that man. He'd come close in 1993, but a bout of flu that may have contributed to his bucking off two horses in Las Vegas derailed his effort. He ended up third in the world behind Canadian Robin Burwash and Montanan Deb Greenough, the third-generation cowboy who won the championship that year. But there had been flashes of brilliance, most notably an 84-point ride in the third round that was the second-highest score of the rodeo.

Marvin's return to the throne was completed in 1994, when he once again put on a fantastic and wonderful show in Las Vegas. As had often been the case, Garrett jumped out in the first round to take an immediate lead with his 79-point victory. He then tied for second with rider Rocky Steagall in round two, and continued his march to the winner's podium by placing in two subsequent rounds. He led the world title race from start to finish. And although he finished only fourth in the 10-round average, it was good enough to help him maintain his No. 1 position and claim the third bejeweled gold and silver buckle of his career.

Marvin Garrett called 1995 "my Cinderella story." Sportswriters usually reserve that phrase for a breakthrough event in which an unlikely, underrated, or unranked athlete emerges as a champion. Garrett, working toward his fourth bareback riding world title, was already the most dominant rider of his era. So, the sense of what he was saying was that he was living out a fairy tale.

After dominating the action at rodeos across the nation, Marvin entered the 1995 National Finals with then-record regular season earnings of $94,713. Typically an explosive force at the NFR, Garrett cashed a third-place check in the first round and then seemed to go into cruise control, watching as his nearest rival, rider Clint Corey, banged out second-place finishes in rounds two and four and a win in round three.

Corey's strong showing ignited a fire in Marvin that awoke him from his trance. In an intense fifth round, all of the top riders drew from a deep pool of award-winning bareback horses. Garrett's ride was outstanding—a 79-point effort aboard the Calgary Stampede bronc River Bubbles—earning him fourth place in what might go down as one of the greatest rounds of bareback riding in the history of the famed rodeo. More importantly, Marvin stopped riding as though his world title were assured and instead began demonstrating the brilliance that had marked his riding all season and, indeed, throughout his career.

Tapped off and "in the zone," Garrett placed in round after round, capping the 10-round match with an 84-point ride aboard the horse Dirt Dancer to capture the average competition with a total score of 775 points. It was one point more than his nearest competitor, his younger brother Mark Garrett.

Trailing in third place was Larry Sandvick, a mischievous and charismatic Wyoming cowboy whose antics, both in and out of the arena, had earned him the nick-name "the Wild Man." When the points were tallied and the money added up, "Marvelous Marvin" had written himself into the rodeo history books with record season earnings of $156,733.

With the fourth world title securely in his grasp, Marvin Garrett was assured of instant acceptance in the ProRodeo Hall of Fame. But his fairy tale career was hardly over. There's no hiding the fact that Garrett was propelled forward by the desire to match Joe Alexander and his old friend Bruce Ford as the only men to have won five bareback world championships.

He very nearly did just that in 1996, when the title bout came down to the very last horse. Going into the final round of the NFR, the world title had yet to be decided. Four riders—Deb Greenough, Sandvick, and both Garrett brothers—had a legitimate shot at winning. The tension was palpable as the four cowboys awaited their rides. What happened next astounded even veteran NFR spectators.

Greenough cracked out of the chute, and officials invalidated his ride for failing to spur the horse out of the gate. Marvin, too, failed to score. Sandvick, it was ruled, had slapped his horse. Only Mark Garrett managed to make eight on his bronc, in the process setting an NFR record for the highest 10-head bareback riding score up to that time. The younger brother of the four-time champ wept in the hallway of the Thomas & Mack, sobbing that the win "wasn't supposed to be that way." But his older brother could hardly contain his satisfaction and pleasure at seeing Mark claim another championship for the Garrett clan.

"The thing that was neat about it was, we all came in there giving it all that we had. The ones who messed up knew why they had messed up. For me, to see [Mark] win the world title, he got to feel what I felt. I was pretty tickled. It was just as good for me. Better, really, than if I had won it," said Marvin afterward.

With so much good fortune visiting the Garrett family, there soon came a stunning turn of fate that would truly test their mettle and their desire to continue in the sport. On

November 5, 1998, Mark, Marvin, bull rider Thad Bothwell, and saddle bronc rider Scott Johnston were traveling in a prop-driven private plane piloted by Johnny Morris, a former bareback rider from Montana who had served as a charter pilot to the Garretts for well over a decade.

The passengers were en route to the Grand National Rodeo at San Francisco's Cow Palace, traditionally the final major competition on the PRCA calendar, and hence the event that often decides who does and does not qualify for the NFR. Marvin needed a big win there.

He'd been sidelined by a broken arm suffered in August at a rodeo in Colorado Springs, an injury that caused him to miss several months of competition during the height of the rodeo season. In the interim, he'd slipped out of the top 15 riders in the world standings. He needed a $5,000 boost if he was to make the season-ending trip to Las Vegas. He'd gotten himself mentally prepared to do battle, and was making the long trip from South Dakota to California with his brother, who also needed to win some cash if he was to compete at the NFR.

Morris' plane was in the shop, so they had borrowed a larger, more powerful Cessna 210 that belonged to saddle bronc champ Dan Mortensen. Unbeknownst to the pilot or his passengers, the plane had developed a fuel pump leak and its rate of fuel consumption was much greater due to a turbocharger installed on the engine—a power boost that Morris' Cessna lacked. Distrustful of gauges, Morris had estimated the plane's flying time based on flight hours and fuel consumption. But when he saw that the plane was indeed at less than one-quarter tank, he decided to make a pit stop in Lodi, Calif., to refuel.

"I remember looking down at the gauge and thinking everything was fine," says Marvin, who sometimes co-piloted the plane. "We were approaching the landing strip in an urban area about the time the engine quit." Morris reached for a switch to activate the auxiliary tank, but the tank was unexplainably empty. With no suitable place to land, Morris aimed the gliding plane toward a gravel road bordered on either side by fruit tree orchards. But the plane nosed down, crashing into the trees.

Morris and Marvin Garrett were immediately knocked unconscious, and both Bothwell and Johnston had sustained broken backs. Only Mark Garrett was relatively unharmed. He began pulling the other riders from the wreckage, amazingly getting assistance from Johnston. Morris, trapped in the cockpit, was badly burned as the wreckage caught fire, although he was pulled from the plane, miraculously still alive. But Morris would perish a week later in the hospital.

Marvin struggled to hold on to his sanity. In addition to a broken back, he had sustained a broken bone in his riding arm, just above the elbow. Due to the extent of the injuries, doctors postponed any attempt to operate on the arm, so they simply put it in a sling and gave the cowboy morphine. The drugs caused him to hallucinate.

"I didn't want to go to sleep, couldn't sleep. It was the worst week I'd spent in my entire life. Eventually, I told them to stop giving me morphine, that I preferred the pain to the drugs," said Marvin. Finally, his head cleared. Then he learned that Morris, with whom he had had a very close and special relationship, was dead.

"Johnny was such a good guy, such a tough cowboy. I knew he was upstairs (in the hospital), and I guess I just felt sure he was gonna make it. We were all devastated by the news," he said.

Garrett finally had the arm repaired, and he returned to his home in a full body cast. For the first time since he could remember, he was completely reliant on others, even for simple things such as picking up the receiver to answer the phone. His three children—son Weston and daughters Kassi and Kaylee—pitched in to help Lisa care for their dad.

Doctors had told him it was doubtful that he'd regain full function, and were even cautious about whether Garrett would walk again. But Marvin could move his legs, and he figured if he could do that, he could walk. And if he could walk, he could ride.

He began a long, arduous rehabilitation program. He'd lost the ability to use his right hand, and when feeling did return, his exercises consisted of tasks that most of us do without thought. Picking up a paper clip or a pen, for instance, or shuffling a deck of cards—something Marvin did over and over again.

"You should have seen me try and do that. I am sure it is the funniest thing you've ever seen," he said. Once he became ambulatory, the depression that had set in from being bedridden and from the grief of losing Johnny Morris began to leave him. One day, he left his room and slowly made his way down to his corral, where Mark and another cowboy were breaking colts.

"It gave me a big laugh and lifted my spirits," he said. By January, the cowboy felt well enough to travel to Denver for the National Western Stock Show to watch his younger brother ride. His face was still puffy, his body encased in its cast, but he was walking, albeit slowly. At the time, it took me about an hour just to cross a street," he said. It would be a full year before he was able to once again mount a horse and compete in his specialty event.

During his convalescence, however, Garrett was invited to serve as a broadcaster at the National Finals. He'd been sitting in the stands watching his brother through two rounds, then got the job doing radio play-by-play with cowboy Roy Lemmel. Having a role to play there, he said, sure beat watching from home.

"I was sure willing to be there in the front row, doing something. I had sat there the first two perfs, and it was a weird feeling not to be able to go down there onto the floor. I'd made my living down there behind the chutes. It felt like my home. To not be able to go down there among the other cowboys, that was sure a weird feeling," he said.

In fact, Marvin was not to be a spectator for long, at least, not in 2000, when he made his triumphal return to the National Finals, giving a credible performance and ending the year as the No. 11 bareback rider in the world standings at season's end. By that time, Garrett had already joined the exclusive club of cowboys inducted into the ProRodeo Hall of Fame in Colorado Springs, as well as crossed the $1 million career earning mark.

Still a tough competitor at an age when many rough-stock riders have already retired, Marvin holds on to his dream of capturing that fifth world title. He's never cared for all the travel, preferring to be

SHARI VAN ALSBURG

Wildmen Garrett and Sandvick take a break at the Deke Latham Memorial Rodeo, Kaycee, Wyoming.

home with his family on the 500-acre ranch he bought in 1989 with his rodeo earnings.

That, and the joy he finds in watching his kids starting to compete in rodeo, might keep him from ever attaining his goal of matching his mentor, Bruce Ford. Only, don't bet on it. Marvin Garrett may be an aging star, but he still has the fighting spirit that made him a heavyweight contender in the rodeo arena.

"All of my world titles were great to win; they all feel really good. But the two I am most proud of are the first and the last," he said, with an impish grin on his face. "And I haven't won that one yet."

DON GAY

AS THE Mesquite High School senior class of '72 sat through graduation on a warm spring evening in Texas, it's a good bet many of them worried about their futures. Not Don Gay.

"I stepped off that graduation stage on a Saturday night and gave my [step] mother a kiss and the diploma, and me and six other guys got into a station wagon and drove all night to a rodeo in Illinois," he remembers.

The following day, Gay won first place in the bull riding and second place in the saddle bronc event. He used a portion of his $422.50 earnings to buy steak dinners for his traveling buddies. Afterward, Gay called his father, stock contractor Neal Gay, and told him not to worry — he'd see him in December at the National Finals Rodeo in Oklahoma City.

Thus began the career of the greatest bull rider in the history of professional rodeo. But Gay's trek began years before, as a young, motherless child growing up around his father's rodeo arena, located about 15 miles east of Dallas. Don's mother died of leukemia when he was still a child. Neal Gay reluctantly quit competing as a bronc rider to take care of Don and his older brother, Pete. To do so, he needed a steady occupation.

With the help of friends and investors who included 16-time world champ Jim

Shoulders, Neal founded Mesquite Championship Rodeo in 1959. At first, Shoulders and Gay struggled to attract even a handful of spectators in the arena's 3,500 seats. It was hard work, requiring Neal Gay's full attention. Many was the time that Shoulders or Harry Tompkins baby-sat the young boys in the years before Neal remarried.

Needless to say, in his father's bachelor days, Pete and Donnie didn't receive much coddling. Before they'd even started grade school, the boys were doing chores around the arena. By the age of 5 or 6, they were loading and sorting calves and steers for the timed events.

But when there was a rare moment that he wasn't busy, Don Gay could almost always be found around the bull pens, watching the huge animals that must have towered over him like skyscrapers. It didn't take long before he was something of an authority on his daddy's livestock, and the adult bull riders came around to ask about the animals they'd drawn for the performances.

"Watching Harry Tompkins listening to a 9-year-old kid tell him what his upcoming bull was going to do, jump for jump, was quite a sight," Neal once remarked. "And Donnie very seldom told them wrong. He knew those bulls inside and out. And he couldn't wait to get on 'em."

Gay's dreams of riding bulls were inspired by Jim Shoulders, the most legendary cowboy of his day. Among Shoulders' 16 world championships were

The eight-time world champ makes a back-bending effort at Cheyenne Frontier Days, 1989.

a record 7 world titles in bull riding. Early on, Gay decided that he would win as many as his hero, mentor, and former baby-sitter.

There is no doubt Shoulders was Donnie's hero as a youth. A *Sports Illustrated* story noted that the young cowboy kept a photo of Shoulders topping a coal-black bull at a rodeo in Burwell, Nebraska.

It was a classic shot of Shoulders. The bull is suspended in midair, its eyes rolled

"Pain just didn't figure in. I hurt, but I stood it because I wanted to win so much. I made the necessary sacrifices."

back in its head, its nose high. Shoulders' legs are splayed out in a "V" shape, chaps flying, his arm taut. It looks almost as though he's lifting the bull like a dumbbell. As the writer notes, Shoulders' face is twisted in a grimace that, upon close inspection, registers a look of contempt for and sheer mastery over the animal.

"[That photo] used to give me chills and

make me want to go out there and get on a bull. It still does," Gay told the reporter.

Don and older brother Pete started riding calves as children. And although Donnie talked a good talk about one day being a world champ, he was fearful when, at age 7, he graduated to riding bucking steers. His father allowed him to chicken out on several head until finally his patience gave out, and he said, "If you don't go ahead and get on, I'm not gonna let you ride anymore."

Don rode.

By the age of 9, that initial fear was gone and Don entered his first rodeo. The competition was for boys 14 and younger, and the precocious Don finished second to his older brother. It's said he nearly wore out his red ribbon showing it to everyone he knew.

Don honed his abilities by riding steers every week. By age 13, he could ride every steer he drew with ease. He got his first chance on a full-size bull at a bull riding clinic at Jim Shoulders' ranch in Henryetta, Oklahoma. Although the bull wasn't even flanked and simply loped across the arena, it made no difference to the young cowboy: He was a bull rider.

Donnie continued to practice diligently, training on a black bull named Diesel Smoke from his father's string. The bull weighed 1,250 pounds, and would jump, kick, and circle in an easy manner. At first, Gay was tossed off the bull so often that he really thought he'd never master the animal. But within a month, he was consistently topping off the bull. That success fueled his desire to clamber aboard yet more challenging animals.

Neal didn't want his boys getting hurt, so he was strict with them. They could ride at home, but weren't allowed to compete elsewhere. Don, however, was allowed to attend summer riding camps at Shoulders' ranch. But he burned to hit the road, and that desire grew stronger with each passing year. Although he'd filled his rookie permit and gained full membership in the Professional

Rodeo Cowboys Association by age 16 (ironically, by riding a bareback horse named Teacher's Pet at a pro rodeo in Waco), his dad still made him stay home and attend to his school work.

"He was so anxious to leave and go rodeoin,' and it was even harder when Pete went out before him. He (Don) wanted to drop out of school," says Neal Gay. "I remember telling him, 'Donnie, if I have to handcuff our wrists together and sit in every class with you, you're going to graduate.'"

But there was never any discussion of college; Don Gay knew where his destiny led, and it wasn't in the bookshelves of some stuffy library but in the mud, muck, and (he hoped) the glory of the rodeo arena.

At 18 Don Gay couldn't be held back any longer, so his father sent him and Pete off with this stern blessing: "Boys, you can make this rodeoin' a good and profitable thing if you take care of business. Just remember, meet your obligations — and don't call me for money."

That year, Don, Pete, and Neal were reunited at the National Finals Rodeo in Oklahoma City. Don finished the season ranked eighth in the world; Pete trailed his younger brother in 13th place. Also among the top 15 bull riders was Jim Shoulders' son, Marvin.

Already, Don was establishing himself as a front-runner, even with just half a season under his belt. The following year, the freckle-face kid with the Howdy-Doody grin would begin to assert his dominance as the best bull rider of the decade — and one of the toughest ever.

In the first round of the 1972 NFR, Gay's bull threw him off. Don's hand was broken, but rather than be daunted by the injury, Gay simply iced it down before each performance and rode. He made qualified rides on seven of his ten bulls, including an 89-point ride that was, at time, the highest mark ever scored at the NFR.

"Pain just didn't figure in. I hurt, but I stood it because I wanted to win so much. I made the necessary sacrifices," he said afterward.

Don Gay again qualified for the National Finals in 1973, but this time he was in contention for a first world championship with Bobby Steiner, who like Gay was the son of a rodeo stock contractor. Gay and Steiner were neck-and-neck for the world title, and the two were virtually

CAREER MILESTONES

Don Gay

born: September 18, 1953
Dallas, Texas

Eight-Time PRCA World Champion Bull Rider (1974-77, 1979-81,1984).

1985 Competes at the NFR for the last time, ending his career after 13 trips to the championship-deciding rodeo.

1984 Comes out of retirement to win a record eighth world championship in bull riding, surpassing the record of his mentor, Jim Shoulders.

1982 Qualifies for his 11th consecutive National Final Rodeo, but is forced out of competition at the Finals due to injury. Citing injuries incurred during his rodeo career, Gay announces his retirement from bull riding at age 29.

1981 Increases the PRCA regular season bull riding earnings record for the eighth consecutive year.

1980 Wins sixth world championship by a margin of $188, surpassing legends Harry Tompkins and Smokey Snyder in titles won.

1979 Among the inaugural class of riders inducted into the ProRodeo Hall of Fame in Colorado Springs, Colo. Despite riding only one bull at the National Finals due to injury, Gay wins the world title on money won over the regular season.

1977 Defeats Randy Magers in a ride-off to win the National Finals Rodeo bull riding title. Tops the bull Oscar at the Cow Palace Rodeo in San Francisco for 97 points, the highest-scored bull ride in PRCA history at the time. Only eight rides were made on the bull, three of them by Gay. Wins first NFR average of his career.

1976 Rides the Kelsey bull Red One for 95 points to set a National Finals Rodeo arena record. Becomes only the second rider in 198 attempts to top the famous bull. Loses the bull riding world title to Butch Kirby under a new system for deciding championships based solely on money earned at the National Finals Rodeo. Gay was named PRCA champion for the most money won over the regular season.

1975 Competes at more than 171 rodeos en route to claiming a second PRCA world title.

1974 Wins his first PRCA bull riding world championship, surpassing the single-season earnings record set by Jim Shoulders in 1954.

1973 After bucking off his final bull at the NFR, Gay finishes as reserve world champion behind Bobby Steiner of Texas.

1972 Graduates from Mesquite High, steps off stage into an awaiting car, and wins his first two events the following day. Qualifies for the National Finals Rodeo in his first full season of competition, finishing eighth in the world.

JAMES FAIN

Gay, on autopilot, makes a huge move to stay atop the Ivy bull #14 at the 1985 NFR.

Harry Tompkins. He was Jim Shoulders' disciple, and he lived by Shoulders' dictum: If everything is going wrong, hold on. "You don't get a check for riding 7 seconds," Gay's mentor would say.

"Jim'd say, 'Stick your hand in there, hold on with your legs, pull up with your arm, and try, dammit,'" said Don Gay. And that, in a nutshell, is how Don Gay rode bulls.

But there was much more to Gay's game than mere toughness and try. One thing stands out in every interview, every story ever done on the rider: a self-confidence that bordered on cockiness. There wasn't a bull Don Gay didn't believe he could ride, nor a competition he didn't think he could win.

"I always intended to win, and there wasn't a day went by that I didn't think I was gonna be the champ. I think Joe Montana was like that — he wasn't physically the best, but he made up his mind. The name of the game is not to get close, the name of the game is to win it," said Don.

In today's top-tier sports, athletes have sports psychologists to help them overcome fear and lack of confidence. Gay had the mental game worked out more than two decades ago.

Early in his career Don traveled with Gary Leffew, a young bull rider from California. Leffew was very impressed with Max Maltz's ground-breaking self-improvement book *Psycho-Cybernetics*. The book stressed the importance of positive thinking and using the subconscious mind to influence one's actions and performance. Although many other cowboys (including Jim Shoulders) scoffed at the ideas that Leffew espoused, Gay took the words of the 1970 world champion to heart.

"Gary Leffew started me in the positive thinking plan when I traveled with him in 1972. I hadn't even won $2,000 by June when I graduated from high school, but I ended up winning $15,000 and making the National Finals that year. I just looked at his books, like *Psycho-Cybernetics*. And he had a little notebook that had little sayings like, 'Every obstacle is only a weakness in your mind. Be great because it is in you, if you only believe,'" quoted Don from his own small

tied for the championship going into the final round.

Gay had drawn the bucking bull of the year, Mr. Bubbles. For the first 6 seconds, the bull turned left, but then he turned back to the right, away from Gay's riding hand, and Gay was unceremoniously dumped to the arena floor.

Don at first thought he'd choked under the pressure, so later the next season, he chartered a plane to a rodeo in Madison, Iowa, just to give that bull another try. That time, the bull dispatched him in less than 2 seconds, and Gay realized that he'd been beat by the bull, fair and square.

But the experience of losing to Steiner made Gay even tougher. Don had never been a pretty, graceful bull rider like

notebook. "A lot of guys think it's silly, but I don't because I've seen it work with Gary, and I knew it would work for me."

According to Gary Leffew, other cowboys confused Gay's confidence with arrogance. But Leffew admired his young compadre's bluster.

"When he won his first title, Donnie walked over and I said, 'Let me look at it.' And he tossed it to me and said, 'Take a good look. That's the first hill on the way to the mountain.' He was the ultimate over-achiever," said Leffew.

One final element set Gay and his traveling partner, childhood friend, and saddle bronc riding champ Monty "Hawkeye" Henson apart: their willingness to ride anywhere and any day of the week to get a chance at a check.

When Don's career began, a cowboy could compete at as many events as he was physically able to enter. It was not unusual for Gay and Henson to enter 200 to 300 rodeos in a season, and compete at two-thirds of those. For instance, in 1975 Don competed at 171 rodeos—which may very well be a record. That year, he handily beat bull rider Randy Magers for the world championship by a margin of $10,000. In other words, Gay won three dollars to every two won by Magers.

Like Larry Mahan, Jim Shoulders, Harry Tompkins, and other top-ranked cowboys who preceded him, Don flew to many of his competitions. He even went so far as to get a pilot's license and bought several airplanes during his career. But when he was on a tight schedule, such as during the Fourth of July, he preferred to hire pilots. That way, Gay could catch some sleep in the plane, often the only sleep he got between rodeos.

"I rodeo hard all the time and I love to fly. But flying is a business just like rodeo," he said in 1978. "There's been some pretty good pilots killed in rodeo." Among them was George Paul, a gifted Texas cowboy Don counts as one of the best to ever straddle a bull. In 1968 Paul was killed flying his own plane in an accident that Gay, at least, believed was due to Paul's inability to

stay awake. Mindful of his own mortality, Don balanced the risks he took in the arena with the risks—like flying—that he was willing to leave to others more skillful (and better rested) than himself.

In the arena, however, Gay proved more than willing to take chances. Small, agile, and full of try, Don matched some of the greatest bulls of his era. Always, Gay hankered for the toughest bulls in the pen. He was known as a rider who saved his greatest rides for moments when all the chips were on the table.

For instance, at the 1976 NFR Don was in a close title race that came down to the final night. That year, a new system for determining the world championship had been put into place. Whereas all previous championships were based on money won over the season plus money won at the National Finals, from 1976 to '78 the contestants' slates were wiped clean at the beginning of

SUE ROSOFF

Gay, mobbed by reporters after setting the record for the highest-scored ride in NFR history.

the event. Whoever won the most at the NFR won the world championship. So, essentially, it was a 10-bull ride-off.

In the final round, Gay knew he needed one of two bulls if he was to win the gold buckle: Jim Shoulders' bull General Isomo (who would be voted top bucking bull of 1977) or Joe Kelsey's bull Red One. He drew Red One. Don was the last to ride.

Out of the chute, Red One twisted, spun, and bucked with remarkable speed, but

Like his mentor, Jim Shoulders, Don Gay didn't always know when to let loose of the rope. Hung up to dry at the '75 NFR.

Gay matched the bull move-for-move and made the whistle.

"I don't know how I stayed on him," said Don later. "Of course, I'm probably prejudiced, but I'd say that ride there is the greatest bull ride that's ever been made."

Indeed, Gay's 95-point score that night was the highest ever recorded at the National Finals up to that point. And, some 23 years later, Don's NFR record for the highest-scored bull ride had yet to be matched or exceeded.

Although Gay considers his bout with Red One as his best bull ride, others might argue that he bested himself the following year. At the Cow Palace Rodeo, which traditionally marks the end of rodeo's regular season, Don drew the bull Oscar, a huge, gray-and-black Brahma-cross bull owned by a group of stock contractors known as RSC Inc. Oscar was said to have thrown more than 200 cowboys in his career. In 1975 at the National Finals, the bull had sent Donnie sprawling on the arena dirt.

But at the Cow Palace, Gay got his revenge. This time, he made the bell and then grabbed his hat off his head and fanned the bull, to the audience's delight. The judges awarded him 97 points, the highest bull riding score up to that time. (In 1979, the score was bested by Denny Flynn, and in 1991, Wade Leslie was awarded a perfect 100-point score aboard the Don Kish bull Wolfman).

A *Sports Illustrated* reporter compared Gay's showy finish aboard Oscar to the moment Muhammed Ali stood over a fallen Sonny Liston, yelling at the defeated champion to get to his feet.

It is an apt comparison, because Don was proud and boastful and, like Ali, able to back up his words with his actions. Typically, rodeo athletes are modest and reserved. Not Gay. He was a darling of the press because he would make bold pronouncements. Whereas another might make a spectacular ride, and chalk the whole thing up to "the luck of the draw," Gay was willing to give himself credit when credit was due.

"I always liked Muhammed Ali," Don once said. "Instead of waiting for everyone else to tell him how tough he was, he told them. I'm more or less the same way," he said.

JERRY GUSTAFSON

Bullfighter Wick Peth steps in to free Gay's trapped hand.

And with his Texas drawl, his engaging smile, and his quotable witticisms, the champ became the media star, the go-to guy whenever a national magazine or television show host wanted to do a story on rodeo.

During his career, Gay made appearances on the *Dick Cavett Show, Good Morning America,* and on *NBC Sports.* He was also profiled in *People Magazine, Sports Illustrated,* and was included in a *New York Times* article on the ProRodeo Hall of Fame.

Speaking about Don and his sidekick, Hawkeye Henson, nationally renowned rodeo photographer Sue Rosoff said, "The thing that was neat about those guys was (that) they had these larger than life personas. They were just so charismatic. I never thought of them as heroes, because I wasn't there in that context. But when you saw how they were in public, they could be so charming. They were the last of that era of people who were rodeo cowboys, versus rodeo athletes."

Although Gay would identify himself as a cowboy first and an athlete second, he certainly bridged a gap that existed between Jim Shoulders' generation of hard-drinking, hard-living bull riders and the generation of college-educated athletes like Tuff Hedeman and Lane Frost.

Don might stay up all night, singing and partying with the band Ricky and the Redstreaks at Cheyenne Frontier Days, but he would get up the next morning, pop Jane Fonda's workout tape into a VCR, and sweat out the poison from the night before.

And although Jane Fonda certainly was no friend of cowboys, most of whom were politically to the right of Ronald Reagan, Gay was swept up by the aerobic exercise craze she helped to create. Just as he'd seen the benefits of Gary Leffew's mind-control exercises early in his career, he saw the benefits of Fonda's exercise program late in his career. In some ways, Fonda can take a small share of credit for Gay's eighth world championship.

By the age of 29, Don was ready to hang up his bull rope. Knee, groin, and shoulder injuries over the years had crippled the rider and made every bull ride painful. In 1979 he'd been gashed by a bull, an accident that resulted in 63 stitches in his left arm and lingering pain. The following season, he injured his groin muscle and had to sit out the final four months of the season. At the 1980 NFR, he was hit in the ribs on his third bull, and though he came back to win the following night, the pain was simply too unbearable for him to go on. Bull rider Denny Flynn very nearly overcame Gay, but Don's lead held and won the 1980 world title by a scant $188 margin.

Each year the injuries were slower to heal, the world title harder to earn. In 1981 Don went into the National Finals with a slim lead over Bobby Delveccio, a colorful bull rider from Bronx, New York. Gay bucked off four of his first five bulls. But with the pressure mounting, he made three

This 1976 ride, on Kelsey's Red One, earned Gay the highest score ever recorded at the NFR: a 95.

COURTESY *RODEO SPORTS NEWS*

spectacular rides on his final bulls, placing in each round to win his seventh championship, thus tying Shoulders' career record.

The following year, injuries continued to plague the cowboy. For the first time in nine years, Gay's name wasn't No. 1 on the list of bull riding's top money-earners. Charles Sampson, the sensational bull rider raised in Watts, Calif., had been topping Don all year. Gay qualified for his 11th NFR in 12 seasons, but finished a desultory fifth in the world standings — the lowest finish since his rookie season. Soon after, he announced his retirement.

"The last three years that I rodeoed, I got to where I didn't really enjoy riding bulls. Even when I was winning, I was hurting," he'd said.

Gay went home to help his father with the Mesquite Championship Rodeo, which had grown immensely. Neal's venture now included a covered arena, weekly barbecues, and an audience that boasted notable film and television celebrities; Dallas business executives; professional football, baseball, and basketball athletes; and prominent local, state, and national politicians. As he helped his family with the rodeos, Don Gay watched from the sidelines as young riders tried his daddy's bulls, riding to make names for themselves as Donnie had done more than a decade ago.

It wasn't long before the champion became restless. Two years before he'd retired, he had stated his intention to earn his eighth world championship. That goal nagged at him. Furthermore, the Professional Rodeo Cowboys Association had changed its rules: The riders had to limit their efforts to 100 rodeos.

Although Donnie didn't like the new rule, it meant he wouldn't have to go after as many bulls in order to win a world title—a fact that just might save him from further injury. And his exercise program was reaping rewards. For the first time in a decade, Gay felt good, healthy, pain-free. After 11 months, he decided to ride a few bulls and see how things went.

He cracked back out of retirement in the fall of 1983 at a special rodeo arranged for

President Ronald Reagan and guests. Don Gay's return to the arena was largely overshadowed by an accident that sent reigning champ Charles Sampson to the hospital with a shattered face. But it was nevertheless the beginning of a storied comeback.

Gay felt good. For the first time in a long time, he'd enjoyed riding a bull. Without the pain, the giddiness and the pure high of riding a bucking animal came rushing back. He felt like he was 20 again. He stepped up his exercise routine, began riding practice bulls, and reconsidered his goals. Perhaps his retirement had been a bit premature.

Don entered a contest in Hobbema, Alta., where he handily defeated a bull named Confusion, voted by cowboys as Canada's bull of the year. By January of 1984, he was back in the thick of things. At Denver's season-opening National Western Stock Show, he topped Steiner's bull Savage Seven, a former bucking bull of the year, then topped out his other two bulls. With a $5,430 paycheck, he had the stake and the confidence to mount a world title bid.

"My goal from that point on was an eighth world title," he said, "taking it one bull at a time. I also vowed I wasn't going to ride hurt, like I'd done all those other years. Riding hurt takes the fun out of it."

Gay continued cashing big checks — $3,536 at Houston, another $5,393 at Reno, more than $4,000 at Tucson. Don was having so much fun, he'd nearly reached the 100-rodeo limit by July. The new 100-rodeo rule forced him to slow down, which was hard for someone who was used to riding nearly every day, all-season long.

At the Cow Palace, the final rodeo of the season, Gay bucked off a bull that he felt wasn't any tougher than the practice bulls back home. So, to hone his edge for the NFR in December, he returned to Mesquite, topped off most of the bulls in his father's herd, threw in a win at a jackpot bull riding event at the famous Fort Worth honky-tonk Billy Bob's Texas, and packed his bags for the NFR.

"I really worked on conditioning my mind the last month going into the National Finals. Riding bulls is not like riding

COURTESY PRCA

Don and his dad, Neal, are both honored in the ProRodeo Hall of Fame in Colorado.

a bicycle. It's chicken one day, feathers the next. When things are going well, you get the feeling you can't do anything wrong, and then suddenly something goes wrong — you're not riding well, you're not placing — and you're bothered."

But Don wasn't troubled by anything — no injuries, no self-doubts — as he vied for his record eighth world championship. At the NFR, he rode seven of his ten bulls, placing in three go-rounds. In the world championship race, Gay handily defeated Charles Sampson by a margin of $11,512. As he walked out of the arena, his hero, his mentor, and yes, his former baby-sitter, stood by the arena gate.

Jim Shoulders was the first to offer his handshake in congratulations.

Don Gay amassed more than $650,000 in his professional rodeo career. His record of eight world titles in bull riding remains unchallenged. He was an original inductee into the ProRodeo Hall of Fame in Colorado Springs, and is honored in the rodeo wing of the Cowboy Hall of Fame in Oklahoma City. Today, Gay works as a stock contractor and serves as a television commentator for the Mesquite Championship Rodeo and the Professional Bull Riders.

FRED NYULASSY

TUFF HEDEMAN

AT THE SUMMIT of every sport are men and women who combine natural athleticism with heart, desire, and mental strength. Often, their appeal transcends their sport and makes them household names, what we call superstars. Athletes such as Tiger Woods, Steffi Graf, John Elway, and Michael Jordan. Then there is the rare athlete who lacks the physical gifts, but nonetheless proves that heart and desire are the most important qualities of all. Tuff Hedeman is just such an athlete.

In a schoolyard filled with kids, Richard Neale Hedeman would have been the last boy you might have picked to become a rodeo bull rider, much less a world champion. A gawky, scrawny, awkward child, Hedeman had Howdy-Doody hair that sprouted a perpetual cowlick, crooked teeth, hand-me-down shirts, and Coke®-bottle-bottom glasses. He was pigeon-toed and so uncoordinated he'd trip over his own feet. Clearly, he lacked the raw physical attributes of an athlete. But he did have one thing that was essential to a rodeo bull rider: toughness. How he got his nickname would later become the stuff of rodeo lore.

One day when he was 6 years old, he went for a ride to the local feed store with a friend of the family, an old rodeo hand named Tater Decker. When Decker closed the passenger door, he saw a pained look on the boy's face and traced the distress down

"Tuff rides ugly," said Don Gay of Hedeman. But what the bull rider lacked in grace he made up for in guts and heart. Hedeman at Salinas, 1990.

to a small hand caught between the door and the jamb. Decker immediately hustled around the pickup to open the door. All the while, the boy made not a peep.

"I had creases in my fingers. He asked me if I was all right. And I said, 'Yeah, I guess so.' I didn't make a fuss about it. And he said, 'Well, I guess you are a pretty tough nut.'"

Decker knew a good nickname when he came on one, so he took to calling the boy "Tough Nut," which eventually was shortened simply to "Tuff." Although he'd later grow into the name and take it as his own, Hedeman wasn't pleased with the nickname at the time.

"It was a name that, as I grew up, I despised. I wouldn't dare tell someone my name was Tuff. I'd tell them it was Richard Neale, or Rick, or Neale. But I wouldn't tell them it was Tuff. It's like, 'So you're Tuff? Well, how tough are you?' Having to fight my way through school was not my idea of a good time" he said.

Still, he wasn't one to back down from a fight either. A young cowboy who was part of the junior rodeo scene remembers the day Tuff showed up at a competition in El Paso. "He had on these glasses that were as thick as they come. We started kidding him, and he didn't like it. And he wanted to fight, those sorts of things. Yeah, he was a tough kid. The name fit him."

Despite their initial hostility, Hedeman and the other young rough-stock rider, Cody Lambert, became close friends and later traveling partners. Like Hedeman's father, Red, Lambert's dad was in the race horse

SUE ROSOFF

fast, and I won first place. I got a blue ribbon. And I was hooked."

The judges might have awarded him first place because he rode that calf well. More likely, they simply felt that he demonstrated the greatest amount of "try," the word cowboys use to describe a heart-bursting desire to succeed. Regardless, what was important was that the recognition would set the course of Hedeman's life. Had he not won that day, we might very well not be telling his story here. Because after that first taste of success, Hedeman would face many disappointments on his way to becoming a rodeo cowboy.

Years later, Hedeman's friend, seven-time world champion all-around cowboy Ty Murray, would say, "Here's a kid who had nothin' going for him. Nothin'. And he goes to this little calf riding and wins first place. I think that made a huge impact on him."

Hedeman remembers the many practice sessions at which he would tag along with his older brother, Roach, and the three Lambert brothers. "We practiced riding bulls every week. If there were six guys, I would have been ranked sixth. If there were eight guys, I would have been ranked eighth. I gave it all I had every time, but I just didn't have it. I was a slow learner," said Hedeman, who reputedly set records in El Paso for lasting only one jump. "Most people would have said, 'Hey, give it up. Take up finger-painting. You know, anything else. It wasn't until I was a junior, senior in high school that I began to have any success."

business. Possessed with great natural talent, Cody served as a mentor and coach to Hedeman and a raft of young cowboys who came out of that area.

It's hard to say why the older boy felt that he should take Hedeman under his wing, for nothing indicated that the gawky kid had any hope of ever becoming a cowboy of Lambert's caliber. The last of seven children, Tuff was born in El Paso, Tex., in 1963. His parents owned a cattle ranch and his father

"I gave it all I had every time, but I just didn't have it. I was a slow learner."

had a keen interest in rodeo, which gave Tuff ample opportunity to ride and rope. Clearly, Tuff wanted to be a cowboy just like dad and his older brother, Roach. But if it were not for a fortuitous event that happened when he was just 4 years old, it's doubtful Tuff would have stuck it out. That was the age at which Tuff competed for the first time, in a calf riding event.

"I was scared to death," he recalls. "The calf ran straight down the arena pretty

Cody Lambert pretty much ignored the younger boy until it became clear to him that Tuff didn't know the word quit. Once he saw the determination in the young kid's eyes, Lambert applied himself to helping Tuff become a better rider. But talk about tough love — Cody nearly loved Tuff to death.

"Cody just wouldn't let me give up. I'd buck off, and other guys would tell me that was okay. But Cody would tell me what I did wrong and say there wasn't any excuse for not trying harder than I was. He expected me to get better. I felt like I had to."

About the time that his riding seemed to click, Tuff's path crossed that of another aspiring bull rider whose star would forever be hitched to Hedeman's wagon. While competing at a national high school rodeo competition in Yakima, Wash., Hedeman met an Oklahoman named Lane Frost. The two were instant natural rivals.

Frost was everything that Tuff was not. Dark-haired with pale blue eyes and long, dark lashes, he was disarmingly handsome, the kind of boy every young girl dreams of dating. His personality was outgoing but never boisterous or egotistical. He exuded a charm that made people want to immediately befriend him. Moreover, Frost was a natural athlete who possessed the fluid grace that Hedeman would never have. In 1981 Tuff was the reserve champion bull rider in the National High School Rodeo Association; Lane was the national champ.

After graduating from high school in 1981, Tuff followed his pal Cody Lambert to Sul Ross State University in Alpine, Texas. John Mahoney headed the rodeo program there. Over the years, Mahoney coached some of rodeo's greatest athletes including Stran Smith, Trevor Brazile, Kory Koontz, Rich Skelton, and Guy Allen. But Mahoney still holds Hedeman up as the standard for hard work and determination.

"Tuff was 18 ... and had more try than talent. You could see the potential, but he didn't have any natural ability," Mahoney remembers.

While practicing at Sul Ross, the other cowboys would typically leave the rankest, most treacherous bulls for Hedeman. The cowboy never complained. Hedeman would often cling to his handhold long after anyone else would have given up, and that impressed Mahoney. When it came time to pick the sixth man for the Sul Ross squad to compete at the 1982 College National Finals Rodeo, Mahoney passed up a senior and chose Tuff instead. The decision caused some of the team members to grumble, but Mahoney felt that the sophomore had earned the honor.

CAREER MILESTONES

Richard "Tuff" Hedeman

born: March 2, 1963
El Paso, Texas

Three-Time PRCA Bull Riding World Champion (1986, '89, '91); PBR Bull Riding champ (1995).

1996 Hedeman repeats as Cheyenne Frontier Days champ and is inducted into the ProRodeo Hall of Fame. He qualifies for his 12th National Finals Rodeo.

1995 In July Hedeman wins the bull riding at Cheyenne Frontier Days. Competing in the Pro Bull Riders finals in October, he is severely injured by the bull Bodacious. However, he claims the PBR world championship with more than $126,000 won. Six weeks later, he draws the bull again at the National Finals Rodeo, but declines to ride. Bodacious is retired later that week.

1994 Helps establish the Professional Bull Riders association, which he serves as president.

1993 Surpasses $1 million in career earnings after finishing third at the famed Calgary Stampede. Conquers the bull Bodacious at a bull riding event in Long Beach, Calif., calling it "the best ride I've ever made." At the NFR, he bucks off in the eighth round and experiences temporary paralysis. Successful neck surgery allows him to return to competition after a year's hiatus from the arena.

1991 Wearing the No. 13 back number at the NFR, Hedeman claims his third-and-final PRCA bull riding world title.

1990 At the NFR, Hedeman bucks off the bull Stinger and gets hung up in his rope for more than 90 seconds. Unscathed, he returns to compete in the closing rounds of competition.

1989 Hedeman wins his second world championship in the final round of the NFR, fanning his bull for an extra 8 seconds in memory of his fallen friend Lane Frost. Winner of the '89 PRCA NFR bull riding average for the highest score on 10 head.

1987 Wins the National Finals Rodeo bull riding average for the highest cumulative score on 10 rides.

1986 Leading the world standings going into the NFR, Hedeman encounters trouble during the finals, but rallies to claim his first world championship in bull riding.

1985 After jumping to the lead in the PRCA world standings with an early-season win at Fort Worth and holding that lead all season, Hedeman loses the world title to Ted Nuce in the final round of the National Finals Rodeo.

1984 Traveling with Cody Lambert, Bart Wilkinson, and Lane Frost, Hedeman qualifies for his first National Finals Rodeo.

1982 Picked for the last spot on his college team, the sophomore leads Sul Ross State University to the National Intercollegiate Rodeo Association men's championship and wins the bull riding.

1981 Receives scholarship to attend Sul Ross State in Alpine, Texas.

1980-1981 Claims New Mexico High School Rodeo all-around and bull riding titles, a reserve championship at the National High School Finals Rodeo, and wins the George Paul Memorial Bull Riding Award at the American Junior Rodeo Association Finals.

As it turned out, the chance to win the national team title rested solely on Tuff's shoulders. It all came down to the final bull on the final night. The bull, 222, was a veteran that had unseated riders throughout the season and gone unridden at the College Finals. Adding to the pressure was the announcer, who pumped the suspense by telling the crowd, "This is it, the whole thing boils down to the last ride."

"I never wanted to get something over with so bad in my life," remembers Hedeman many years later.

With the tenacity of a bulldog, Hedeman rode the bull to the bell to clinch the title for Sul Ross State. While the rest of the team gave each other high-fives in celebration, Hedeman went off to be alone behind the chutes. Mahoney went to him.

"It was a pretty emotional moment, and Tuff said to me, 'You're one of the first guys who ever believed in me.' To that, Mahoney replied, 'It doesn't matter if you'd ridden that last bull or not. I'd have believed in you anyway."

The following year, Hedeman was a full-fledged team member at Sul Ross. On the last night of the College Finals, he topped off the Marvin Brookman bull C14 to win the bull riding average, the bull riding championship, and give Sul Ross the national title for the second consecutive year.

Throughout his college career, Hedeman squared off against his nemesis, Lane Frost. And although Frost seldom voiced his cravings to beat the raw-boned Texan, Hedeman was outspoken in his desire to beat Frost like a dirty rug.

"Lane was the guy I wanted to be and to beat. In my eyes, he was a lot prettier and rode better," said Hedeman. In an event where half the points go to the rider and the other half to the animal, Hedeman was at a disadvantage. Whereas a stylist like Lane Frost could make an average bull look fantastic, Hedeman shined brightest on the bulls that wanted to plant a cowboy deep in the dirt, then come back to dig a grave. His style was different than most of the bull riders, and it took some time for judges to recognize his talent and reward him for mastering the toughest bulls.

Eight-time world champ Don Gay said it best: "Tuff rides ugly." Whereas Frost eased into his rides like a surfer dropping into a wave, Hedeman's style was ham-fisted and chunky. Most riders at the time wrapped the barrel of the bull with their legs dangling and their feet turned out. Instead, Hedeman hitched his legs up on the bull's shoulders like a jockey. His long torso extended out over the bulls' heads like a buzzard perching on a tree branch. But on the rankest bulls, Hedeman seldom faltered. Many times he would get pulled over onto his side, his body parallel with the ground, seemingly poised to fall, and then right himself to make the bell. He was living proof of the bull rider's credo: The guy who tries the hardest wins.

Hedeman, Frost, and another up-and-comer, a soft-spoken Texan named Jim Sharp, elevated the level of bull riding in the 1980s. Cody Lambert, the fourth wheel of their rolling caravan, said of his younger peers, "They rode like you wouldn't believe. Some people go on streaks and win

Though not known as a bronc rider, Tuff could make a respectable ride.

GALLAGHER

Hedeman convened an impromptu clown convention when he got hung up on the Vold bull Stinger at the 1990 NFR.

a few rodeos. But those guys did it for years. Up to that point, if you rode 50 or 60 percent of your bulls, you were a top guy. If you wanted to be a contender against Tuff, Lane, and Jim, you had to ride 90 percent of your bulls."

Frost and Hedeman qualified for their first National Finals in 1984, finishing ninth and tenth in the world, respectively. Hedeman had left his ugly duckling past behind. He gave up the thick glasses for contacts, got his teeth straightened, and wore stylish shirts. He was competing against his heroes and was proud to be among them. And he'd met a beautiful young woman named Tracy at the National Finals, and the two were soon engaged to be married.

Tuff partnered up with Lane Frost in 1985, and the duo laid siege to the bull riding standings. Tuff's $10,000 win at the first major rodeo of the year in Denver was followed by a $9,000 victory at Fort Worth. Hedeman seemed to be propelling himself toward the inevitable world title in

December. The National Finals Rodeo was moving that year to Las Vegas, where the prize money was bigger than it had ever been. Winning became a habit, and when the newlywed cowboy and his sparkling wife rolled into the neon glow of Vegas in December, his confidence was soaring.

"1985 was the year I felt 99.9 percent sure I was gonna be the world champion," he said. Midway through the 10-round rodeo, Hedeman had won a round and finished second in another, and it appeared that the championship would indeed be his.

But his carefully woven season began to unravel in rounds six and seven, when Hedeman bucked off his bulls. Still, as he taped up for the final round, he maintained a narrow lead in the world title race that he'd led for 364 days, 23 hours. Then, Hedeman bucked off his tenth and final bull. Ted Nuce kept his seat, winning the 10-round average, which was the bump he needed to pass Hedeman and snatch the lead in the world standings.

The next year, Hedeman again led the world title race going into the season-ending NFR. After bucking off in the first two rounds, it once more appeared that the title would slip through his fingers. Rodeo pundits recalled how he had "choked" the previous year, wondering if Hedeman had the right stuff when the pressure was extreme. Hedeman answered the critics by rallying, cashing checks in six of the remaining eight rounds to place second in the average behind his buddy, Lane, and first in the world ahead of Ted Nuce.

At 23 Hedeman was a champion. It was more than a dream come true for a once-awkward kid who dared not to even think that one day he'd be hailed as one of the greatest cowboys to ever straddle a bull.

"When you walk up on the stage and they hand you a beautiful gold buckle with diamonds in it, that's great. But when that buckle says you're the world champion, it doesn't get any better than that," said Tuff.

In 1987 Lane Frost got to taste the champagne and strap on the gold buckle. Again,

GAVIN EHRINGER

Tuff took the loss of the Bud Light Cup championship in 1996 hard, saying, "It hurt worse than getting hit in the head by that white bull (Bodacious)."

Ted Nuce was the loser. In the final round, Nuce had been unceremoniously dumped in the dirt by a bull named Red Rock, an assist that helped hand Frost the win. The baby-faced Californian had entered the rodeo with a $1,000 lead over Frost, but walked away trailing Lane by more than $4,000.

The next year was Sharp's turn to win the title, which he accomplished in thrilling style by riding 10 straight bulls—the first time anyone had ridden all 10 bulls at the NFR. Sharp, who had enjoyed regular season strings of 57 consecutive rides in 1986 and 51 straight in 1987, scarcely realized the magnitude of what he had accomplished. But he shared the credit for his amazing successes with his traveling mates.

"The good old days really started for me in 1986, when Tuff asked me at Denver if I wanted to rodeo with him, Cody, and Lane. I thought that was the neatest thing in the world. It was nearly as neat for me as winning the world," he said in a memorial article he wrote about the 1988 NFR. "We had so much fun together, and when we showed up, we always won something. They say you're as good as the company you keep, and I couldn't have kept any better company than that."

Indeed, the quartet of Hedeman, Frost, Clint Branger, and Sharp were like rock stars when they arrived at rodeos. But it was Frost, as always, who attracted the biggest crowd of buckle bunnies and auto-graph-seeking kids. It sometimes bothered the other guys when, after a rodeo, Frost would sign autographs for an hour or more while they waited by their van, impatient to get to the next competition or just to catch some sleep at the Holiday Inn. Frost, however, was not bothered by the yoke of stardom—something that Hedeman, who could be curt at times with fans, would later come to understand and even appreciate.

Frost's fame did not diminish as a result of Sharp's victory. If anything, he'd become even more beloved as a result of a series of matched rides held in 1988 that pitted him against the bull Red Rock, considered by many to be the greatest bull in rodeo history. During the 1988 season, stock contractor

John Growney had taken the bull out of retirement, staking the bull's history of 309 unridden trips against the popular and handsome Oklahoma champ. Frost had managed to crack the code, beating the bull four to three in the best-of-seven series. The much-publicized contest earned both rider and bull recognition on national news television and in numerous magazine articles, including a feature in *Sports Illustrated*. Nothing that season would eclipse what many feel was the greatest bull riding match-up in the history of the sport.

When they weren't on the road competing, Tuff and Lane vacationed together with their wives, Tracy and Kellie. Theirs was a special friendship, said Tracy years later. "Lane was a great guy; he was fun to be around. We got to do a lot with him and his wife, Kellie. I can't say I ever had a friend who was as good a friend as Tuff was to Lane. It was just fun to watch them."

On July 30, 1989, that friendship ended in one of the worst tragedies ever to visit rodeo's tight-knit family. It was a drizzly, gray afternoon at Cheyenne's Frontier Park. Lane Frost was riding in the finals on a bull named Taking Care of Business. He made the whistle and bailed off but slipped as he tried to flee from the bull. Taking Care of Business turned and hooked Frost in the back with a horn in what seemed like a harmless pass.

Ty Murray, who witnessed the goring, said of the accident, "The bull put his head on Lane and smashed him and went on. It looked like no big deal. Only Lane didn't get up. And you knew with Lane Frost, if he didn't get up, he was hurt bad 'cause he was one of the toughest guys."

Frost finally rose to his feet, indicating toward the chutes that he needed help. Hedeman knew immediately that something was seriously wrong. Lane had suffered a torn artery. An ambulance carried the fallen hero to the hospital, but doctors were unable to stop the bleeding. Lane Frost died in the ER. Heartbroken, Tuff went into Lane's room to spend a little time with his friend and to say goodbye. He gave his friend a final hug.

"It was the toughest thing I've ever done in my life. It wasn't that I didn't know that we were in a dangerous business, in a dangerous sport. But you don't expect a guy who is a world's champion, the best at what he does, to have something like this happen to him. It was a difficult pill to swallow," said Tuff.

Lane Frost was laid to rest in Oklahoma,

JEFF BELDEN

Tuff gives son Robert Lane a kiss following round eight of the 1995 NFR.

next to the grave of Freckles Brown, a legendary bull riding champ who had seen the boy's potential and helped coach him to greatness. Afterward, Hedeman found it difficult to perform, afraid that he couldn't give himself fully to the job of riding bulls. With little joy, he persevered, if only because that was all he knew to do.

Once again, the world championship in Las Vegas came down to the final bull. The battle was between Hedeman and Jim Sharp, who had extended his NFR riding streak to 20 by topping off his first 9 bulls at the 1989 Finals. Hedeman had faltered in the third round, and a familiar and heavy weight seemed to rest on his broad shoulders, for he'd already called his shot: He intended to win the world title in memory of his fallen friend.

When the bull riders checked the day sheet to see which animals they were matched against that fateful Sunday, many gave a low whistle when they saw Jim

Sharp's draw—Mr. T, a black-and-white bull considered a worthy successor to Red Rock as the most difficult bull in the business. Prior to the finals, Mr. T had only been ridden once in PRCA competition, ironically on the very day and in the very same arena where Lane Frost had lost his life. If Sharp could ride the bull, he would top Hedeman in the average race and defend his world championship from the previous year. If he toppled, Hedeman had only to make an 8-second ride to claim his second gold buckle.

Sharp screwed himself down tight onto the back of the bull, but three massive jumps

"By 1991, I'd finally figured out that if I won it, I wouldn't be the happiest man in the world, and if I didn't, I wouldn't be the most miserable."

were all it took to dislodge the sticky rider and end his epic streak. Hedeman knew he had to score to claim the buckle. Adding to the pressure were the intonations of announcer Bob Tallman, who proclaimed to the audience that "He's not riding alone."

Hedeman rode the bull in spectacular fashion for the regulation 8 seconds, then grabbed his hat and fanned the bull for another 8, in honor of his fallen friend.

Hedeman tied Sharp for the 10-round bull riding average, winning the world title with the highest single-event earnings, $122,765. Reluctantly, he assumed the mantle of stardom that had formerly been worn by his friend. It wouldn't be fair to assert that Hedeman climbed out from behind Frost's shadow, for their talents were equally great. But in the eyes of fans, Hedeman was now "the man," and he would learn to embrace and even take pleasure in the growing attention that they lavished on him. Years later, the story of their tragic friendship became the basis for the film *Eight Seconds*.

Hedeman's poignant win in memory of his best friend was indeed a moment worthy of a Hollywood film. But the following year, the script very nearly cast Tuff in the tragic role. Poised to defend his world championship, Hedeman entered the NFR's seventh round matched against the Harry Vold bull Stinger, a 1,700-pound behemoth with a 4-foot vertical leap and horns the size of baseball bats. Six seconds into the ride, Hedeman got tipped into his hand and fell into the "well," the bull riders' term for the vortex of the whirling animal's spin. Hedeman flipped over his rope, trapping his hand in the plaited handle.

For the next minute, Hedeman ran along and was dragged beside the bull, trying to free his imprisoned hand. A dozen off-duty bullfighters led by Tuff's older brother, Roach, leapt into the arena to aid the rider. Mercifully, the bull's batteries finally ran down and Tuff's death grip with the rope was broken.

Miraculously, Hedeman was winded but not seriously injured. His faith in himself was not shaken either. The following night, Hedeman topped off his bull to tie for first place. But he failed to make the bell on his final bull, and the world title again went to his traveling partner Jim Sharp.

Hedeman's gold buckle ambitions hardly dimmed, but his priorities had begun to shift as the 1991 season ground on. In May he received the first major injury of his career, tearing the ligaments in his right knee at the Helldorado Days Rodeo in Las Vegas. Hedeman was forced to take time off.

It was a blessing of sorts—Tuff was home when his wife gave birth to their first son, Robert Lane, that June. Gradually Hedeman recognized that winning world titles was not the sole purpose of his life, that proving himself was no longer the necessity it had once been to him. Later that month, he struck out once again and made up lost ground to qualify for the NFR.

Gone were the self-doubts and anger that had plagued Hedeman earlier in his career.

His first world title, he'd won to prove himself to the doubters. The second, he'd won for Lane. This title would be for his family. It would be no cakewalk—in the sixth round of that year's National Finals, the bull Dr. J slammed against the chute gate, shearing the rowel off Tuff's spur and twisting his ankle backward, causing a severe sprain. But the pain, which must have been agonizing, was nothing but an inconvenience to the determined rider. On Friday, Dec. 13th, the unsuperstitious Hedeman (who was also wearing the No. 13 back number) won the round on the bull Playboy Bunny, scoring 91 points—one of the highest marks of his career.

Again, the title came down to Sunday's final round. Hedeman drew from the rank eliminator pen a bull named Thumper that had snookered rider Clint Branger in the sixth round. The bull cracked out spinning left, then cut back. Hedeman countered, but he overcorrected. The bull threw him a belly roll, and Hedeman tilted off to the side, his body hopelessly out of position, off-center, and at the bull's mercy. Had the bull spun to the right, Hedeman would likely have fallen, but the bull instead lunged forward, and Hedeman gathered his strength, pulled himself upright, and managed to stay aboard long enough to hear the air horn. It was not a pretty ride, and the judges marked him a modest 76 points. But it was classic Hedeman—he rode ugly, like a battle-scarred boxer, shaken but unbowed. Like a champion.

As he claimed the gold buckle that evening, Hedeman reflected on how his views on winning the world championship had changed.

"By 1991, I'd finally figured out that if I won it, I wouldn't be the happiest man in the world, and if I didn't, I wouldn't be the most miserable. Losing the closest friend I'll ever have and having a baby changed my outlook on life."

Implicit in Hedeman's words was an acceptance that he'd reached an apogee of his career, that there was nothing more to prove to anyone, even himself. Win or lose, he was no longer the geeky kid struggling for recognition. Besides, Hedeman was beginning to move away from his role as rodeo's biggest star to create his own theater. In 1993, he and 30 other bull riders got together to create a new organization called Professional Bull Riders. Their goal was to sanction independent bull riding events, produce their own line of products, gather corporate sponsors, and in the end take bull riding from the dusty environs that had nurtured the sport to big-city arenas and television sets across America.

But as Hedeman labored to organize the sport of bull riding, he continued to compete almost full time in the PRCA. At the '93 Calgary Stampede, he crossed the $1 million career earnings mark in the PRCA. Also that year, at a bull riding competition in Long Beach, Calif., he mastered one of the most difficult bulls ever to buck: Bodacious, a butter-colored behemoth who regularly unseated the best riders in the business. Hedeman scored 95 points that night, and he remembers that ride as the best he's ever made.

It would not be the last time the two would meet.

ROBERT A. JOHNSON

After years of misfortune at Cheyenne Frontier Days, Hedeman earned back-to-back bull riding titles at the rodeo in 1995-96. Here he's making an 83-point ride on the bull 40RV in Frontier Park.

By season's end, Tuff was once more among the front-runners going into the NFR. Once there, however, his desire to stay in the bull riding game would be severely tested. Riding in the eighth round, Hedeman was slammed into the arena dirt by the bull Dodge Magnum Power of the Western Rodeo's string. He laid motionless, unable to move for nearly 10 minutes as paramedics and physicians with the Justin® SportsMedicine program attended him.

Hedeman's paralysis, it turned out, was only temporary, the result of a bulging disk in his neck impinging on his spinal nerves. But while performing spinal surgery to fuse two of the disks, the surgeon noted that Hedeman had an unusually narrow spinal canal and that he would remain at risk for debilitating injury for

as long as he continued to ride. That wasn't anything new to Tuff.

"You're always in danger riding bulls. I don't think bull riding was ever considered totally intelligent in the first place," he said.

Tuff spent the entire 1994 season recuperating, using the time productively to help organize the fledgling bull riding outfit, practicing team roping, and making appearances for his numerous corporate sponsors. He had plenty of time to consider life beyond rodeo, and he listened and absorbed the advice of his close friends and family members, who pointed out that his place among rodeo's greatest stars was already assured, that he had nothing left to prove.

But after a year, he grew restless. The lure of bull riding proved simply too great. That January, he made an 11th-hour decision to ride at the first major rodeo of the season, Denver's National Western Stock Show. He rode his first bull, bucked off his second. Then he headed up to Steamboat Springs to compete in the famous "Cowboy Downhill," a sort of Grand Prix-style free-for-all race involving 50 cowboys clad in chaps, hats, and skis going full-blast, en masse, first across the line wins. Hedeman won.

Hedeman's 1995 season might be the most memorable of his career, for reasons both good and bad. At the Lazy E Arena, Hedeman won the Bullnanza bull riding, the crown jewel of the Professional Bull Riders events. In July he won Cheyenne Frontier Days with an 83-point ride in the finals—exactly six years to the day that Frost had died. "I knew if I had a chance to do something great, not only for myself but for (Lane), this was the place to do it," he said.

In October, at the Pro Bull Rider Finals in Las Vegas, Hedeman faced a familiar adversary: Bodacious. Hedeman looked forward to the match. He considered Bodacious to be "the most dangerous, most difficult bull I've ever seen." And he relished the challenge.

But this was a different bull than Hedeman had faced two years previously. After a layoff following an injury, Bodacious had rejoined the rodeo trail with a new—and potentially fatal—trick. When the duo

Hedeman slaps a high five on NFR bullfighter Rob Smets in celebration of winning the 1986 world championship.

SUE ROSOF

cracked out of the chute, Hedeman extended his torso out over the massive skull. Bodacious made a small stutter step, then brought his wrecking ball of a skull into direct contact with Hedeman's face. After taking one more massive sucker punch, Hedeman crumpled to the ground, his facial bones shattered. His friend Cody Lambert had been nearby, watching.

"He should have been knocked out, but he wasn't. He was trying to get up, and he looked up. It looked awful to me. I have a pretty strong stomach and can stand a little blood. But when I looked at him, it looked like his nose was gone," said Lambert. "He looked 10 times worse than Rocky (in the movie) did."

Hedeman walked out of the arena and was taken to the hospital. He underwent reconstructive surgery to repair his broken facial bones, a cracked jaw, missing teeth, and damaged sinus cavities. When Tuff finally returned home, his son, Lane, at first did not recognize his daddy. Then, he climbed up in Tuff's lap and said, "Dad, you know if you draw Bodacious again, you're gonna have to chicken out." And Tuff replied, "You've got a deal."

Six weeks later, Hedeman amazingly was back, competing at the NFR. He had lost 20 pounds and his face looked like a Salvador Dali painting, but he rode nevertheless. Then, an astounding thing happened: Hedeman drew Bodacious in the seventh round.

"I knew I had a one in fifteen chance of drawing him. And I thought, 'There's no way I will draw him again.' Surprise!"

Good to his promise, Hedeman sat down on the bull's back, then allowed himself to be lifted off the bull as the gate swung open, a strategy to keep from being exempted from the following nights' competitions. As Bodacious galloped out into the arena, riderless, Hedeman lifted his hat off his head in salute to the great bucking bull.

Two days later, bull rider Scott Breding attempted to ride the bull wearing a baseball catcher's mask for protection. Bodacious used his sucker-punch stumble, smashing Breding's face so violently that the rider's eye

Hedeman's young fans flock to the champ after his victory at Cheyenne Frontier Days.

socket shattered. The bull's owner, Sammy Andrews, retired the two-time bucking bull of the year on the final day of the rodeo.

Although prudence might have dictated that Hedeman retire, he still proved unwilling to hang up his bull rope. After the accident, he continued to compete in both the PBR and the PRCA. More and more, though, the bull rider seemed to be letting loose of his place as bull riding's Great One to assume the role of bull riding ambassador and president of the PBR. With his strong guidance, the organization grew tremendously throughout the 1990s, eventually overtaking the PRCA in terms of television audience share, prize money for the bull riders, and sponsorship clout. In 1996, Hedeman finished second in the PBR/Bud Light Cup standings and was inducted into the ProRodeo Hall of Fame in Colorado Springs. Hedeman was also the subject of a TNN Documentary, *The Life and Times of Tuff Hedeman*. This was how he summarized his own career:

"For me to turn a dream, a love of a sport, into a career and a profession is the coolest thing in the world. Riding bulls is my love, what I dreamed of doing. If someone had told me when I was 12 years old, 'You are going to be a world champion bull rider,' not only would I have laughed at them, but everyone else would have too. It took me awhile to get it, but there's one thing I am extremely proud of: That's what I wanted to do, and I never gave up."

KENNETH SPRINGER

CHARMAYNE JAMES

SINCE THE first National Finals Rodeo was held in 1959, there have been many legendary moments in the history of the event. Some that come immediately to mind are Freckles Brown's successful trip aboard the formerly unridden bull Tornado in 1967, Dean Oliver's unfortunate loss of the calf roping world championship when he broke two ropes at the 1966 NFR, bull rider Jim Sharp's 10-straight qualified rides at the '88 Finals, and the seventh performance of the 1997 Finals in which three calf ropers successively beat the arena record.

But perhaps the most legendary and amazing of all NFR moments belonged to a skinny, straw-haired, teenage girl from the hinterlands of New Mexico and a plain-Jane Quarter Horse she called Scamper.

The girl was Charmayne James, the year was 1985, and the December day, Friday the 13th.

Just 15 years old, James was nonetheless the defending world champion. She'd claimed the world title the previous year as a rookie, shocking and surprising the rodeo world with major wins at San Antonio and Houston, then defeating Lee Ann Guilkey in Oklahoma City to decisively claim the world title.

In 1985 the NFR abandoned the Sooner State for a new home in Las Vegas, and James and her horse were the odds-on favorites to win the gold buckle. Early in

Scamper and Charmayne's domination of the barrel event made them the highest-profile team in the horse world by the early 1990s.

the rodeo, the duo only strengthened their bid, placing five times in the first six rounds, including three first-place finishes. But as they prepared to dash into the arena in round seven, Scamper got excited and bumped his head into a concrete wall in what seemed to be a rather insignificant incident. It was anything but that.

"When he hit his head, it must have knocked the Chicago screw in his bridle loose. When he lunged forward to make his run into the arena, his headstall took off and hit me right in the eye, and I knew it was off," remembers Charmayne.

James and Scamper hit the arena bridleless, with Charmayne holding the bit in the horse's mouth with nothing but her reins. With no means of exerting pressure or control over her horse's head, James simply told herself to be calm and act as if nothing was wrong.

Scamper cleared the first and the second barrels without incident. But as they rounded the third barrel, Scamper spit out the bit. With reins, headstall, and bridle hanging off his throat like a necklace, the horse sprinted for the arena exit. It was a flawless run... so flawless, in fact, that Charmayne put quirt to hide as they dashed toward the electronic timers.

"Oh, no!" thought Charmayne as she cleared the exit, "now I have to stop!"

Partway up the alley was a gate, and the two looked about to hit it at full speed. Fortunately, several people in the arena hollered to the gatekeepers to keep the gateway open, and they left just enough of a gap

that James was able to pull her knees up as Scamper blasted through the narrow hole.

Beyond the gate, however, was a long, broad alley leading to the arena's huge concrete parking lot. Barrel racer Sherry Altizer, who must have been watching the run on the tiny video monitor outside, positioned her horse to block the alley. This slowed Scamper, and Charmayne's uncle was able to throw his arms around the horse's neck, bringing him to a halt.

"So, my dad said there was a little bay gelding in the pens, and he said I should ride him and see what I thought. "

Somewhat shaken but never panicked, Charmayne didn't immediately register the cheers that had erupted from inside the Thomas & Mack Center arena. Then, someone told her to hustle up and get on the victory horse to take a lap. "Charmayne, hurry up. You won the round."

"No I didn't," she said incredulously. "His bridle came off!"

But Scamper, running free, had stopped the clock in 14.40 seconds — the fastest time in the round and the second-fastest time up to that point in the entire rodeo. Charmayne and Scamper had turned a potential disaster into an accomplishment that no one who witnessed it would ever forget. At that moment the James legend truly began.

Charmayne's story, however, began some years earlier in the tiny New Mexico outpost of Clayton. The youngest of four girls, Charmayne was actually born a Texan: The nearest large hospital was in Amarillo, two hours south and east of tiny Clayton.

Horses were a part of her life nearly from the time she could walk. Her parents, Charlie and Gloria James, operated Clayton Cattle Feeders, and Charmayne and her three older sisters all pitched in to help manage the daily chores.

Charmayne proved handy with a horse as a girl. At age 8 she acquired her first barrel horse, Bardo, an unruly Thoroughbred who had come off the racetrack. According to Charmayne, Bardo was "a bit crazy," and inclined to run sideways, and jump. She admits to being a little afraid of the horse at first, but she spent an entire summer riding him all day long in feedlot pens and the pastures that adjoined them. After that, Bardo became as calm as a western pleasure horse, and Charmayne began winning some rodeos.

Charmayne's parents were fairly strict about their daughter's competitive ambitions, for her father had told her, "If you're gonna rodeo, you'll have to pay your own way. It's not worth it to go and have the family away from home if you don't do well." Competitive by nature, Charmayne replied, "Well, that's fine with me. If I don't win, I don't want to go anyway."

In two years the diminutive girl who preferred raw onions to sweets had amassed close to $15,000 on Bardo in open amateur events in the tri-state area of Oklahoma, Texas, and New Mexico. But then a freak accident put a stop to her activities.

Charmayne's sister was to use Bardo for the National High School Rodeo Finals. She was practicing pole bending at home when the horse broke his leg and had to be put down. Once over the grief, Charmayne began pestering her parents for a new horse.

"We went to the racetrack in Raton and to various ranches, but I just didn't find anything I liked. So, my dad said there was a little bay gelding in the pens, and he said I should ride him and see what I thought. Dad warned me that he had a reputation for bucking, that I should warm him up on the ground a little. Of course, I got right on him and kicked him out, and he kinda crow-hopped on me. I giggled," she says. "And that was that."

Charmayne rode the horse for three days solid, forming a bond that would last for many years. Had she known more about the little bay's ornery reputation, she might have been a little more reluctant to goose him.

The horse, whose registered name was Gills Bay Boy, had been bred by Buddy Draper of Wetmore, Colorado. As a colt the horse had bucked Draper off and broken his back. After that, the horse went through a series of owners and sale barns in La Junta, Colo.; Guymon, Okla.; Clovis, N.M.; and finally Clayton, before landing in the capable hands of Ron Holland, the head cowboy at Clayton Cattle Feeders. When Holland decided it was time to move on, he put the horse up for sale, and that's how he came to the attention of Charlie James.

Charlie thought the $1,100 price tag on the bay was too high, but he knew his daughter liked the horse and that the two got on well. Holland had put a nice finish on the once-ornery horse. At 4 the gelding could perform a sliding stop, rollback, and spin like a working cow horse. He also had cow sense, a mighty handy trait in a feedlot. And when Charmayne began taking him around the barrels, he proved to be a natural.

"Dad watched me go around the barrels, and when it came time to name him, he said to me, 'Well, he kinda scampers around the barrels. Why don't you name him Scamper?'"

CAREER MILESTONES

Charmayne James

born: June 23, 1970
Amarillo, Texas

10-Time Women's Pro Rodeo Association Barrel Racing World Champion (1984-93).

2000 Wins Cheyenne Frontier Days on Cruiser, also qualifies for the National Finals, her 17th consecutive trip, stretching her records for most NFR qualifications in barrel racing and most consecutive qualifications.

1996 Scamper is the first barrel racing horse inducted into the ProRodeo Hall of Fame.

1993 James surpasses the $1 million mark in earnings and qualifies for 10th straight NFR. Charmayne claims her record 10th world championship.

1992 James fends off Twila Haller at the National Finals to claim her ninth straight world title. With the win she surpasses bull rider Don Gay's record for the most single-event world titles ever won in rodeo.

1991 James and Scamper sweep the Houston Livestock Show Rodeo, winning all rounds for the second time in their careers.

1990 After winning Houston, Scamper undergoes knee surgery to remove a bone slab that had troubled him throughout much of his career. Despite the layoff, James comes back to again dominate the NFR, winning the event's average title and racking up season earnings of $130,328.

1989 James again wins the NFR average en route to her sixth world title.

1988 Again wearing the No. 1 back number at the NFR, James tops the men's all-around champ in money earned for the year, winning $130,540. James marries team roper Walt Rodman, leaving her childhood home to live in California.

1987 James completes the regular season as the highest money-earning contestant in rodeo with $80,314, becoming the first woman barrel racer to enter the National Finals wearing the No. 1 back number. Again she dominates the NFR barrel racing average, placing seven times.

1986 Charmayne wins more than $151,969. It is more money than any rodeo competitor had ever won in a single event in a single year, and just $15,000 short of the money won by men's all-around champ Lewis Feild. At the finals she clocks a time of 138.93 seconds over 10 runs, the fastest average time in barrel racing history.

1985 As the reigning world champ, James continues dominating the regular season, claiming her second Houston title. At the NFR James hits a barrel in the ninth round—the only barrel she would hit during her amazing string of 10 consecutive world titles. Despite finishing second in the average, she claims her second world championship by a margin of nearly $10,000. In round seven she makes her famous "bridleless" run on Scamper, winning the round in the time of 14.40 seconds.

1984 In her maiden year in professional rodeo, James wins both the San Antonio Stock Show and the Houston Livestock Show Rodeo to become a front-runner in the world title race and ensure a trip to the National Finals Rodeo in Oklahoma City. James wins the barrel racing rookie of the year title, qualifying second in the world among barrel racers for the NFR. There, she defeats first-place qualifier Lee Ann Guilkey by winning the 10-round average competition to claim her first WPRA World Championship with earnings of $53,449.

Pam Minick of the WPRA compared Charmayne's record 10 wins at Houston to an NFL team winning 10 Super Bowl titles.

Charmayne worked Scamper daily in the feedlot, using lunch breaks to introduce him to barrels. After three weeks she entered him in an amateur event in Texline, Texas. In his first competition (albeit a small one), Scamper won the fastest time in the junior event and the third-fastest time in the open. As Charmayne later said, "Scamper stopped the clocks from the get-go."

For two years Charmayne ran the horse in amateur events, placing in most of the competitions. Scamper's impressive speed and natural ability got Charmayne thinking about turning professional, so at 13, her mother helped her apply for a Women's Professional Rodeo Association permit. They hauled the horse to Dodge City, and Scamper won in his professional rodeo debut.

Since it was already midsummer, the Jameses decided to wait out the season and go for the rookie title in 1984. They went through the run of big winter rodeos: Kansas City, Kan.; Denver; Scottsdale, Ariz.; and El Paso, Texas.

Although Charmayne placed in a few rounds, she hit so many barrels that she failed to make the finals at any of the events. Scamper was skittish—he had never competed indoors—and Charmayne admits that she was intimidated by the big arena crowds and the big-name riders whose names she had heard listening to the NFR broadcasts on the radio.

Finally, her parents sat her down and told her if she didn't start winning, they would try something different.

Charmayne's next rodeo was the San Antonio Stock Show, one of the top five rodeos in prize money. She won that handily, then traveled on to Houston, the biggest regular season rodeo, winning that too. The wins thrust her into second place in the world standings, assuring her of a trip to the National Finals as the top rookie. There, of course, she earned her first world title.

Houston proved to be a favorite competition for both Charmayne and Scamper. In 11 years they won that competition an amazing 10 times. But at first Scamper liked the huge arena, which has often been likened to a pasture, much more than Charmayne did.

"Scamper loved it there. He made great runs there. But I was scared to death," she admits. "All the people, the fans, and the media terrified me. In any interviews I did, I came off sounding like a moron. I couldn't even talk. There was no reason for it, really. I was just shy."

Eventually, she would grow out of that shyness. She had to. Over the next few years, as Charmayne continued winning world title upon world title, she appeared in a raft of magazines and news shows that included *PEOPLE Weekly, US Magazine, Seventeen, Sports Illustrated, ESPN,* and *ABC's Wide World of Sports,* and nearly every newspaper in every town and city, big and small, wherever she appeared.

Although Charmayne's youth was not without precedent in barrel racing (in 1968 Ann Lewis won the world championship at age 10), the sport wasn't exactly geared toward such a young star. After winning her first world title, Charmayne was given the keys to a new Dodge pickup. But at 14, it would be two years before she could legally drive it.

Still, on her way back from Oklahoma City, her mother stopped in Texline and asked if Charmayne wanted to drive her new pickup the 20 or so miles home. She gave her mom an enthusiastic "Heck yes!," and got behind the wheel. But they'd barely gotten underway when the New Mexico State Patrol pulled her over.

"It's okay," said her mom, "we cleared it with them already."

Charmayne suspected something was afoot and, indeed, as Charmayne pulled into Clayton (accompanied by two state trooper cars), there was a giant party going in the grocery store parking lot. Nearly the entire town was there to cheer her victory, and as she unloaded Scamper from the trailer for all to see, she and her horse were awarded roses.

Given their growing success, it was inevitable that she and Scamper would spend less and less time in their hometown. Realizing that a horse such as Scamper represented a rare opportunity that might come but once in their daughter's lifetime, the James family pulled together to make the sacrifices necessary to keep her on the road.

Charmayne's mom, Gloria, drove and accompanied her daughter on the road, tending to the business details of a professional rodeo athlete. Meanwhile, Charmayne's sisters handled their mother's duties at home and helped their father run the feedlot.

Whenever she could, Charmayne hurried home so she could spend time with friends and sleep in her own bed. But the demands of the road made it impossible to maintain a normal school schedule, so she began taking correspondence courses. That freed her to stay at major rodeo events spanning days and weeks, but kept Gloria from spending the additional time with her husband and her other daughters.

"Everyone was just so good. They all made major sacrifices for me, and I felt an obligation to all of them to keep winning," said Charmayne.

And win she did. In 1986 Charmayne was in her second year as a Winston Pro Tour contestant. At the time elite competitors were formed into teams to compete at select events featuring purses in excess of $100,000. Charmayne—the girl who ate onions as a kid—ironically ended up on the Jolly Rancher candy team. "I got all the free candy I could ever want," she said, laughing.

The format of the competitions suited Scamper's style. The contestants typically ran three times in a day, and as he figured out the barrel pattern and arena conditions, he went faster and faster. All the money earned at these special events applied toward the world standings, and Charmayne banked check after check. She began to get over some of her shyness as fans flocked around her at autograph sessions at each venue. By the end of the regular season, she was so far ahead in the world standings, she could not be beaten if her nearest competitor won everything at the National Finals and Charmayne failed to win a dime.

But in typical fashion Charmayne cleaned up at the NFR, placing in every single round and handily winning the 10-round average in the record time of 138.93 seconds. The record stands today, although with an asterisk that denotes a different, shortened pattern was run in Las Vegas that year.

When her earnings were computed, she'd toted up more money than any single-event contestant in any rodeo event ($151,969), and had fallen just short of the mark set by men's all-around champ Lewis Feild.

KENNETH SPRINGER

James credits her Paint barrel horse Magic with helping her to clinch her 10th barrel racing world title.

With the demise of the Pro Tour in 1987, James' earnings declined sharply, but she remained by far the most successful barrel racer in the history of the sport.

Again she entered the finals with the world title statistically decided, then piled up winnings throughout the rodeo. She placed in all but three rounds, again win-

While still in her teens, James had amassed a pirate's hoard of trucks, saddles, buckles, and bucks.

SUE ROSOFF

ning the rodeo's average title and again surpassing the $100,000 annual earnings mark. In round eight she and Scamper combined to run the fastest time of the entire rodeo.

Lewis Feild again surpassed all other competitors in total earnings, but Charmayne topped all the other cowboys in single-event money earned for the season. That, she said, caused a bit of consternation among rodeo's leadership.

"I don't recall if it was 1987 or 1988, but the PRCA board considered a vote that would have taken the barrel race event out of the race for the No. 1 back number at the National Finals," said Charmayne. Awarded to the contestant with the largest single-season earnings, the No. 1 back number represented a considerable honor, one that James felt belonged rightfully to her and her horse.

"The year I won the No. 1 back number (1988), I won more money than the all-around cowboy (Dave Appleton). And I felt like we'd worked really hard for this and that Scamper was the greatest horse in rodeo at that or any time, in any event."

Although the rule change was never implemented, Charmayne had become energized in what would become a campaign to put barrel racing on equal footing with the men's rodeo events. In interviews with reporters, she would later make the point that although fans regarded barrel racing as one of rodeo's favorite events (a popularity that her success helped to cause), the women didn't receive prize money equal to the men at rodeos and at the NFR. Eventually she helped to lead a threatened walkout of women barrel racers that caused the NFR committee to equalize prize money in the barrel racing.

For five years James had seemed to sleep-walk to the world championship. But 1989 would truly test her desire as a competitor and as a horsewoman. First, she failed to win Houston for the first time in her career. And secondly, she went into the National Finals in first place, but within easy striking distance of Marlene Eddleman, the Colorado barrel racer who had been the last to hold the world title before Charmayne had come on the scene.

Furthermore, Scamper had suffered from a knee injury through much of his career. The injury had steadily calcified, creating a large bone spur. In the early rounds at the NFR, the horse had sored up and was running poorly. He placed only once—a check for fourth place.

Meanwhile, Eddleman was placing consistently, clocking first place in the opener and placing in three of the next four rounds.

Midway through the rodeo, James ran into rodeo announcer Bob Tallman, who gave her a peck on the cheek and said, "Well darlin', we all knew this day would come." To which Charmayne replied, "Don't count me out yet!" Then she turned on her heel and walked away.

In the sixth round Eddleman knocked over a barrel and took a 5-second penalty;

at the same time, Scamper found his stride and turned in a run of 14.42 seconds to take first place. Both women placed in the next round, although Scamper again posted the fastest time. When Eddleman and her horse struck another barrel in round nine, effectively taking them out of the 10-round average competition, Charmayne was indeed back in the hunt.

To win, Charmayne and Scamper had to keep all the cans standing and win the average. This was easily within their abilities: Scamper and Charmayne hadn't knocked down a barrel at the NFR since 1985, which must have represented an unofficial record. Although they didn't place in either of the last two rounds, they did win the average to maintain their lead over Eddleman, defeating her by $4,000—the thinnest margin of victory in Charmayne's career.

If Tallman or anyone else thought that Scamper had lost a step, any doubts were erased in 1990. Again the horse dominated the winter rodeos, including Houston. After that, James decided to have Scamper's troublesome right knee operated on. Veterinary surgeons removed a large slab fracture from the knee, forcing the barrel racer to lay off for a time. But when Scamper returned to the arena, he was his old self, racing and winning with that familiar consistency. James won her seventh world title in 1990 with more than twice the money earned by her nearest competitor, Deb Mohon.

The amazing Cinderella story of Charmayne and Scamper inevitably had to come to a close. By 1992 the horse had begun to show his age. Although Charmayne and Scamper continued to compete, other women were steadily gaining and challenging for the crown. In 1992 for example, Montanan Twila Haller gave Charmayne a scare when she won first place in the first three rounds of the NFR and continued snaring checks throughout the 10-round extravaganza.

Meanwhile, Charmayne and Scamper placed a mere three times, winning but one round. Consistency, rather than speed, was becoming Scamper's most dangerous weapon: His streak of not hitting a barrel went unblemished, and Charmayne finished second in the average, two spots ahead of Haller. Were it not for that, Charmayne's streak of world championships, now numbering nine, would have come to an end.

Charmayne realized that 1993 would probably represent Scamper's farewell tour. Rodeo fans were a bit stunned to see Charmayne competing that season on a bold, flashy Paint gelding named Magic. It was all part of her strategy: Charmayne had bought the Paint as a replacement for Scamper. She was seasoning him in smaller pens, such as the Cow Palace in San Francisco, breaking him in to the rodeo scene while allowing Scamper to rest and avoid bad arena conditions or pens where he had traditionally not run well.

Magic was an interesting acquisition: Charmayne had looked at many, many horses in her quest to find a backup runner to eventually step up and take Scamper's place. Trainer Larry Stevens told her that he felt he'd found just such a horse and invited her over to his place to take a look.

When she got there, she saw a Paint gelding tied in the barn, and she said to Stevens, "So where is this horse you wanted me to see?"

And Stevens replied, "You're looking at him. I knew if I told you he was a Paint, you'd never come look at him."

Indeed, very few Paints had proven themselves in rodeo competition, but Charmayne was willing to take a gamble after winning a jackpot race on her first trip out with the horse. Though the two would not cash any paychecks immediately, James felt that if Stevens got along on the horse, so would she.

With the help of both Magic and Scamper, James qualified for her 10th consecutive NFR in 1993. She brought both horses to the NFR, and many people speculated as to whether Magic would get his chance to dash through the arena.

Benched throughout most of the rodeo, the Paint got his chance in the seventh round when Scamper came up a bit sore, and Charmayne decided to give him a rest. Riding a new horse in the tricky Thomas & Mack Center made James nervous.

"I was scared to death because my big

chance was in the average and a bad ride could have killed us, but I felt like I had to give Scamper the night off," she said.

The Paint, however, proved himself, placing second in the round despite being the final horse to run that night, a position often regarded as a disadvantage because the ground tends to get hard and slick with each passing barrel racer. The second-place check they earned would be the only day money won by James in the entire rodeo.

In the next round Scamper came back on the top of the ground (a barrel racing term meaning "first to run"), and James held firmly to her lead in the 10-round average.

Meanwhile, Coloradan Kristie Peterson, a former county jail clerk and mother of three who was tearing up the barrel racing records on a gelding she'd bought for $400, was applying considerable pressure on James.

Peterson's horse, Bozo, was already proving himself to be barrel racing's next superhorse and a fitting successor to Scamper. At the 1993 NFR, Peterson had placed in six of the first eight rounds and was piling up money to challenge James for the world title. But James was determined to win a 10th world championship, feeling that Scamper needed to go out at the very summit of the game that he'd dominated for so long.

Again, consistency proved to be the key. Like Eddleman five years earlier, Peterson clipped a barrel in round nine. That one flaw proved Kristie's undoing. To retain the title, James only had to keep all the cans standing in the 10th round. For the sixth time in 10 years, James and Scamper won the NFR average, a victory that was crucial to their winning their record tenth world championship.

For the first time in the barrel racer's career, though, she had a second horse to thank: Scamper's backup, Magic.

"Magic helped us win that 10th world title," said Charmayne.

But the night belonged to Scamper. Charmayne, once a girl who had been the pride of her small town, was now a mature woman and the pride of rodeo fans across the United States. She'd been the first woman to earn more than $1 million in the arena and the first to surpass the men in individual world titles won. Along the way she had met a U.S. president, competed in a special exhibit at the Olympic Games, and appeared on the covers of magazines, in newspapers, and on news and sports programs throughout the country.

Sensing that they would not see Scamper again, the NFR audience gave the horse a standing ovation as Charmayne brought him into the arena. In a ceremony reminiscent of the party held in a Safeway parking lot in Clayton, N.M., a decade before, Scamper was presented a huge garland of roses as the audience insisted that he be paraded once more through the arena.

In a special ceremony Scamper was inducted into the ProRodeo Hall of Fame in 1996—the only barrel horse to be so honored.

In the ensuing years, Charmayne would prove that her great fortune was not entirely due to her great horse. Riding Magic, she returned to the NFR in 1994, and she has qualified in every NFR through 2000. Sloopy, another horse she acquired after Scamper, helped her to win close to $250,000 over the span of several years. Although neither horse was at the level of Scamper, Charmayne proved that she was a great trainer with the ability to take a good horse and make him a great horse capable of taking his rider to rodeo's biggest showcase.

But life after Scamper wasn't easy for Charmayne. Her marriage to roper Walt Rodman fell apart after seven years, and she relocated from California, where Rodman's family lived, to a small ranch in Stephenville, Texas. She continued to search for a fitting replacement for Scamper, sensing that although Sloopy and Magic were quite good horses, they lacked the ability to take her back to the No. 1 position. Charmayne says that she was a bit disillusioned, unsure of what she wanted to do.

"I was at a loss for what to do, what not to do. I got divorced, and at that point I was struggling financially," she says. "For a few years I was glad to be out of the limelight. After a while, it grows old. I was starting anew, I was finding and making good horses, and I had a lot of work to do to get back to the top."

James has done the work, and she feels she has found a fitting superhorse to replace Scamper. And amazingly, his story is oddly reminiscent of the horse who first carried James to fame.

Charmayne bought the horse for the bargain-basement price of $2,000 from Bill Dodgin, a semiretired race horse trainer from Amarillo. Like Scamper, the horse had an ornery disposition. When Charmayne and her mother, Gloria, first went to see the horse, he pinned his ears back and ran after them. By the racing sire Streakin Six and out of a Lady Bugs Moon mare, the horse had proven to be a washout on the track, but had the size and heart that Charmayne was looking for in a barrel prospect.

Despite having little time to train the horse while she was campaigning Sloopy, James began to sense that she really had something when she entered the horse, whom she named Cruiser, in a jackpot event in Mineral Wells, Texas. Much like Scamper years before, Cruiser won the novice class and posted one of the fastest times in the open class.

"After that, I thought, 'Wow, that's pretty neat,'" said Charmayne. "Magic and Sloopy were both great horses, but it was work for them. It's a lot easier for Cruiser. Not only that, but I trained him. And if you train a horse yourself, the timing and coordination between rider and horse are already there."

In December 1999 the duo paired for the National Finals, placing in three of ten rounds and piling up winnings of $40,253. That, despite the fact that the horse had some soundness problems in his left hind leg midway through the rodeo. In January 2000 they won the Denver National Western Stock Show, beginning a run that reminded many of the triumphant campaigns Charmayne had made aboard Scamper.

One of the few contests Scamper never won was Cheyenne Frontier Days. To be fair, the rodeo did not hold barrel races while Scamper was at the height of his career, but the bay did get a couple of chances at the famed Wyoming rodeo when barrel racing was reinstated. In 2000 Charmayne and Cruiser streaked to victory at Cheyenne, adding another award to Charmayne's bursting trophy case.

In 2000 James and Cruiser again made the trip to the NFR, marking the 17th time that the young woman had competed there. Despite leading the world standings,

KENNETH SPRINGER

Three of rodeo's biggest stars, Ty Murray, Scamper, and Charmayne.

they lost the world title when red-hot barrel racer Kappy Allen simply decimated the competition aboard her 8-year-old gelding Risky Chris.

Still, Charmayne's second-place finish in the world standings portended a new era for rodeo's winningest barrel jockey.

Are there more world titles in her future? Only time will tell. But win or lose, barrel racers past, present, and future will always look up to the woman from Clayton, N.M., with a measure of awe.

"Charmayne is like the grandmother of women's barrel racing, even though she is still so young," said three-time world champion Kristie Peterson. "When I went to the National Finals, I looked to her for advice. She was always so cool, calm, and collected. She made money when there wasn't much money to be made, and the publicity she earned helped to elevate the fortunes of all barrel racers.

"Charmayne is blessed with the talent and the grace of a champion — not to mention the luck of the Irish!"

DEVERE

BILL LINDERMAN

AS AMERICA'S fascination with its native hero, the cowboy, reached its crescendo in the 1950s, more than a few competed for the title "King of the Cowboys." Most, of course, were Hollywood stars who earned their titles from studio publicists or the press. Then there was Bill "The King" Linderman, who earned his nickname from the cowboys themselves.

Nobody is sure when Linderman became "The King." Most of his contemporaries say that it was sometime in the early 1950s, probably the year he became the first cowboy ever to win three world titles in one season. Linderman wasn't the type of cowboy to strum a guitar although he often did sport a white hat. He was a tough guy— some would say the toughest. But he was also a good man, generous with his money, his advice, and his time.

Admired, of course, for his six world titles won between 1943 and 1953, Linderman was probably admired even more for his leadership. As a board member and later president of the Rodeo Cowboys Association, he played a pivotal role in the sport's history during a time of rapid change and growth. Using his level-headed sense and a work ethic that was largely the reason for his arena accomplishments, he helped boost the sport to national recognition, solidify its business structure, and resolve many of the conflicts that inevitably

At Great Falls, Mont., native son
Bill Linderman scores points on
the bronc Speckled Boy.

arose among the cowboys, livestock owners, and rodeo committees. All the while, he remained one of the most successful cowboys in the sport, earning nearly a half-million dollars during a career that spanned three decades.

Born in 1920, Bill came of age during the difficult times of the Great Depression. His family had settled in the area of Red Lodge, Mont., where ranching and mining competed as the main sources of income. Bill took part in both. He built his formidable strength and size as a hard-rock miner, and he learned the skills of a cowboy working on ranches with his brothers.

His older brothers, John and Doug, were widely regarded as good hands, especially when it came to taming broncs. Bill admired them, and he worked hard to match their skills. But it was his younger brother, Bud, who typically gets credit for steering Bill towards rodeo.

Of the four brothers, Bill was the least gifted in natural ability, and Bud the most. All the brothers, of course, were accustomed to riding the rough off a horse. In their neck of the woods, horses were pretty much left to run wild until they were 4 or 5 years old, when the cowboys put them through a rapid training program. Breaking a full-grown range horse, who had scarcely seen a man at this point, was a dusty battle of wills, and all the boys were adept at it.

But Bud, it was said, had a great natural spurring lick that gave his rides style— something that rodeo judges were eager to reward. Bill, on the other hand, was some-

a showy and well-regarded bronc named McArthur, who was owned by stock contractor Earl Anderson. Linderman made the whistle, which set him up for a trip to the pay window.

"I got paid in dollar bills, a roll of more than 300 of 'em. I never had seen so much money at one time. I just had to go on and rodeo from there," he said.

Although saddle bronc riding was Bill's favorite event, he didn't limit himself to the broncs. He also entered team roping, steer wrestling, calf roping, and occasionally the bull riding. If there was money in it, he'd even enter the wild horse race and the wild cow milking, two events common at rodeos in those days and at which Linderman was said to have excelled. Although reporters sometimes noted that the cowboy didn't contest in the bull riding, photos made early in Linderman's career prove otherwise.

Linderman won his first world title in 1943 in bareback riding. That year Bill was the standout bareback rider at the most important competition of the season — the Madison Square Garden Rodeo. The month-long competition was roughly comparable to the National Finals Rodeo of today in terms of its importance and stature among the cowboys. As the last major rodeo competition of the year and as the rodeo with the biggest payout, it proved critical to the world-title races. Linderman's victory there effectively put the title on ice for the 23-year-old competitor.

what more awkward and mechanical in his riding, and he had to work extremely hard to improve. But he possessed a great competitiveness that made him want to do better than his talented younger brother, and that helped carry him through the hours and hours of hard practice required for him to master each and every rodeo event.

It's difficult to say just when Bill decided to become a roving rodeo gypsy, for all of the Linderman boys competed in small rodeos

It's often said that rodeo cowboys of that era were hard-drinking brawlers intent on having a good time. Although Linderman was certainly respected for his powerful fists, he was also a prototype of the rodeo cowboy as a professional athlete. He made a study of the sport, always looking for an edge that might help him win. It is said that he had an encyclopedic memory of the bucking horses of his era, that he knew their names, their histories, and their normal bucking patterns. But he didn't hide this useful intelligence from his fellow

"There weren't as many rodeos, and what there were put up so little money that even the big winners could hardly afford to keep at it."

in their home state. But by several accounts Bill's rodeo saga truly began in 1942 when he was traveling through Colorado on his way to a ranching job in Montana.

He stopped by the Greeley Independence Stampede, one of the larger summer rodeo events, and decided to enter the saddle bronc riding. That decision would alter the course of his life. One of his two draws was

riders. When a cowboy asked him what he knew about a given animal, Linderman would give him a quick and accurate scouting report. This was especially true among the young riders, who, until they had proven themselves, were otherwise ostracized by the older, more experienced hands.

It is said that Linderman entered every rodeo intent on leaving with a check. He was an intense competitor, and he hated to lose. The other cowboys soon learned to avoid Bill if he bucked off a bronc or failed to turf a steer.

When Linderman came on the scene, World War II was raging overseas, and many of the best cowboys were conscripted into military service. Many of those who remained home were too battered and beat up to pass the military's medical entrance exams. And although the cowboys undoubtedly would have liked to serve, they were often perceived as draft dodgers through no fault of their own. Not only did the cowboys suffer from a negative public image, they were often taken advantage of by the rodeo promoters too.

"In those days, things were tough," said Linderman. "There weren't as many rodeos, and what there were put up so little money that even the big winners could hardly afford to keep at it. Lots of times the entry fees added up to more than the prize money, and the rodeo made money off the cowboys if they didn't sell a single seat.

"There was no insurance. If a man got hurt, it was his tough luck unless his buddies passed the hat for him. The judges sometimes weren't competent to mark a calf scramble, and the rules were different just about every place you entered."

Linderman foresaw a better future for the sport. Almost from the start, he joined the R.C.A.'s board as contestant director for bareback riding. At first Bill was a strongly opinionated fighter who defied others to challenge his opinions. At board meetings he would raise his voice until it shook the windows and pound his fist on the table when he wanted to make an emphatic point. He often prevailed by sheer intimidation.

But over time it was clear that his ideas were good ones. In 1951 he was promoted to the vice presidency of the rodeo board. Not long after that, the reigning president of the R.C.A., Toots Mansfield, announced that he was resigning from the job, and Linderman became the president. Being in a position of ultimate authority changed Linderman's negotiating skills from confrontation to consolidation and consensus.

"He became the force that seized the plans and thinking of his 10-man board, composing, smoothing, and welding the various (recommendations) into R.C.A. policies and rules," said one of his fellow board members.

Under Linderman's direction the sport prospered immensely. Rodeos were added

CAREER MILESTONES

Bill Linderman

born: April 13, 1920
Bridger, Montana

Six-time World Champion Cowboy (All-Around, 1950, '53; Bareback, 1943; Saddle Bronc, 1945, '50; Steer Wrestling, 1950).

1970 Bill Linderman is inducted into the Colorado Sports Hall of Fame.

1966 An 8-foot bronze statue of Bill Linderman is unveiled at the entrance to the Cowboy Hall of Fame in Oklahoma City.

1965 Linderman wins the steer wrestling at the Pendleton Round-Up at age 45. Just one month later, he is killed in a commercial plane wreck in Salt Lake City, Nov. 11, 1965. At the time, he is the highest money-earner in the history of the rodeo association.

1959 Linderman serves as arena director at the first National Finals Rodeo in Dallas, forfeiting the chance to compete at the inaugural event.

1957 Linderman finishes among the top 10 all-around contestants for the 10th consecutive year.

1953 Linderman wins his second all-around world championship.

1951 Linderman succeeds Toots Mansfield as president of the Rodeo Cowboys Association. He serves as president for six years, before finally handing over the reins to Harley May.

1950 The cowboy celebrates his greatest season, winning world titles in bareback riding and steer wrestling as well as the all-around cowboy title.

1945 Linderman wins the title of world champion saddle bronc rider, defeating Ken Roberts by a margin of $1,500. He also wins more money from all events over the season than anyone in rodeo.

1943 Linderman claims his first world title, in bareback riding, based on season earnings.

1940 Competes at his first R.C.A. rodeo, the Greeley Stampede in Colo., winning the saddle bronc average and $300.

Bulldogging a steer before the hometown crowd, Red Lodge, Mont., 1964.

FOXIE

across the nation, eventually topping more than 500 events scattered from San Francisco to Manhattan, and from Homestead on the southern tip of Florida to Edmonton in the northern Canadian Rockies. By the late 1950s when Linderman finally stepped down from the office of president, the sport boasted more than 14 million annual spectators and prize money in excess of $22 million. Top riders like Jim Shoulders and Casey Tibbs were earning salaries that rivaled those of professional baseball players. And it was, first and foremost, Bill Linderman they had to thank for their prosperity.

But even as he helped shape the future of pro rodeo, Bill Linderman was himself cutting a wide swath in the field of competition. In 1945 he claimed his second event title, defeating Ken Roberts in the saddle bronc riding event by roughly $1,500. That same year, he was second to his younger brother, Bud, in the bareback riding standings, with nearly $7,000 won during the season. Although no all-around champion was named that year, Bill Linderman, as the biggest money-winner in rodeo for 1945, justifiably should be acknowledged as that year's top overall contestant.

Bill Linderman's next big season was 1950. That year the cowboy defeated a rising young star named Casey Tibbs to win the saddle bronc riding world championship. He also won the steer wrestling world title, defeating Homer Pettigrew, who holds the record for the most world titles in steer wrestling, with six. And finally Bill claimed

the all-around title as the biggest money-winner for the year, with $30,715. Before that time, no one had ever won three world titles in a single season, a feat often referred to as "rodeo's Triple Crown."

Even more amazing, though, is that Linderman managed to accomplish that while competing at opposite ends of the arena. Generally speaking, cowboys of his era were not the single-event specialists who would come to characterize rodeo in decades to come. However, it was rare to find a cowboy who could compete at the highest levels in both the timed events and the rough-stock events.

Obviously the skills that enabled a cowboy to be an adept bareback rider were not that different from the skills that made him competitive in bull riding. But one could ride a bucking bronc or bull without the horsemanship skills necessary for, say, calf roping or team roping. That's what made Bill an amazing and respected rodeo hand: He had worked tirelessly to develop his skills in nearly every discipline, and he was competitive in each at the very highest level.

He paid a heavy price for competing in all those events, however. Like another famous Montanan, Evel Kneivel, Linderman was known as much for his wrecks and injuries as he was for his successes. During his career he broke his neck and his back steer wrestling at a rodeo in Deadwood, S.D.; fractured his skull at the Colorado State Fair in Pueblo; broke his hand at the Madison Square Garden Rodeo in New York; broke his leg three times at various rodeos; and broke his riding arm below the elbow four times.

Despite these setbacks, Bill never tired of rodeo competition. He again proved his formidable talent by winning the all-around title in 1953, setting a record for money won ($33,674). That year he finished third overall in the saddle bronc event and second in the steer wrestling.

By then, however, a whole new generation of young cowboys had arrived on the scene: Jim Shoulders, Harry Tompkins, and Linderman's prankster friend Casey Tibbs principal among them. Immensely gifted in several events, these younger riders poured the coals to the furnace, competing at more rodeos than their predecessors. Meanwhile, Bill was busy toiling in the unpaid job of rodeo president, which often took him away from major events while he presided over the quarterly meetings of the R.C.A. and attended to the myriad tasks of running a burgeoning sports association.

After earning his sixth world title in 1953, Linderman would never again lead the world standings in bareback riding, saddle bronc riding, and steer wrestling. Nor would he claim the all-around title again. But even amid the hungry new generation of post-war riders, Bill remained The King.

After turning 30, an age when many competitors' careers were winding down, Linderman continued competing for an additional 15 years. For the first eight of those years, Linderman never failed to finish among the top ten riders in the all-around competition, and he was a consistent top-five rider in at least one of his three specialty events.

In 1955 when he broke his arm twice over the course of the season, he still managed to win more than $19,000—a sizeable sum at the time. He wound up ninth in total earnings that year, a testament to his toughness. And that was his worst finish in the all-around standings since the R.C.A. originated the award in 1947.

Bill didn't limit his competitive enjoyment to the rodeo arena. He was also known to be an avid golfer. And just as in the rodeo arena, Linderman was not afraid to litter the air with purple prose when things weren't to his liking. One story has it that Bill was having a bad day on the course, and one of his cowboy buddies offered a piece of advice. "Bill," he said, "maybe you aren't addressing the ball properly."

Bill walked up to the tee and said, "Dear ball, you S.O.B., when I hit ya, why don't you go straight!"

Although his antics might not have earned him the admiration of the country club crowd, he certainly was loved and respected among his peers. It may be cliché to say that he was generous to a fault. But, well, he was. He loaned his fellow cowboys

BUSTER RUETTEN

Linderman's statue by artist Bob Scriver now greets visitors to the Cowboy Hall of Fame in Oklahoma City.

COURTESY PRCA

In addition to the PRCA's annual Linderman Award presented to the top prize winner who earned money at both ends of the arena, many rodeos honor the champ with their own trophies and awards.

thousands of dollars to help pay medical bills when they were injured or to pay their entry fees when they had gone into a slump.

"Bill would hogtie me and hook me with spurs if he knew I told you this," said one of his friends to a *Denver Post* reporter, "But he tore up $10,000 worth of IOUs in one bundle. He'd loaned it to hard-up cow-

DEVERE

Though not known as a bull rider, this photo taken at Phoenix in 1943 proves Linderman did indeed compete in every event.

boys. He figured the $10,000 wasn't lost. He'd invested it in rodeo."

Linderman was also quick to help young cowboys out by giving them advice or encouragement. But increasingly his discussions with fellow cowboys behind the bucking chutes or at the hot dog stand were not about the competition going on at the moment, but about decisions and policies made by the R.C.A. board. Everyone, it seemed, had a different opinion to share about how the rodeo business could best be run.

Bill Linderman had also struggled for years with the rodeos themselves. Initially the rodeo committees had been very distrustful of the R.C.A. and had done everything in their power to undermine the upstart rodeo association. Whereas the individuals who organized the rodeos would liked to have choked the R.C.A. in its infancy, they came to respect and admire the association during Linderman's reign as president. It was through his efforts and those of the rodeo board that the sport had gone

from being a loose confederation of hundreds of independent rodeos to a strong and unified sports association with standardized rules and procedures.

Writing for the *Denver Post*, sports columnist Robert Marranzino said of Linderman, "He was the great emancipator of the waddie. He brought them up from slavery, and he brought the rodeo game up from a rowdy competition among cowboys to a national sport."

But after fighting many battles over the years, Linderman eventually grew weary of the presidency. On two separate occasions he tried to get his name taken off the annual ballot. But his supporters would not let him. Finally in 1957 his will prevailed. A young, college-educated competitor named Harley May was elected to take his place. Relaxing at his home in Idaho, Linderman seemed relieved to finally be free of the responsibility.

"It's great to have those S.O.B.s hollering at somebody else," he said.

But Linderman could hardly stay away from a leadership role for long. In 1958 a commission was formed to undertake a project — to create a new, championship-deciding rodeo finale, in essence a rodeo World Series.

When it came to selecting an arena director, there was no other choice for the National Finals Rodeo than Bill Linderman. He was picked by unanimous vote of the NFR commission, which consisted of cowboys, stock contractors, and rodeo committee members from across the United States. Harley May, who chaired the new commission, said of the position, "The job requires a man who has the unqualified support of the entire sport of rodeo, a man used to getting things done with a minimum of fussing, and a man thoroughly experienced in all phases of contest rodeo.

"More than any other man in rodeo, The King fills all those qualifications."

Linderman forfeited his own chance to compete in steer wrestling at that first NFR in order to attend to all the details necessary to complete a successful event. It was no easy task, coordinating the livestock from nearly every stock contractor in the business, making sure that the right animal was in the proper chute, and that the right calf was lined up for a particular calf roper. But Linderman, with his exceptional memory for livestock, his eye for detail, and his monster work ethic, handled the first NFR with scarcely a hitch.

Linderman continued to serve as treasurer-secretary of the Rodeo Cowboys Association in the years to come. He was 45 when he competed in a major event for the last time. He won the steer wrestling at the '65 Pendleton (Ore.) Round-Up Rodeo. At the time, his career earnings stood at just over $480,000, a record.

He might have continued competing for several more years if tragedy had not intervened. Linderman was en route from Denver to Spokane, Wash., to attend a series of awards banquets and do some promotion for the rodeo association. Having crossed over the snow-laden Uintah Mountains of Utah, his plane was on the final approach to the runway in Salt Lake City when it nosed down abruptly, striking the ground short of the tarmac. The landing gear collapsed, and the plane skidded more than a half-mile before coming to rest. Fuel lines apparently ruptured in the crash, and the plane burst into flame. Linderman, along with 41 other passengers, perished in the fire. Fifty more survived.

A memorial fund was created in Linderman's honor, and in 1966 his friends gathered at the Cowboy Hall of Fame in Oklahoma City to witness the unveiling of an 8-foot bronze statue of The King. Undoubtedly, a large portion of the $12,000 raised came from cowboys who had been down on their luck and received a "loan" from Linderman. The year prior to his death, he was said to have paid more than $1,300 in entry fees for cowboys headed to the National Western Stock Show in Denver. Noted one rodeo association official, "They paid him back for sure if they got lucky. But he carried a lot of chits with him when the plane burned in Salt Lake City."

Among the many close friends in attendance was Gene Pruett, who had served for years alongside Linderman on the R.C.A. board. In his presentation speech Pruett said, "(Bill) was a man of great physical strength, with personal convictions and opinions to match. Bill has a host of friends who swore by him, and some enemies who swore against him. If an issue arose concerning the sport of rodeo, he was never a fence-straddler. He took a side, and spoke out about it.

"I was proud to call him a friend."

Bill Linderman is remembered not only as an inductee into both the Cowboy Hall of Fame in Oklahoma City and the ProRodeo Hall of Fame in Colorado Springs, but in the Professional Rodeo Cowboys Association's annual Linderman Award. The trophy is awarded to the cowboy who wins at least $1,000 in each of three (or more) events, including a rough-stock and a timed event. It is considered among the toughest rodeo awards to win and the mark of rodeo's best true all-around hand.

COURTESY PRCA

Linderman's contributions to rodeo, both as a contestant and an administrator, earned him a fitting nickname: The King.

LARRY MAHAN

"TO BE A winner in rodeo, you have to be above the ordinary. You're not just the fellow who is out there competing. You are a guy who has more going for him. You're the kind of a guy who will push himself and keep pushing ... it's tough on you physically, it's tough on you mentally. But if you have that desire to win, that means you have to win."

Those words, spoken by Larry Mahan in 1972 during the filming of the Academy Award-winning documentary *The Great American Cowboy*, summarize the philosophy of the greatest all-around cowboy of his era. Even more succinctly, Mahan once said, "Winning to me is what alcohol is to an alcoholic, what dope is to an addict. I've got to have it."

That was philosophy. Here is the poetry.

Mahan is sitting astride a white bareback bronc, his body inclined backward, his face masked by a dirt-stained silverbelly hat with a flattened brim that juts like an awning over his forehead.

He nods almost imperceptibly, an anonymous hand reaches down to unlatch the gate, and the bronc rears out of the chute. The cowboy catches the horse's neck with his spurs, and rider and horse blow skyward in a leap that would make Michael Jordan nod knowingly. The horse takes another mighty leap into the arena, then

Mahan shakes out his spurs and pulls them up the horse's neck. Then he resets the spurs just as the horse sets back down.

Seeming shocked that the small man is still perched solidly on his back, the horse rears upward, until both he and Mahan are held at the peak of balance, that delicate point at which the horse is just a featherweight away from tipping over backward.

The camera freezes horse and rider, leaving us with the indelible image of a movie-star handsome cowboy in the prime of his life doing battle with a powerful and treacherous bucking horse, also in his prime. And making it all look like ballet.

Larry Mahan grew up in the rain-soaked, verdant mountain country of the Pacific Coast. Although his family owned a couple of acres when he was very young, it certainly couldn't be described as a ranch, but they always had a few horses around the place.

"My first love was the horses," Mahan recalls. "I got my first horse, Sheba, when I was 8, and I spent several days riding her night and day." The boy rode in a local drill team, holding a flag while Sheba fretted, dancing in place as the other riders wove around them. Later, Mahan used the half-Arab pony as a roping horse, and he also used her to practice his bareback spurring licks. Although Sheba didn't buck, Larry would lie back on her, imagining that he was champion Eddy Akridge.

Ray and Riva Mahan divorced while the boy was still quite young. Ray had been a heavy equipment operator and a farrier and had done some rodeoing in his younger

Mahan liked this shot (taken in Australia) so much, he used it for his clothing company ads. The horse actually flipped over, pinning Mahan underneath him.

entered his first contest in 1957, a kids' calf riding competition in Redmond. He claimed the buckle for first place plus a whopping $6.

"Winning that youth rodeo event planted the seed for what I wanted to do with my life," he said. "Even at that age, I found out what it was like to compete. To win."

In middle school and high school, most of Mahan's friends were other boys who hoped to become rodeo hands. When his parents couldn't take him to the youth rodeos, he caught rides to rodeos with his buddies. He went to as many as he could in the summers, but he was no hard-core competitor by any measure, making eight or ten rodeos a summer.

At the time, youth rodeo riders didn't ride bulls, only calves and steers. By the time he was 16, Mahan felt he was ready to get on some man-sized livestock. He went to a few competitions contracted by the Christensen Bros. Rodeo Co., and because there were fewer bareback and bull riders, he was able to get some practice on the stock that was turned out at the end of each event.

A couple weeks later he went to a rodeo in Klamath Falls, Ore., and entered the bull riding. There were two go-rounds, and Mahan's first draw was an old gray fighting bull named Tony Lama.

"I don't think anybody had ever won anything on him, but of course I was a nervous wreck," he said. "He skinned out through there, started to turn back. Then he stopped and stood there, trying to hook the clowns with his horns. So I got a reride on a nice bull named One Punch, and he was just a nice easy bull. I made the ride.

"Then, in the next round, I drew a bull named Top Rail. He was a perfect draw."

In his heyday Top Rail was one of the top bulls in the Christensen Bros. string, and Larry bested him to win the round and the rodeo's average.

"Winning that rodeo was a big carrot dangling out there in front of me," he said of the experience. The kid, who was said

days. But Riva had put a stop to that. In the uncertain economic times of the 1940s, she felt it was simply too dangerous an activity for a family man to be involved with.

After the divorce, however, Riva remarried, this time to a horse trainer and farrier who also had some rodeo experience. Both father and stepfather were supportive of Larry's interest in horses in general and rodeo competition in particular.

By age 12 Larry had become very involved with a local saddle club that held roping events and practices on Tuesdays and

"... Mostly, though, sports taught me to get in the moment, to focus on what I was doing at the time."

Sundays at the state fairgrounds in Salem. Larry would help load calves and steers, sometimes clambering aboard a calf while he herded the others through the pens.

"The ropers saw that I was such a little maniac that they began letting me get on a couple of calves at the end of the night's roping," he recalls.

That experience paid off when Mahan

to be a good, natural bronc rider as well as a bull rider, caught the attention of Bob Cook, a rodeo hand who worked for Christensen Bros.

Cook was known as a guy who would help a fledgling rodeo cowboy with talent, and he recognized something special in this young want-to-be from Brooks, Oregon. Cook got the stock contracting firm to loan Mahan some practice bulls. Actually, there was an agreement with the saddle club that Larry and three other boys would share in caring for the animals, but it was Mahan who showed up with the rake, the feed bucket, and the water hose night after night.

Larry went to the saddle club four or five days a week and at the end of the night, he'd run the bulls into the chutes and practice on them. He gained additional experience mounting the turn-out animals at the nearby rodeos. He also contested in the team roping.

Larry was also a good, if not outstanding, wrestler in high school. Although he did well at district meets, he didn't excel at the state level. No matter. The discipline and the physical training, he felt, played an important role in his development as a rodeo athlete.

"I learned a lot from [wrestling]. I learned body control. And I liked the fact that it was one-on-one, that if you won, you had no one else to thank and if you lost, you had no one else to blame. Mostly, though, sports taught me to get in the moment, to focus on what I was doing at the time," he said.

As his high school graduation neared, Mahan learned firsthand the dangers of his chosen career path. At a rodeo in Stockton, Calif., he was bucked off a bull named Rattler. Rattler stepped on Larry's jaw, breaking it in five places. For two months Mahan had to take his meals through a straw.

"I've got to admit, I had a few chickens in my gas tank after that," recalls the cowboy. But on the positive side, Mahan gained his slightly quirky, crooked grin that to this day causes women's hearts to flutter. Larry, however, already had his heart set on a girl he'd met at the fairgrounds arena in Salem:

CAREER MILESTONES

Larry Mahan

born: November 21, 1943
Salem, Oregon

Six-time World Champion All-Around Cowboy (1966-70, '73); two-time World Champion Bull Rider (1965, '67).

1994 After doing rodeo telecasts, television commercials, TV movies, and his own series called *Horseworld*, Mahan appears as Blue Hannigan in the Tommy Lee Jones film *The Good Old Boys*.

1975 Mahan co-stars in two feature films, *Six Pack Annie* and Roy Rogers' *Makintosh and T.J.* Teams with Billy Kidd in Steamboat, Colo., to hold the first-ever Cowboy Downhill ski race. He competes in the NFR for the final time in saddle bronc and bareback riding. Those qualifications bring his total to 26.

1973 Mahan again qualifies for the NFR in three events, winning a record sixth all-around championship with record earnings of $64,447. Mahan enters the clothing business.

1972 Mounting a comeback, Mahan rips his right bicep loose from a tendon in his arm, forcing surgery. Although he returns to action less than two months later, he fails to make the NFR in any of his three events. His year is recorded in the documentary *The Great American Cowboy*, which goes on to earn an Academy Award for best documentary the following year.

1971 After breaking a leg at a rodeo in Ellensburg, Wash., Mahan is forced to sit out the NFR for the first time since his debut there in 1964.

1968-1970 Mahan maintains his streak of all-around championships, drawing even in the record books with Jim Shoulders in 1970. Between 1966 and 1970, he qualifies in all three rough-stock events each year.

1967 Mahan becomes the first cowboy to surpass the $50,000 mark in season earnings. At the NFR the cowboy wins the saddle bronc ride, and finishes the year with $51,966. In round two, he also tops the rank saddle bronc Descent for 79 points, the highest scored ride of any NFR rough-stock event that year. Mahan also wins his second bull riding title with $21,653.

1966 Coming off a phenomenal season, he qualifies for the NFR in all three rough-stock events. He handily claims the world all-around cowboy title and cracks the $40,000 season-earnings mark. Mahan also claims a second bull riding world championship.

1965 Mahan wins the bull riding world championship despite bucking off all but one of his bulls at the NFR.

1964 Mahan qualifies for his first NFR, competing in the saddle bronc riding in Los Angeles. When the rodeo closes, he is ranked 15th in the world in the event.

1963 He fills his R.C.A. rookie permit with an $852, second-place finish in El Paso, Texas.

1962 Mahan moves his family to Arizona, where he finishes out his final year of high school rodeo by winning both the Arizona State High School Rodeo Association bareback and steer wrestling championships, as well as the state's all-around cowboy title.

1960 At his second R.C.A.-sanctioned rodeo, a small competition in Klamath Falls, Ore., the 16-year-old high school student wins the bull riding.

1957 Mahan competes in his first rodeo, a kids' calf riding in Redmond, Ore., winning $6 and a belt buckle.

AL LONG

Mahan grabs a handful of Red Mud at Dallas, Tex., in 1974.

ment in an auction barn, he competed in amateur events to build a nest egg that would enable him to finance a run in the Rodeo Cowboys Association.

Still only an R.C.A. permit-holder and not allowed to compete in most of the major pro rodeo events, he went to El Paso, Tex., in February of 1963 and entered the rodeo there. He placed second overall in the bull riding, winning $852. The earnings enabled him to fill his permit and become a full-fledged member of the Rodeo Cowboys Association.

"From that day on, I became a 'Roads Scholar,'" says Mahan, enjoying what is obviously a favorite pun.

Like most rookies, Mahan was just another face in the crowd, struggling to make enough scratch to pay his entry fees. He saw big-name riders like Jim Shoulders and Casey Tibbs, the men he'd admired when he was a boy. At one rodeo he watched as Shoulders, who was considered the top bull man in the 1950s, was dumped off the back of a Beutler Bros. bull. A few weeks later at La Fiesta de los Vaqueros rodeo in Tucson, Larry drew that same bull. This time Shoulders was watching.

Before getting down on the animal, Mahan recalls that he asked Shoulders if the older man had any advice about how to handle the bull. Shoulders just said, "Good luck, Kid."

"I got thrown off right at the latch," Larry said, just like Shoulders had.

While Shoulders may not have had much to say to the young rider at the time, Mahan's talent was praised by one rodeo sage, announcer Mel Lambert. At the Oregon State Fair rodeo, Lambert advised the crowd to keep an eye on the local cowboy because "Someday he is going to be the all-around world champion."

"You could just see it," Lambert recalled in a *Sports Illustrated* article some years later. "The way he sat on a horse and spurred, he was all business, and he had the try to get him wherever he wanted to go."

Where he wanted to go was to any rodeo, anytime, anywhere. Tearing up the road, Larry began competing at a frenetic

Darlene Weisz, a willowy, dark-haired beauty of a horsewoman.

In 1962 Mahan and his bride moved to Phoenix, Ariz., where his father was living at that time. The couple's first child, Lisa Renèe, was born in the fall. Larry competed in some high school rodeos that summer (he was still eligible), winning the Arizona High School Association all-around crown as well as the bareback and steer wrestling championships.

He'd intended to enroll in Arizona State that fall and join the school's rodeo squad. But he was stunned when he found out that out-of-state residents paid considerably more than in-state students. With a wife and child to support and marginal employ-

pace that was to characterize his career both in and out of the arena. Nothing, it seemed, could slow the ambitious young cowboy, not even injury.

Mahan recounts the story of how, at a rodeo in Helena, Mont., he was jerked down on the bull's head in an unequal meeting of the minds. The bull was unscathed, but Larry suffered a broken nose and cracked upper teeth. Not enough to keep him off his schedule.

Later, at another rodeo, Mahan's neck was mauled by a bull. The doctor looked at the X-ray rather hastily, assuring the rider that everything was okay. But the cowboy's neck remained sore for some weeks afterward. A month later a rodeo cowboy caught up with Larry and asked if he'd spoken with the doctor, who had been trying to reach him.

"No," Mahan replied. "Why?" When the doctor had a moment to review the X-ray more carefully, he discovered three cracked vertebrae in the back, just below the neck bones. "I guess they just healed themselves," he said. "At least it stopped bothering me."

Larry adopted the attitude that the best way to fix a riding weakness was more practice. At one point he enrolled in a school held by bronc rider and Canadian all-around champ Kenny McLean. According to McLean, the young rider came to the clinic hoping to improve his consistency and spurring style and technique. He got on 49 broncs in a week.

"I was so sore, I could hardly leave Canada," Mahan said.

That first year of rodeoing full time, the cowboy concentrated on the saddle broncs.

Larry was so focused on bronc riding that he bought a practice horse and hauled it with him throughout the rodeo season. It was, he said, the perfect practice bronc.

"He was well-mannered in the chute. You could even ride him like a saddle horse. But if you put a flank on him, he'd jump and kick just perfect. After six or seven seconds, he'd just stop and I would just climb off. I practiced on him for a span of a few months, and when I got

back to Arizona that fall, he had stopped bucking. So I sold him to some kids as a saddle horse," he remembers, cracking a crooked smile. "He was a great kids' horse by then. But you didn't want to get anything near his rear feet."

Concentrating on broncs, Mahan earned his first trip to the National Finals Rodeo in 1964. After the event wrapped up in Los Angeles, however, Larry had made only $343, finishing the year ranked 15th in the event with a sum of $6,473. Clearly, the cautious approach wasn't going to make him the kind of living he foresaw as a rodeo star. The following year, he returned to riding all three rough-stock events with equal fervor.

What he gave up in arena conservatism, however, he made up for in fiscal conservatism. Mahan began investing his money. That very businesslike approach to "the game," as Larry to this day refers to rodeo, would earn him a great deal of attention as a new breed of cowboy: a cowboy athlete.

By 1968 "Super Saddle," caught here making a ride on Major Reno, was rodeo's top draw.

FERRELL BUTLER

"The business aspect came into play very early in my career. I realized that I'd better hang on to every nickel because if misfortune ever visited me, the money would stop right then. I give Lisa credit for that. If she had not been born in 1962, I would have been a little too much of a wild child," he said. "As it was, I walked, talked, ate, slept, and breathed the game."

Mahan had other peculiarities that set him apart from the stereotypical hard-drinking, hard-living, tobacco-spitting cowboys of old. For example, at a rodeo in Sterling, Colo., he crossed paths with Enoch Walker, a world champion bronc rider he admired very much. Mahan had a container in his hand, and he was tipping it back and taking a hit off it when Walker spied him behind the bucking chutes.

"He asked me to give him a swig, I guess

Mahan, weathering the storm on Hurricane at the Cow Palace, 1966.

BEN ALLEN

figuring it was whisky. So I handed him the bottle. And he said, 'What in God's name is this? Honey! What in the hell has rodeo come to?'" Mahan was indeed holding a plastic honey bear in his paw, using the amber fluid to get his energy level up before riding.

Larry Mahan also began to pilot his own plane, a practice that, although not exactly new to rodeo, was considerably more efficient than traveling by car or commercial aircraft. Despite having "a real fear" of flying, he rationalized that flying to the rodeos beat driving all night and arriving the next day bone-tired.

On one chartered flight Larry asked the pilot if he would teach him to fly. For two weeks Mahan and the certified flight instructor, Arnold Kolb, traded time at the controls. When they arrived in Burwell, Neb., the two rented a J-3 Cub trainer, and Larry learned takeoffs and landings. By fall he traded a pickup truck he'd acquired for a 1946 Cessna 120 that belonged to Jim Madland. He worked on his flight training at the last major regular season rodeo of the year, the 1965 San Francisco Grand National. As his career progressed and his income grew, Mahan upgraded to better, more powerful planes.

That season Larry returned to the NFR, this time in the bull riding. The event had moved to Oklahoma City, and it was to stay there throughout Mahan's career. Many will remember 1965 as a watershed year for rodeo. Every single world champ that year would go on to be an original inductee into the ProRodeo Hall of Fame in Colorado Springs, as would two of the great bucking animals from that era: Jim Shoulder's legendary bull Tornado and a bucking horse named Descent. Among that outstanding class of champs, of course, was Mahan.

After taking a break from bull riding after the broken jaw incident, Mahan had come back to the event with a vengeance. He later credited bull riding with helping him deal with fear, a handy trick for all of the rough-stock events. Early in 1965 Larry got on a bovine hot streak, winning more than

$9,000 in three months at the big indoor rodeos. That gave him the lead in the bull riding world standings that held all the way through the year and into the NFR.

Mahan's finals was anything but notable, however. In eight rounds the cowboy only rode one bull for a measly 60 points. In contrast, the defending champ, Ronnie Rossen, topped seven of his bulls to handily win the NFR bull riding average. But the $1,848 Rossen received wasn't enough to close the gap that separated him from Larry, who claimed the title by a margin of just over $1,000.

"I felt like I had backed into the world title," said Mahan. "After such a big start, I'd gone into a slump in July. It got so bad that Bill Linderman (a great all-arounder who worked both ends of the arena) approached me at Douglas, Wyo., after I had bucked off a perfect bull and said, 'Young man, can I give you some advice?'"

"And I said, 'Sure.'"

"'If you want to win it, you've got to quit falling off.'"

Mahan did his best to heed the older rider's advice that next year. Larry's rapid rise to rodeo fame truly began in 1966. With an exceptional showing all season in all three of his specialty events, he would prove to be a verifiable iron man by season's end. At 23 Mahan accomplished something that had never been done: He qualified for the NFR in all three rough-stock events.

Certainly, there had been other strong multievent cowboys. Principal among the rough-stock riders were Casey Tibbs, the famed South Dakota bronc rider, and Jim Shoulders, the 16-time world champ from Oklahoma. But, as any rodeo veteran of their era will acknowledge, both had weaknesses. Shoulders didn't really contest the saddle bronc event, and Tibbs for the most part stayed off the bulls.

In Mahan, rodeo had a true three-event rough-stock rider who was equally adept at each of the events. Going into the NFR, he already had a lock on the all-around title, the most coveted of rodeo championships. And that, coupled with an obvious star power, made him the big draw of the 1966 Finals.

Larry had good performances in both the horse events, placing four times in eight rounds of bareback riding (including a win in the final round) and twice in the saddle bronc riding. But bull riding at the NFR was, once again, a bugaboo for him. He tasted Oklahoma soil in his first four rounds, a truly embarrassing start for the reigning world champion bull rider.

Whether it was pure luck or merely the end of a slump, Larry finally connected in round five aboard a big brown bull that had bedeviled the other riders throughout the season. After that, Mahan won another

Mahan's image as a clean-cut professional is evident in the suit and tie he wore as he took possession of his fourth all-around champion's saddle.

check for a 70-point ride in round six. Although he finished off his next two bulls with qualified rides, neither effort proved good enough to garner additional cash. Still, something had clicked in Larry's mind, and that set in motion a new approach to rodeo the following year.

Whereas most athletes at the time thought that sports success came from physical preparedness and conditioning, Mahan started realizing that mental attitude and preparedness were at least as important, if not paramount. On the advice of Gary Leffew he began studying works like *Psycho Cybernetics*, which

Mahan's singing career gave him the chance to hob-nob with his singing idol, Waylon Jennings, who he opened for at several concerts.

taught that subconscious mental processes were what trained the body to perform under stress, and that those subconscious thoughts could be mastered and harnessed to improve performance.

Mahan competed with even greater energy than he had in the past, and by Sep-

tember he had surpassed Jim Shoulders' all-time record for rodeo earnings. Without doubt, the all-around title was in Larry's hands. But the question on everyone's mind in Oklahoma City was if he could surpass the milestone of earning more than $50,000 in a single season.

By the eighth round, he was so close to the $50,000 target that he could feel it. But in the saddle bronc riding, he drew a humdinger named Red Pepper, who served up a little spice. Larry went all-out, clicking his heels with every leap and then arcing his boots forward in time with the horse's ground-pounding hoof beats. The dance earned the duo 70 points on the judges' cards, and $387.49 for first place. That brought Mahan to within $96 of reaching his income goal.

When Larry's turn in the bull riding came, silence gripped the normally boisterous cowboys. In fact, the entire arena became oddly quiet in anticipation of the moment. Mahan's bull, a big black and white Brahma-cross named Hamp, cracked out and began spinning hard to the left. Suddenly the bull cranked back out of the spin, seemingly defying the rules of momentum. He leapt skyward, floated briefly, then fell to the earth with a stiff-legged crash that drove the cowpoke down onto his bony spine like a 155-pound sack of cement. Larry stuck with Hamp to the whistle, then dismounted and scrambled for the fence. His efforts earned him fourth place and a check for $98.89, bringing his prize money to $50,000.75.

All told, Mahan topped 24 of the 27 animals thrown at him at the '67 NFR, a performance that would have earned him an MVP in most other sports. He won the NFR saddle bronc riding average for the highest score on nine head, including a 79-point ride on the great bronc Descent in the second round that would go down as the highest scored ride in any NFR roughstock event that year. (Freckles Brown's legendary ride on Tornado at that same finals earned him only 73 points under the less generous scoring of the time.)

Once the final round and the average

COURTESY PRCA

In his singing debut, Mahan rode in on this steer singing, "Mommas, Don't Let Your Babies Grow Up To Be Cowboys," and was dismayed to hear the audience chuckling. After the song, he stepped off and discovered the puddle.

award was figured in, Larry's total earnings that year were $51,966. In addition to winning his second straight all-around crown, he also claimed his second bull riding world championship with more than $21,000 won in that event. Mahan also placed among the top five riders in both of the horse events to close out a rodeo season for the ages. Adding to Larry's near-perfect season, the Mahans added a second child to their family, John Ty, who had been born in January.

Not much changed in 1968. Again, Larry was a dominant force in all three rough-stock events throughout the season. Again, he went to the NFR with the all-around title sewn up. This year, he shined brightest in the bareback riding, placing second in the average behind his occasional traveling partner Jim Houston. In the world standings he failed to win an event championship, but he did complete the year as the reserve

champion in the saddle bronc riding behind another outstanding young gun, Shawn Davis, who claimed his third world title in four years. In the all-around race Mahan nearly matched his previous year's earnings record, falling just shy of the $50,000 mark.

Larry's riding caught the attention and admiration of the cowboys he'd looked up to in his youth. They recognized the one intangible that separated Larry Mahan from the other cowboys of his generation: star quality. Of Mahan, Jim Shoulders said, "Larry does have great coordination, and he does work hard at his trade. But so do a lot of cowboys. You can look at them and tell right off they have it and that they are dedicated to rodeoing. And yet they don't make it. Larry's different. Why? I don't know."

But by the late 1960s Mahan's fame, which had seeped beyond the brim of the rodeo world the first year he won the all-around, was flooding outward. In addition to a *Sports Illustrated* profile, he appeared on the Johnny Carson show, in the pages of *The New York Times, PEOPLE Weekly*, in the then-popular men's magazine *True*, and even in the *Wall Street Journal*. Journalists dubbed him "Goldfinger," "Super Saddle," and one even called him "the cowboy in the gray flannel suit."

But the cowboys themselves were to honor him with the title that best expressed their admiration. They called him simply "Bull."

What appealed to the press, however, was the differences that set him apart from other cowboys. He didn't smoke and he rarely drank. He didn't spend all his time with the tight clique of cowboys, instead getting to know rodeo committee members and sponsor representatives who might help him advance the sport of rodeo. He was a rodeo cowboy, the best of his era. But he was also a personality, one whose charisma shined from the first row all the way to the top tier of seats.

For some years Larry had been in the running for the title of Oregon Athlete of the Year. Finally, in 1970, the sportswriters

"When I started winning a lot, everybody seemed to wear their hair short. As my hair started to grow, I was terrorized because of it."

of his home state conceded that rodeo was indeed a legitimate sport and that Mahan was its reigning king. He beat out baseball great Harmon Killebrew, which brought the cowboy to the attention of the Oregon-based sportswear manufacturer Jantzen.

A Jantzen representative called Bull and explained to him that Jantzen worked with top athletes as part of its International Sports Club. Though the pay was paltry, the company put together two photo shoots each year, bringing together outstanding athletes from a wide variety of sports. This year's shoot was to be in Majorca, and would Mahan be interested?

"I didn't even know where Majorca was," said Larry. "I figured it was somewhere south of Dallas. But I signed on, figuring it would be fun."

Soon Mahan was jetting off to Spain with athletes of the day who included Dallas Cowboy Don Meredith, hockey's Bobby Hull, Los Angeles Laker Jerry West, and surfing legend Corky Carroll. Hanging out with so many outstanding and successful athletes opened Larry's eyes to a bigger world. And that began to change the way he looked at himself.

"When I got into the game, I looked, talked, and walked like everybody else. I heard the banter the rodeo announcers all used about how the cowboy represented freedom and independence and the American spirit. But we were the first to judge anyone who didn't fit neatly into our little box. We were talking out the sides of our mouths," he realized.

Of course, America was embroiled in a losing foreign war, and young people everywhere were challenging the values of traditional society. Rodeo, however, had remained largely quarantined from society in general, floating along as if in a 1950s time warp. An incident that happened at the Mayflower Hotel sometime in the late 1960s helped awaken Mahan to the conflicts that gripped the nation and to how out of sync the cowboys were with the society at large.

A big cowboy grabbed a hippie and proceeded to cut the youth's long hair with a pocketknife. Larry remembers that, "I'd always been so involved in the game that although I had heard about such things, they always had happened at arm's length."

He perceived the incongruity of rodeo committees trying to attract people to their events, then having the rodeo announcers say things like "this is a place where you could still tell the boys from the girls."

A shaky Mahan ropes Billy Kidd, Lorie Bryngelson, and J.C. Trujillo at the Cowboy Downhill in Steamboat Springs, Colorado.

"That just struck me as wrong. Here we were trying to get people to come and pay for a ticket so that we could offend their long-haired, 16-year-old son," was how Mahan saw things. "We should reach to all fields of the public to get rodeo fans. You can't just depend on cattlemen."

So, around 1970, he began to grow his hair and sideburns long (by rodeo standards) and wear flashy clothing, such as broad-collared print shirts, hats with ornate bands, and a puka shell necklace. He'd long tucked his jeans into his boots, a throwback to an older western fashion, but now those boot tops were flashy and more attention-grabbing. The older rodeo hands, and some of the younger ones, didn't like it.

"When I started winning a lot, everybody seemed to wear their hair short. As my hair started to grow, I was terrorized because of it," he said. But the new generation of riders who looked up to Mahan soon followed his fashion lead, and puka shell necklaces and flashy hatbands became a common sight behind the chutes.

Meanwhile, Larry kept on winning. In 1969 he maintained his streak, qualifying for the NFR in all three of his events. At the NFR he placed in the average in all three events to finish the season by besting his record for the all-around with earnings of $57,726.

The next year Mahan's season began much like the weather in the Rockies — cold. For the first time in several years, he failed to crack into the top-five standings in the all-around race by March. He attributed his bad fortune to the luck of the draw (or rather, the lack of it), saying that the animals he'd contested on "couldn't throw a loose saddle blanket."

But fortune turned in his favor as the weather warmed, and Larry climbed to his accustomed place at the top of the all-around pile. Despite suffering a cracked vertebra that sidelined him for a portion of the season, he maintained an insurmountable lead in the all-around to draw even with Jim Shoulders' record of five all-around world titles by season's end, topping the other cowboys with earnings of $41,493.

At the NFR the 27-year-old mounted an astounding 33 animals, placing on roughly one-third of them.

Ty Murray made it his life's goal to surpass Mahan's record of six world titles. Mahan was the first to shake Murray's hand when he did so in 1998.

In a game where injuries inevitably take their toll, Larry's good fortune finally deserted him in 1971. At one point he was asked what advice he might give to aspiring rodeo cowboys. He replied, "Be prepared to spend several months of your life in plaster of Paris."

Although he had sustained such injuries in the past, they weren't the type that had kept him down for large chunks of the season. In 1971 that would change.

Mahan was in contention for the all-around title with a bright young talent who worked both ends of the arena, Phil Lyne of Texas. But late in the season, Larry broke his leg at a rodeo in Ellensburg and was forced to watch the NFR from the sidelines for the first time in his career.

The following season he mounted a comeback, optimistic that he would be able to win a sixth all-around title and thus surpass Jim Shoulders' record. Around that time, a documentary film-maker, who was following the rodeo trail,

began to pick up on the "rivalry" between Mahan and Phil Lyne, the young multi-event hand from George West, Tex., who had stepped up to claim the all-around title during Mahan's absence in 1971.

The film followed the two as they traveled from rodeo to rodeo, swapping leads in the all-around title race. The filmmaker tried to create a strong contrast between the slow-talking Lyne, who traveled from rodeo to rodeo in an old station wagon and two-horse trailer, and Mahan, the flashy all-around champ who flew from rodeo to rodeo in his own private plane. In fact, the contrast wasn't as black and white, for Lyne was also a pilot and a good friend of Larry's.

The third star of the movie was a bull named Oscar, who was considered the top bull in rodeo at the time. In July Mahan tore his biceps muscle at Cheyenne Frontier Days, an injury that effectively took him out of six weeks of competition and the all-around title race. This was bad news for the filmmakers, because much of the tension of the film involved the title race.

Looking for an alternate Hollywood ending, the producers later matched Larry against Oscar. Setting the scene for the contrived contest, the announcer informed the filmgoer that Mahan "was riding for no money, no title." Just the primitive contest of man against beast. Larry cracked out of the chute, the bull began turning back to the left, and rider and animal were frozen in a statue-like pose as the credits rolled.

"It's a good thing they didn't show the next couple of seconds," says Mahan, a sly grin crossing his face. Despite stretching the definition of the term "documentary," the film went on to win an Academy Award. Larry's already great popularity soared even higher in the wake of what was, admittedly, a moving and attention-grabbing film.

By this time Mahan was involved in a western clothing line and was making plans to ride the wave of documentary fame to a career in Hollywood. His marriage to Darlene was beginning to disintegrate, and the cowboy contemplated plans to move to Hollywood and prospect for television, film, and commercial work. But first, he had to win a sixth all-around title and put that goal to rest.

"I felt like 1973 would be my last year of being totally involved in the game. I was moving into the apparel line, and I needed to find some way of advancing my business and preparing for my future," he said.

So, at 30, Mahan prepared for another frantic year of two-a-day rodeos, 100,000 miles of travel, and literally hundreds of broncs and bulls. By September he was back atop the all-around standings with a lead of more than $15,000. Though reluctant to predict his all-but-inevitable sixth all-around championship, Larry's confidence grew larger and larger as December approached. In his own recap of that memorable finals, Larry wrote about his favorite three-event rider: himself.

"In retrospect, I rode well at the '73 NFR. I placed more than ever before. Seven broncs helped provide checks … missed one out and won third in the average. Made money on two bareback horses, rode the rest, and won second in the average. In the bull riding I won money on four bulls and fell off four … I didn't want to put too much pressure on the champ, Bobby Steiner, and runner-up Donnie Gay.

"I left the '73 NFR with that sixth world champion all-around cowboy buckle. The goal had been reached, but in my heart I knew that I would never rodeo again with that fire in my belly."

At the awards dinner that followed, Jim Shoulders introduced Larry. As the man who had succeeded him as rodeo's greatest all-around cowboy mounted the stage, Shoulders pulled two dollars from his pocket … handing it to Mahan and jokingly telling him to get a haircut. Almost two decades later in 1998, when Ty Murray captured his seventh all-around title and thus reached his goal of surpassing Mahan's record, Bull was the first to offer a handshake and congratulate him, thus continuing a tradition among men who rodeo fans will always remember as simply "the Greatest."

Larry Mahan withdrew from serious rodeo competition after the 1975 season.

When his marriage with Darlene dissolved in 1974, he made the move to Los Angeles where he found work in several films and television projects. Some music industry friends convinced him to try a singing career, and Mahan toured for several years and released an album titled *Larry Mahan: The King of the Rodeo*. That career reached its apogee when he opened for Waylon Jennings at the famed Red Rocks Amphitheater in Colorado, where he said, "I was sure all those people who showed up were there to see me." Soon after, the band leader fired himself from his own band, content that all the hard work had made him a better entertainer, if not a chart-topper.

He fathered a third child with his new wife, Robin, and continued building his own highly successful brand of western apparel. For eight years he starred as the host of the acclaimed television program *Horseworld*. When his second marriage failed, Mahan settled on his 680-acre ranch in Guffey, Colo., west of Colorado Springs, where he continues training horses and conducting riding clinics with his significant other, Diana McNab, a former Canadian ski team member and a sports psychologist. The two of them conduct equine wellness programs that utilize horses in teaching stress management and optimizing human potential.

In a sense, he has come full circle: His love for horses, which got him involved in the rodeo business and set the stage for an amazing career, is now where he finds his passion and purpose. He says he no longer misses the excitement of "the game," finding that his goal of earning his Ph.D. in horses provides challenges enough.

Visiting with him on his ranch, which has an amazing view to the east of the famous Pikes Peak, it's hard to believe that this gentle, gray-haired, contemplative man is the same person who once proclaimed, "Winning to me is what alcohol is to an alcoholic, what dope is to an addict. I've got to have it." Still, Mahan remains a man driven to succeed.

Only now, he doesn't define success in 8-second intervals, but in the hours spent in pursuit of a zen-like unity with horses.

TY MURRAY

JOY MURRAY pumped her fist and shouted her support as her son stepped onto center stage at the Thomas & Mack Center in Las Vegas—and into rodeo history.

On Sunday, December 13, 1998, PRCA Commissioner Steve Hatchell shook the hand of Ty Murray before 17,500 rodeo spectators at the National Finals Rodeo and congratulated him on earning his seventh world champion all-around cowboy title.

With the seventh victory of his incredible career, Murray had eclipsed six-time winner Tom Ferguson and, more importantly to the then-29-year-old cowboy, the career of Larry Mahan. For, as Joy would proudly tell anyone who happened to be near her at that moment, topping the achievements of Larry Mahan had been her son's dream for nearly his entire life.

In fact, the proud mom said, she'd saved an assignment from Ty's third-grade teacher that asked the school kids, "If you could do anything in your life, what would it be?"

While other children stated their hopes of one day becoming astronauts, firefighters, doctors, nurses, or other careers, Ty had answered, "I want to beat Larry Mahan's record."

Appropriately, the man who had been Murray's inspiration and his mentor was there at the Las Vegas arena gate, offering his handshake to Ty as the cowboy stepped

out of the arena at the conclusion of the 10th round of NFR bull riding.

Mahan congratulated his protegé, who had just secured his second bull riding world title and surpassed Mahan's six all-around awards. But Mahan, like numerous others, had recognized Murray's greatness many many years before that momentous day.

"I remember watching a 13-year-old warming up for the bull riding event at the National Little Britches Rodeo Finals in Colorado Springs," said the legendary man cowboys referred to as "Bull." "And I thought to myself, 'My God, he's riding bulls better than I did as a world champion.'

"Mentally, I could see that he had total concentration and dedication to his sport. I felt that, barring injury, this young man was going to be one of rodeo's greatest champions," remembers Mahan. "When I heard he was going to compete in all three riding events, that was intriguing. I wanted to meet someone who was as out of his mind as I'd been."

For Murray, meeting Mahan was akin to having an audience with Babe Ruth. His elation was even greater when the rodeo legend called him that spring and invited him to spend part of the summer at his tidy spread just a few miles west of Colorado's famous Pikes Peak.

"I barely knew Larry Mahan. I thought he was God. I didn't have any idea what he was gonna do with me. I thought maybe he was going to work me," said Ty.

"Work him?" said Mahan with a laugh. "I knew enough about rodeo cowboys not to

think I could have gotten any decent work out of him." Mahan also felt there was little he could offer the boy as instruction. But what he did give to Ty was an abiding friendship and a sense of what it meant to be a champion. Murray was especially impressed with Mahan's ease around people and his natural public relations skills.

"I didn't learn hardly anything from him about riding, but I learned a lot about people," said Murray of his summer expe-

"I can't remember a day in my life when I didn't want to ride in a rodeo."

rience with "Bull" Mahan. Those same skills would come in handy years later, when Murray became rodeo's most recognized star.

Almost from birth, Ty Murray had been preparing for his future. Born October 11, 1969, in Phoenix, Ty was to grow up in a rodeo-rich environment. His father, Butch, was raised on the famous 101 Ranch in Oklahoma, and had started colts since he was old enough to sling himself up into a saddle.

When Ty was born, his father was working as a racetrack starter and had

enjoyed a long if not particularly distinguished career as a multievent rodeo hand. His mother, Joy, was the sister of Butch Myers, one of the best timed-event hands in the rodeo business. Furthermore, she had her own rodeo credentials that, amazingly, included successes as a bull rider in the National Little Britches Rodeo Association.

Joy and Butch weren't worried about their baby growing up to be a cowboy: When Ty was 2½ years old, his father loaded him onto a calf and ran alongside the toddler, holding onto the boy's belt. When he reached the age of 4, Ty told his dad, "You don't need to hold on to my belt anymore, Dad.

"I fell pretty hard, but that's how I learned," he remembers.

When he wasn't riding calves, Ty rode his mom's sewing machine case. His mother would pin a number on the back of his shirt, and Ty would mentally blow the living room up to the size of the National Finals arena in Oklahoma City.

"He plumb wore his mom's sewing machine case out from sitting on that sucker and spurring it," says his dad.

Before he even went to grade school, Ty had entered his first rodeo. Not surprisingly, he won. Ty was handed a check for $44, but he handed it back and told them to keep it. His real prize was the bright buckle he held in his hands.

His first-grade teacher, Mary Flynn, remembers that even at that young age, Murray spent his weekends at rodeos or practicing for them. "Ty wasn't like most of the students. He knew what he wanted to do, even at that age. He daydreamed about rodeo and drew pictures of bucking horses," she said.

"I can't remember a day in my life when I didn't want to ride in a rodeo," says Murray.

By age 8, Ty was helping his father break horses, who arrived at the Murray's place by the semitrailer-load. At age 9, Ty rode his first bull, an 1,800-pound brindle, at a Little Britches rodeo.

His second bull bucked him off, stepped on his face, and broke his jaw.

Ty accepted that, knowing that injury and pain were the price of admission in the very dangerous game he'd chosen to play. His commitment was complete. His only concern was that he might miss the junior rodeo finals.

A rodeo-friendly physician wired up Ty's jaw and, a few weeks later, the cowboy rode in the finals with a helmet perched atop his head. He won both rounds and the event title.

At age 12, Murray began breaking colts for money, saving his cash to buy a mechanical bucking machine. The first day the machine was installed, Ty rode it until his legs were chapped and bleeding.

Nearly everything Murray did was intended to make him a better competitor. He learned to ride a unicycle to improve his balance, then added juggling to his routine to enhance his timing. He walked the entire pipe rail fence at the racetrack.

In high school he trained with the gymnastics squad, yet never competed in a meet — no time on the weekends, what with so many rodeos to get to. That training would remain apparent in Murray's flying dismounts and the fluid, almost acrobatic way he rode.

Ty's intensive preparations had their intended effect: By the time he was a regular competitor in the National Little Britches Rodeo Association, he was already a stand-out rider. Murray claimed National High School Rodeo Association all-around and bareback riding titles in 1987 as well as the National Little Britches Rodeo Association senior men's all-around title.

As he awaited his 18th birthday (the age at which he was able to join the Professional Rodeo Cowboys Association), Murray competed in amateur and open rodeos, typically besting the adult riders. The money he made enabled him to bankroll his first pro season, and Murray enjoyed a life of relative luxury compared with most first-year competitors. "I like a comfortable place to sleep and a good steak, and I plan on riding well enough to afford them," he said at the time. Simultaneously, Murray was setting fire to the collegiate record books.

Swayed by the aggressive recruiting of Odessa (Tex.) College coach Jim Watkins, Ty had joined the two-year college's rodeo squad in 1988. Among the school's former team

CAREER MILESTONES

Ty Murray

born: October 11, 1969
Phoenix, Arizona

Seven-Time PRCA World Champion All-Around Cowboy (1989-94, 1998); two-time Pro Rodeo Cowboys Association World Champion Bull Rider (1993, '98).

1998 Murray becomes the first-and-only seven-time PRCA world champion all-around cowboy and claims a second PRCA event championship in bull riding with record season earnings of $167,154. In July Murray wins the Calgary Stampede bull riding and all-around titles, as well as claiming $50,000 in the Calgary "sudden-death" bonus round. Murray also claims the Houston all-around title and sets an Astrodome arena record for his 90-point ride on Sammy Andrews' bull Erkel.

1995 Cumulative injuries suffered over his career force Murray to take a season off from competition. Returning to the arena in 1996, he again suffers injury setbacks that force additional surgeries and recuperation. He does not return to full-time rodeo competition until the 1998 season although he does compete in Pro Bull Rider events.

1994 Murray tallies his sixth consecutive world champion all-around cowboy title to draw even with timed-event ace Tom Ferguson in consecutive all-around championships. Murray also wins his second straight Dodge National Circuit Finals all-around title.

1993 En route to his fifth consecutive PRCA all-around championship, Murray stretches the PRCA single-season earnings record to $297,896 and sets an NFR earnings record ($124,821) for the most money won. At 23 becomes the youngest cowboy to reach $1 million in career earnings in PRCA history. Wins Houston to claim a $21,714 check; the following year, he tops that record with a $31,010 win at Houston.

1992 Murray repeats his all-around championship.

1991 Murray repeats as all-around champ. At San Francisco's Cow Palace, Murray scores 92 points on Flying Five Rodeo's Bordertown, then the second-highest bareback riding score in rodeo history.

1990 Murray qualifies for the National Finals Rodeo in all three rough-stock events, becoming the first to do so since Larry Mahan in 1973. Murray tops the bull "Mr. T," becoming only the third rider to master pro rodeo's 1986 Bucking Bull of the Year. He also becomes the first rodeo cowboy in PRCA history to surpass $200,000 in a single season, wins all-around.

1989 PRCA world champion all-around cowboy (youngest in association history); National Intercollegiate Rodeo Association all-around champ; member, NIRA champion men's team (Odessa [Tex.] College); National Little Britches Rodeo Association all-around champ.

1988 PRCA all-around and bareback rookie of the year.

1987 National High School Rodeo Association all-around and bareback riding champ.

members was Jim Sharp, a formidably talented bull rider who had won the 1986 Pro Rodeo Cowboys Association Rookie of the Year title, earned a trip to the NFR, and proceeded to win more money than any rookie in history up to that time. Coach Watkins hoped that Murray would bring the college's fledgling rodeo program another NIRA national title, as Sharp had done in 1986.

Murray would do that, and more.

The multievent phenomenon snared the National Intercollegiate Rodeo Association titles in saddle bronc riding and bull riding en route to the 1989 NIRA all-around

Though he always claimed that he just wanted to be remembered as a good cowboy, Murray clearly loved bull riding best.

crown. His points alone were enough to ensure the team's national victory.

Although academics concerned him less than rodeo accomplishments, he was nevertheless a hard-working student. Watkins recalls that Ty "worked on his physical conditioning constantly and handled his business here at school well. A very responsible student, when he (was) going to be gone for three or four days, he (would) see all his teachers and get the work assignments ahead of time."

Despite a heavy college schedule of rodeos and academics, Ty also enjoyed success as a rookie in the Pro Rodeo Cowboys Association. In 1988 he followed college roommate Jim Sharp's example, earning the title of PRCA overall rookie of the year by virtue of his earnings ($45,977) spread evenly between bareback riding, bull riding, and saddle bronc riding. Despite his exceptional performance, Ty missed competing at the National Finals Rodeo that year, primarily because he'd spread himself so evenly among his three events.

By 1989 pro rodeo insiders were well aware of the cowboy everyone called "the Kid." Never before had rodeo seen a cowboy who brought such equal ability to all three rough-stock disciplines. Even Mahan recognized that there was weakness in his own game (namely his bareback riding) that was absent in Murray's.

If there were any doubts that a new king had come to rule the rodeo realm, Ty laid them to rest at the 1989 NFR. Murray had qualified for his first NFR in saddle bronc and bareback riding. Only one other competitor, Ty's uncle Butch Myers, had managed to make the cut in two events, and what shaped up was an interesting family contest for the all-around championship.

Both Myers and Murray trailed team roper Clay O'Brien Cooper going into the championship-deciding finale, but their advantages over the team roper were twofold. First, they each had two chances each night to win money (O'Brien Cooper had only made the cut in team roping), and they stood to earn more money, since team roping paid roughly one-third less than the other events.

FRED NYULASSY

That Ty and his uncle would compete head-to-head for the championship was a story tailor-made for the scribes. When Butch had won the world championship in steer wrestling in 1980, he'd sat his young nephew on his knee and let him look at the bejeweled gold-and-silver trophy buckle. Murray had said, "I can't wait to get my own."

Ty wasted no time going after his prize. In the first four rounds of saddle bronc riding, he captured a first- and two second-place finishes. In the first six rounds of bareback riding, he garnered a win and two third-place checks.

When the dust settled, Murray had ridden all 10 of his bareback horses, finishing in a tie for second place in the 10-round average competition, and earned sixth place overall in the saddle bronc average, despite bucking off a horse in round three. All told, Murray had banked $58,000 at the NFR, giving him $134,806 for the year.

At 20, he was the youngest cowboy in rodeo history to win the coveted PRCA all-around title, usurping that distinction from the legendary Jim Shoulders, who'd won the title in 1949 at 21. Murray was also the first and so far, the only, all-around hand to win both the National Intercollegiate Rodeo Association men's title and the PRCA all-around world championship in the same year.

Mounting the stage to claim the world champion's buckle, Ty looked at it speechlessly. Finally, and with tears in his eyes, he broke the silence and said, "It sure is pretty."

Murray had but one regret on looking back at his break-out season: He hadn't qualified for the NFR bull riding. "I'd like to compete in the National Finals in the bull riding. It seems if you don't make it to the NFR in that event, people forget that you ever rode bulls," he said. Ty had often professed his love of all three events, but it was clear that distinguishing himself in the bull riding meant a great deal to him. Not long after winning his first all-around

Ty (left) confers with his buddy Cody Lambert following a bull ride at Cheyenne in 1994.

DAN HUBBELL

championship, Murray would prove himself the equal of peers such as Tuff Hedeman, Jim Sharp, and the late Lane Frost.

It was at Rapid City, S.D., that next January that Ty matched moves with one of the most legendary bulls in rodeo history. Mr. T, so named by stock contractor Pete Burns because he was "big, black, mean, and ugly," had twice been voted top bull at the NFR by rodeo stock contractors. In T's career, only one cowboy — Marty Staneart — had managed to weather 8 seconds on his back.

At the '89 NFR, Mr. T had ended Jim Sharp's record string of 23 consecutive NFR bull rides, thus enabling Tuff Hedeman to win the title in honor of his closest friend, Lane Frost. Many say it was Sharp's defeat that earned the animal the title of best bull at the 1989 NFR.

Now, it was Murray's turn to try the beast. Riding with consummate skill, Murray rode Mr. T commandingly to the whistle, the ride earning him 84 points, the Rapid City bull riding victory, and a win in the rodeo's all-around competition.

Murray was modest in victory, saying, "He's a great bull. He bucks really hard, and he's a smart bull—I got lucky."

Ty Murray's story began to attract mainstream press attention—both positive and negative. Denver AP reporter Dirk Johnson visited Murray and Jim Sharp on moving day—the pair were leaving behind their college digs for Stephenville, Texas. Johnson made the day out to be a rollicking party in which the boys drank beer and destroyed property—allegations that Murray vehemently denied.

The negative article made Murray somewhat wary of the press, but his undeniable talent prevented him from ducking the public eye. Although he remained somewhat curt with reporters, he never turned away a kid who wanted an autograph or a photo with Ty. He'd had his idols as a kid, so he knew what a kind word and a scribble on a rodeo program meant to a child's dreams.

Murray motored through the remainder of 1990 at a breathtaking clip, earning checks at nearly every rodeo he entered. At Houston Murray claimed an astounding $16,500 en route to the all-around title there. Of that princely sum, $13,532 came from his win in the bull riding, which Murray was concentrating on to ensure that he'd make the NFR in all three of his events.

Ty was sidetracked for five weeks when, in May, he hung up for an instant in the stirrup of a saddle bronc, whose hind hoof clipped the rider's elbow as he fell. But he roared back in July, winning the all-around title at "the Daddy of 'Em All," Cheyenne Frontier Days Rodeo.

Murray enjoyed an exceptional season, qualifying for the NFR in all three roughstock events—something no one had done since Mahan in 1973. By the National Finals, of course, the comparisons between Mahan and Murray had become inevitable. The Bull, ever gracious with the press, commented with droll humor, "I'm glad I didn't have to compete against that little rascal."

Murray and Mahan crossed paths at the Thomas & Mack Center on the evening of the eighth round, and Mahan asked the one question that only he could: "Fun, isn't it?" Murray just nodded his head, saying "You're right about that. I'd do this for free."

Murray, however, was making his banker in Stephenville very happy, spurring his way to $72,818 in NFR earnings for a season-smashing record of $213,772. It was the first time a cowboy had crossed the $200,000 season's earnings mark and nearly $50,000 more than the next closest earnings mark set by rough-stock cowboy Lewis Feild.

It's probable that Murray would have earned even more were it not for a freak accident in round nine in which his saddle bronc, Bo of Don Gay's All-Star Rodeo, flipped over right out the chute gate, mashing Murray's knee in the fall. Ty's knee swelled to the size of a football, and he chose not to try his remaining five head of bucking stock. Later, photos of the accident would grace a six-page *Sports Illustrated* article on Murray titled "Yipee Ty Yay!"

By 1991, Murray's dominance as the all-around cowboy was all but complete. The futility of trying to pursue Murray in the all-around chase had been proven at year's end, when Murray eclipsed his previous record for season earnings, winning $244,231.

This time, though, Murray stayed healthy through 10 rounds, placing deep and often in all 3 of his specialty events. In his 30 arena trips, Murray cashed checks 13 times and banked more than $100,000, smashing Feild's record for NFR earnings by more than $25,000.

So far in his career, Murray had managed to dodge the odds and avoid serious injury. His luck, however, went sour in August of 1992 after he dismounted from a bull and twisted his knee, damaging ligaments. He strapped on a leg brace, stayed home, and devoted hours and hours to physical rehabilitation exercises. By October he was back to riding. Ty's determination and willingness to work through the pain enabled him to qualify for the NFR in all three events—and sew up his fourth consecutive all-around title with total earnings of $225,992.

Murray's focus from the beginning had always been the all-around title, but by 1993 he was beginning to assert his domi-nance in the one event that meant the most to him—bull riding.

Since childhood, Ty had always been taken by the bull riding. "The bulls would tickle Ty the most—he won't say it, but it's true. He walked and talked and lived and breathed them," said his mother.

That season, Ty would take his bull riding to the highest plateau. Although he competed at a mere 58 rodeos, he placed in the bull riding 51 times—a heretofore unheard-of riding percentage. Among those matchups was a "mano-a-toro" battle with three-time

SUSAN LAMBETH

Joy Murray shares the love with her son following his record-smashing seventh world all-around win.

PRCA bull of the year Pacific Bell of Western Rodeos, a bovine whose reputation put him alongside Mr. T and Red Rock as one of the greatest bulls to challenge Murray's generation.

"That's the rankest bull I've ever seen since I've been around rodeo," said the cowboy, who matched moves with the bull at the Red Bluff (Calif.) Roundup. "He could have bucked me off at any moment from the first jump. But when the whistle blew, that's a feeling that can't be described."

In July Ty became only the seventh cowboy in PRCA history to cross the $1 million earnings threshold, and he'd done it in half the time that anyone before him had. His buddy Tuff Hedeman, who also crossed the $1 million mark that summer at age 30, was the nearest in age to Ty, who was 23 at the time. Ty was also the dominant force in the bull riding standings. Come October, Hedeman was ranked second in the bull riding world standings, but was nearly $30,000 behind Murray in the world title race.

Ty's riding in the horse events all season had been spectacular, of course, but all the talk at the '93 NFR was about the bull riding competition. At first blush, it seemed that nobody had any chance of coming close to Murray, who'd been tapped off all season long and riding like the ghosts of all the legendary bull riders were sitting on his broad shoulders, guiding his every move.

Murray checks the scoreboard at the Pikes Peak or Bust Rodeo in Colorado Springs.

COURTESY PRCA

But early during the 10-round prize fight, Murray hit rough going. Twice in the first four rounds, Ty was bucked off. Then, in the fifth round, Murray's bull had a bad trip. A bull that earlier in the year had earned him 92 points and the win at Nampa tried a little too hard, fell on its side, and left Ty to struggle and hold on while the animal scrambled to his feet, costing Ty precious seconds. Judges awarded him only 65 points—and the option of a reride.

Even with that score, Murray was assured of a check because only three of the remaining fourteen bull riders made it to the bell that night. But, as Ty said, "I came here to try and win first. I'd rather win nothin' than settle for fourth."

He wrapped his rope around the reride bull, Edward Scissorhands of the Wayne Vold Rodeo string, nodded for the gate, and sat tight for what may have been one of the bravest, riskiest, and potentially foolhardy gambles in Vegas that night. Murray made the bell and earned 80 points—good for second place in the round.

Five days later, Ty finished second in the average behind Canada's Daryl Mills, who'd emerged as Ty's strongest challenger. When the prize money was added up, Murray had defeated Mills by a mere $95.

Were it not for his dice roll in the fifth round, Ty would have watched the buckle go north of the border.

Ty Murray didn't win a single go-round in any of his events, but not a night passed when he didn't cash a paycheck. At the rodeo's end, he had won the bareback riding average, the bull riding world title, and his fifth PRCA all-around title. His season earnings were $297,836—a sum that would not be surpassed before the new millennium dawned, and probably for many years afterward.

Ty's single-minded pursuit of rodeo greatness had led to a career of records smashed like gnats on a windshield as he motored at breakneck speed past one milestone after another.

He'd set arena records at rodeos all across the country and won event titles and all-around awards at every major competition too. All that remained was the one goal he'd wanted to achieve since he was a school kid: that of the most all-around titles ever won.

Murray's chance to tie the record came in 1994; after winning five consecutive all-around titles, he needed one more to draw even with Ferguson, who'd won his six in sequence. Once again, Murray had made the cut for the NFR in all three rough-stock events, virtually assuring that he would claim the all-around. And he did this despite competing at fewer rodeos (70) than almost every one of his fellow NFR competitors.

Murray had a fairly conservative finals, by his standards, topping 31 head (including a reride in the bareback event) and placing 8 times. His bull riding was atrocious — Ty bucked off five bulls in succession, rode but four of his ten, and placed but once, in the final round, to earn a mere $9,503 for the event. Daryl Mills, Murray's nemesis the year before at the NFR, claimed a well-deserved bull riding championship. Still, Ty was the man of the week, drawing even with Ferguson and Mahan in all-around titles won.

In the midst of these great accomplishments, Murray gained a bit of national attention he might not have wanted but that made for a great story years later. That January at Denver, Ty again made the papers when he was served an arrest warrant by officers of the Colorado State Department of Fish & Wildlife.

Murray had been invited to visit the ranch of a Colorado outfitter. Later the outfitter was incriminated for holding hunts out of season though Ty did not take part in these. However, during the investigation, officers found photos of Ty Murray allegedly bulldogging an elk. Seems that the cowboys had chased some elk through the hills on snowmobiles, and Murray had dropped one, then climbed aboard and rode it. Murray paid a fine — and added support to people's beliefs that the kid could ride anything with hair on it.

During his career, Ty had often parroted the often-heard saying that in rodeo, it's not a question of if you will get hurt, but when and how badly. Up to that time, Murray

MIKE COPEMAN

Murray's mastery of bulls led to two PRCA event titles.

had been fortunate to escape career-threatening injuries despite the rigors of competing in three of rodeo's toughest and most dangerous events.

By the 90s, stand-alone bull riding events began to compete aggressively with rodeos for the spectator audience. Ty had become involved on the ground-floor level as a founding member of Professional Bull Riders, a sanctioning body organized by the bull riders themselves to gain more control over their sport.

That spring, Murray was competing at a PBR event in Rancho Murrietta, Calif.,

COURTESY PRCA

Not since Larry Mahan had a cowboy qualified for the NFR in all three rough-stock events. Then came "the Kid."

to mount a comeback in 1997, only to get sidelined once again when a shoulder injury sent him back to the hospital and under the knife. Over the course of three years, Ty underwent even more reconstruction.

He spent much of his down time with martial arts trainer Jesse Marquez, who had been introduced to him by his friend Jim Sharp. Murray spent two hours a day in the gym conditioning his body and readying himself for his lifetime goal: to surpass Mahan's record. While much of his focus after 1995 had been on PBR bull ridings, he decided to go after one last PRCA all-around world title in 1998. By all accounts, it was to be a storybook year for the veteran champ.

On his third bull ride out, Ty cracked the 90-point barrier. Then he scored back-to-back all-around wins at two of the biggest rodeos of the season—the Houston Livestock Show (where he also won the bull riding) and the Southwestern Expo and Livestock Show in Fort Worth, where he won the saddle bronc riding.

Those wins catapulted him to the lead in the all-around race, a lead he was not to relinquish throughout the regular season. He dominated the bull riding event all season, too, topping off two of the best bulls in rodeo, Grasshopper and Red Wolf, and made a run at the Pro Bull Riders world championship.

Despite his huge successes at virtually every major rodeo, Murray had never won an event title at Canada's premier rodeo, the Calgary Stampede. In July he finally knocked off that rodeo, placing in three rounds of bull riding to capture the Calgary event title, then returning on Sunday for the famous "sudden death" bonus round. Ty rode both his bulls and, as the only rider to qualify a ride in the final-four round, netted himself a tidy check for $50,000.

Ty qualified for the 1998 NFR in both the bull riding and saddle bronc riding. But for whatever reason—and even Murray couldn't sort it out—the early rounds went against him. In the first half of the 10-round rodeo, Ty was thrown off three bulls and four saddle broncs. Timed event hand Herbert

when he felt his knee explode in pain. The strain from his efforts had torn the posterior cruciate ligament. After learning that surgery and rehabilitation would be necessary, Murray decided to take time off from his rodeo career and have his other injured knee repaired as well.

The hiatus had come at a good time. "I've been battling with bad knees for two or three years—I'm sick of it," he said. Ty had also tired of the grind of constant travel and figured he could use his time off to fulfill obligations to his many sponsors, attend to his growing fan club, and most importantly, rebuild his body and spirit. Little did he realize, his time away from the arena would stretch out over the next two years.

After recuperating and rehabilitating from the two knee surgeries, Murray tried

Theriot had steadily gained ground on Murray, throwing into question what had seemed like Ty's inexorable march to the podium. Murray waived off the skeptics, saying, "Mark McGwire doesn't hit it over the fence every time. But he tries to."

Finally, late in the rodeo, Murray started belting home runs. Ty kept Theriot at bay in the all-around, but staving off relatively unknown bull rider Blu Bryant in the bull riding proved more difficult.

Bryant, who'd gotten red-hot at the finals, forced the contest for the world title down to a one-header in the final round. To win, Murray needed a qualified ride. He drew the Harper and Morgan bull Hard Copy, an "eliminator" bull with a high buck-off percentage.

But Ty screwed himself on tight, nodded for the gate, and topped off the bull as if there were no pressure on him whatsoever. Judges marked him 79 points, good enough to share fifth place in the round with Bryant. Ty closed out his year with $167,154 in bull riding; Bryant earned $147,674.

Mahan met him at the gate. The two locked eyes, then hands. Mahan's mischievous eyes twinkled. Come January, the Bull and the Kid met once again when, in a special awards ceremony at the ProRodeo Hall of Fame, Mahan handed Murray the engraved trophy buckle proclaiming Murray the seven-time all-around champ.

Mahan would say of Murray, "I'm sick of looking in the mirror and trying to tell myself that I am looking at the greatest living rodeo cowboy. That title belongs to Ty Murray."

Having achieved his goal of topping Mahan in all-around titles, Ty began to shift his focus to riding bulls in the Professional Bull Riders. In 1999 he won the PBR Finals in record-shattering fashion, earning $265,000 at the championship (a record figure for any rodeo event) to pump his year-end total to $395,724.

He finished second in the PBR Bud Light Cup Tour World Championship, vowing to dedicate himself to winning that title one day. In 2000 he was inducted into the ProRodeo Hall of Fame.

GAVIN EHRINGER

All-around good guys Jim Shoulders, Ty Murray, and Larry Mahan, ProRodeo Hall of Fame, 2001.

GAVIN EHRINGER

Pop singer Jewel accompanied her boyfriend to a gala honoring rodeo's greatest all-around champs at the ProRodeo Hall of Fame.

DEVERE

DEAN OLIVER

LARRY MAHAN once said of his rodeo contemporaries, "Most of us never had it easy. It's hard to become a champion if you always had change in your pockets."

Dean Oliver had it tougher than most, if not all, of his fellow rodeo legends.

When Vesper Oliver gave birth to her fifth son, he weighed a mere 3½ pounds and was what doctors termed a "blue baby." His red blood cells were under attack from his mother's, and his survival hung on a thread for days. But survive he did, and his mother named him Dennis Dean.

Dean's father was a private pilot as well as an airplane and auto parts salesman. He traveled almost continuously. By the time the family took up residence in Burley, Ida., during the heart of the Great Depression, there were two more kids, and the family had spent time in 40 states. Eventually, they left Burley for Nampa, a rodeo community near Boise. Verne Oliver bought an abandoned airfield, opened a flying school, and flew chartered hunting trips into the bush country of the Salmon River basin.

An avid hunter, Verne Oliver took a contract from the Idaho Woolgrowers Association to rid the area around Arco of coyotes that were preying on local flocks of sheep. While Verne flew, his partner would shoot coyotes from the open door of the plane. On one of their close passes, they crashed into the side of a snow-covered mountain. Verne Oliver died in February 1940, leaving his widowed wife to raise the seven Oliver children.

Vesper Oliver made do as best she could on a modest stenographer's salary. She dressed her kids in Goodwill castoffs, and the children remember standing in line every day to get raisins, beans, and discarded clothing from the Mormon-run Aid for Dependent Children in Nampa. The school kids taunted the Oliver children for wearing threadbare hand-me-downs and gave them withering looks as they carried the charity foodstuffs home. In the sixth grade, Dean won a marbles championship. A picture taken at the time shows him holding the flopping sole of his shoe while kneeling down to shoot marbles with his other hand.

Chronic breathing problems added to Dean's childhood woes, and it was later discovered that he had a damaged heart. If that were not enough, the introverted child also developed a speech impediment that made him unable to pronounce the letter "R." So, the word "rodeo" came out "wodeo," and rope was "wope."

School was further torture for the boy. Frail, friendless, and withdrawn, he frittered away the hours daydreaming of being a cowboy, with a proper ranch and his own herd of cattle. Oliver dropped out of school in the ninth grade and went off to seek ways to make money for his family. He got a job on a dairy farm milking cows, putting up hay, and doing basic farm

Still a newcomer on the pro scene, Oliver is shown roping at Prineville, Ore., in 1955, the first year he won the calf roping world title.

nearly all of his free hours riding. He rode her nearly everywhere he went, to work or hunting small game in the Owyhee Mountains. He rode bareback with a rope he'd fashioned into a hackamore bridle, but borrowed a saddle once from a sympathetic horseman so that he could ride in the Nampa rodeo parade. He had to hitchhike back to the man's home to return the saddle, and continued to ride bareback for several years to come.

Although ill-equipped at the time, Dean started the hard work of becoming a cowboy. According to Dean's brother Dale, "No milk cow or calf was safe after dark. The horse Dean bought was no good, so we'd run on foot after a calf, grab it, and Dean would try to throw it. But then a neighbor saw what we were up to and called the police. I can still picture the two of us lying in the bottom of a drainage ditch with the cops searching for us with flashlights."

At age 19 Dean took up work in the beet fields of Nampa for Alex Reisenstein. He began dating the man's eldest daughter, Martha, who worked alongside the men in the beet fields. Martha remembers the first day she met the now-strapping young man who'd just joined the crew.

"I eased over to get a look at him, and just as he turned around, I stumbled into an irrigation ditch and got sopping wet. It wasn't exactly what you'd call romantic."

When Dean began discussing his plans to wed Martha, his mother and brother tried to make him give up his dream of being a rodeo calf roper.

"I was sure the marriage wouldn't work out," Vesper recalled. "He had this crazy idea in his head about roping, and I just couldn't see Martha putting up with it for long."

Despite his family's misgivings, Martha proved to be his greatest supporter. She even postponed their marriage for several years, allowing Oliver to save up $400 to buy a green-broke mare named Brandy. In 1950 the couple finally tied the knot—and

chores. For his work, he earned $15 a month plus room and board.

That summer he and his brother went to the Snake River Stampede in Nampa. Dean had never seen a rodeo, and he was greatly impressed with the cowboys' fancy hats and boots and their shiny Quarter Horses. Instantly, Oliver realized his destiny in life was to be a rodeo cowboy.

"That night at the Nampa rodeo, I saw a little guy who was wearing glasses—I think he was a schoolteacher from New Mexico—win $300 in calf roping. That seemed like

"But at age 20, when most calf ropers had already started on their pro careers, he had yet to rope a calf."

$3,000 to me, sitting there broke and hungry and wearing secondhand clothes. I figured if he could do it, so could I."

Getting started wasn't easy. Dean moved from farm to farm, doing chores and saving his money for a horse. He found one for $50, but she had a large boil on her side. He carefully ministered to the mare until the sore had healed completely, and then spent

Dean bought his first saddle straight out of a Sears Roebuck catalog. When they wed, Martha, who had been working as a waitress in town, had $12 dollars to her name. Dean was flat broke.

Nevertheless, the newlyweds relocated to Kuna, Ida., where Dean again found work on a dairy farm. He had picked up a few tattered ropes and was practicing his throws on fence posts. At an age when most calf ropers had already started on their pro careers, he had yet to rope a calf.

It was his hope that Brandy could be made into a suitable mount, but he had no calves to practice on and precious little time for practice anyway. Work began at 4:30 in the morning, and on a typical day Dean worked until 7:30 at night.

After hours he would slip into the pens and practice roping, throwing, and tying milk calves in the muck. During lunch breaks, he roped bales of hay. Rather than falling straight into bed when he got home, he roped more bales under a porch light.

Finally, he bought a practice calf for the princely sum of $10. With no proper arena to practice in, he'd have Martha hold the calf and release it when he was ready. Having little experience training roping horses, Dean didn't have any idea how to get the mare to work the rope. So, when he dismounted, the horse would circle around the calf, yanking it around the arena while Oliver did his level best to catch it, throw it, and tie it down.

Dean sought the help of a local rodeo hero, Larry Finley, whose specialty event was bronc riding. With Finley's encouragement, Dean entered the saddle bronc riding event at the Snake River Stampede in Nampa, where he drew two of the best broncs. Finley warned him that, although an experienced rider could count on those broncs carrying him to the bank, Oliver was likely to gain nothing but a mouthful of dirt.

"He was right. Both horses flattened me," Dean recalls.

Unbowed, Oliver decided to forget the rough-stock events and concentrate on roping calves instead. On Sundays he rode 12 miles to the arena of roper and friend

CAREER MILESTONES

Dean Oliver

born: November 17, 1929
Dodge City, Kansas

Three-time World Champion All-Around Cowboy (1963-65); Eight-time World Champion Calf Roper (1955, '58, '60-64, '69).

1976 Oliver competes in his 16th NFR, setting the record for calf ropers. That record is later matched by contemporaries Ronnye Sewalt (in 1978) and Barry Burk (in 1980), and is later surpassed by Roy Cooper.

1973 Oliver wins the Idaho Open Golf tournament in Boise, expanding the meaning of the phrase "all-around cowboy." In addition to becoming a legend in rodeo, Oliver becomes something of a local legend as a senior golfer after playing the game for a mere seven years.

1969 Wins his eighth calf roping world title, besting the record of Toots Mansfield.

1966 Roping at the NFR, Oliver seemingly has the world title sewn up when, in the seventh round, his rope breaks. In the eighth and final round, he breaks another rope, causing his horse to run free in the arena and ultimately causing him to lose the title race by $96.

1964-1965 Oliver defends his all-around championship, becoming one of the most decorated all-around champs in rodeo history.

1963 In addition to winning the calf roping title, Oliver claims the title of world champion all-around cowboy with the help of money earned steer wrestling.

1962 Oliver narrowly loses the all-around title to timed-event competitor Tom Nesmith.

1961 At the National Finals, Oliver wins the calf roping average as well as being awarded the world title. It is the only NFR average that he wins in his career, despite roping at the rodeo an amazing 16 times.

1960 He stretches the single-season calf roping earnings record to $28,841, earning nearly $3 to every $2 won by any other competitor in one event.

1960-1964 Oliver wins a record five consecutive world titles, drawing even with Toots Mansfield for the most calf roping titles won (seven).

1958 He earns a second RCA calf roping world championship.

1956 Oliver competes for the first time in steer wrestling.

1955 He wins his first RCA world title, just five years after taking up the sport.

1954 Oliver vaults to third place in the calf roping world standings with $11,158 won for the year.

1952 Oliver buys his first roping horse. He joins the Rodeo Cowboys Association, and enters his first pro rodeo in Filer, Idaho.

1950 At Nampa, Ida., Oliver, 20, competes at his first rodeo.

1947 At age 17, Oliver attends his first rodeo with his brother. After seeing a schoolteacher win $300 calf roping, he sets his sights on becoming a rodeo cowboy.

DEVERE

With the big Lee Riders clock ticking behind him in Cheyenne's Frontier Park, Oliver goes under the rope, the common style in 1962.

Jake Dyer, one of a handful of accomplished ropers who'd settled in Nampa. Dyer's coaching got Oliver started on the intricacies of training a roping horse.

"I didn't think he would amount to much that first year," Dyer said of his eager but very green pupil. "He'd swing an awful big loop — 'peared to be 20 feet across. Only things he had goin' for him was speed and strength. And Dean was so anxious to get to tyin' he never let Brandy develop as a rope horse.

"Course, the big money's won in those last seconds when you're tyin'. Dean's learning not to rely too much on a horse is probably one of the biggest reasons behind his greatness," concluded Dyer.

Dean began to enter local amateur rodeos and, although he failed to place at his first nine events, he bagged an $80 check at his tenth rodeo. He was earning just $165 a month at the dairy at the time, and he was so elated with his success he began thinking of quitting the dairy and competing full time.

His boss offered to give him a raise, and at month's end Oliver was given a check for $170. Disgusted with the paltry raise, he gave his notice. As he left, the enraged boss hollered, "What makes you think you can be a rodeo star? You can't even walk a straight line!"

Dyer staked the prodigal roper the entry fee for a rodeo in Winnemucca, Nev., and

Dean agreed to give him a split of whatever he won. The cowboy claimed a $450 check for second place. That was Oliver's first big win, and it did much to affirm his conviction that he could succeed as a rodeo roper.

But times were not easy. Not yet, anyway. Dean cobbled together a homemade trailer that he pulled behind a decrepit pickup truck. He carried a 50-gallon drum of gasoline in the truck bed to save money. When he was winning, Martha would accompany him. They would search for a good spot near the rodeo grounds and camp in the back of the horse trailer.

"When Dean didn't make enough to make entrance fees, we'd both go to work," recalled Martha. "Harvest time was best. We'd stop somewhere and chop beets or pick peas until we had enough for Dean to enter another rodeo."

"She'd do anything for me," Dean remembered with pride. "Sometimes she would even go clear back to Boise to work in a laundry to keep me on the road."

By the end of the summer of 1952, Dean Oliver was easily beating the competition in the Pacific Northwest. He had won $4,000 in two years in jackpots and amateur rodeos, but he wasn't content.

"He just kept driving himself unmercifully," said Martha.

His old friend and mentor Jake Dyer was astonished by Oliver's progress.

"Each run was smoother than the one before. His ability on the ground was exceptional. All that practice in the dark and the manure paid off. He could tie with the best of them."

In the fall of 1952, Dean was turned away from an amateur jackpot event in Winnemucca. He surmised that the local amateur cowboys didn't want someone with a reputation coming in and taking money off them. He decided it was time to join the ranks of the professional cowboys, where he would not be turned away again.

Oliver's first pro competition was at Filer, Ida., where he won the calf roping. Soon after, he competed in St. George, Utah, where he placed. Having realized that the horse he trained was inadequate for serious rodeo competition, he was riding other cowboys' calf horses, agreeing to pay them one-fourth of the prize money he won.

Dean went to a rodeo in Denver. He used someone else's horse and placed second in the average, winning $1,700. He had some additional money won a week earlier in Albuquerque, but he'd had to pay $625 between the two rodeos in mount money. Oliver felt it was time to get a horse of his own.

Hearing that the green kid with a pocket full of money was hunting for a horse, a veteran cowboy offered to sell him a buckskin calf horse with a gimpy knee. Although the cowboy told him the horse was 10, he was actually closer to 16. Dean paid the man $1,000 and promised another $750 for Buck, his first real rodeo horse. He built stock racks for his pickup and hauled the horse back to San Francisco for the Grand National Rodeo.

At San Francisco's Cow Palace, Dean placed second in a round at the first professional rodeo he contested aboard the aging but still savvy rope horse, taking home $550. That winter he entered the 1953 Denver National Western Stock Show Rodeo, the first major pro event on the calendar. He hoped for a big paycheck there to cover his expenses for a winter run, having already invested his earlier winnings in a new truck and trailer and making the payments on Buck.

But after missing both calves, Oliver slithered back home in a massive snowstorm with a mere $21 left in his britches, crestfallen that he couldn't continue to the other big winter indoor rodeos.

Back home, he sought employment as a cattle feeder, moving into a trailer home provided by his new employer. By now, he and Martha had a 2-month-old baby girl, and Dean felt the pressure to start winning more regularly.

After a year of roping in which hot streaks were followed by blustery cold spells, he returned to Boise and to the practice pen. Texas roper Dan Taylor helped Oliver improve his skills, and the next season, Dean returned to rodeo with new ability and confidence.

His fortunes took off at a gallop. That year he won just over $11,000, finishing third in the world standings, much to the surprise of his southwestern counterparts. Finances were still difficult for the Oliver family, but at least Dean had finally come out a little ahead and had hope of a better life to come.

Oliver continued to practice hard, falling in with Dee Burk during the winter of 1954-55, paying the famed Oklahoma roping champ $125 a month for the privilege of practicing with him. The investment in coaching paid off handsomely in Denver in January 1955, when Dean returned to the

Rogue's gallery: world champs Leo Camarillo, Dee Pickett, Oliver, and Roy Cooper in 1980.

JIMMIE HURLEY

A man who didn't own a saddle until he was 20, Oliver collected his share in the years to come.

National Western and won $1,250. He continued to the other big indoor rodeos, striking pay dirt in Fort Worth, Baton Rouge, San Antonio, and Chandler, Arizona.

Oliver moved to the lead in the world standings with $5,500, and he plowed some of the money back into a herd of 25 practice calves when he returned to Boise.

"That was when I learned to rope," said Dean emphatically. "With the practice I got on those calves, I was prepared whenever I went to a rodeo."

Finally, the years of struggle began to pay off for the Olivers. Still riding Buck as well as several other horses "not worth a week's feedbill," as one rodeo wag described them, Dean shredded the professional ranks throughout the 1955 season, cashing checks at major rodeos throughout the United States.

He and Martha celebrated the birth of their second daughter, DeAnn, but maintained a steady schedule that kept them on the road nearly the entire year. By late fall Oliver had a lock on the world championship, winning the title with earnings of $19,963.

It was a stunning victory, especially considering that the calf roping had not been won by a cowboy from the Northwest since

pro rodeo began naming world champs way back in 1929. Until Dean came along, Texans and Oklahomans had claimed the lion's share of world titles, with a few stray awards going to ropers from the warm-weather states of California, Arizona, and New Mexico. In those warm climes ropers could practice the year around, staying sharp for the big winter rodeos that were critical to winning the world title.

Oliver wintered in a part of the country where it was next to impossible to rope for six months out of the year due to the cold and snow. Furthermore, he wasn't mounted on a $3,000 roping-bred Quarter Horse, as were most of the "toughs" from Texas and Oklahoma. But what chafed the hides of the prideful Texas calf ropers the most was that Oliver hadn't even come up through a traditional ranching background, but as a city boy turned dairyman.

Besides the occasional speech problems, there were few remaining signs of his painful childhood: Dean had grown to be a large man, 6 feet 3 inches in stature and tipping the scales at an even 200 pounds. The years of dairy work had made him strong, too, a big advantage because the calves used in his early days weighed as much as 350 pounds. Still, Oliver found it difficult to fit in among the other cowboys.

"It wasn't easy to like Dean in those days," said one of his fellow ropers. "Most times after a rodeo, the winner'll buy all the guys a steak or a drink. And there's always a party everyone goes to. But not Dean. He'd always get dressed and head off to the next rodeo town. Stayed to himself most of the time.

"He just wasn't one of us," the older roper concluded.

If Oliver was a little tight-fisted, well, that was understandable. But none of his fellow calf ropers knew of his difficult upbringing, and they took offense at his standoffish behavior.

Rodeo announcers began to refer to the new champion as "The Rope." Somewhat cruelly, a few of the rodeo cowboys corrupted that to "The Wope," poking fun at Dean's occasional lapses into his childhood speech problem. Oliver took their overheard taunts in stride, contenting himself by beating them in the arena.

1956 didn't go so well for The Rope. He slipped to 10th in the world standings, finishing the year with earnings of just over $9,300. But one of the veteran cowboys, Casey Tibbs, began to take a shine to the serious youth from Idaho. And Dean's personal stock among the cowboys began to rise.

"One of the signs that points to a fellow's being accepted is when the guys start pulling stunts on him," said Tibbs a few years later. "I guess I was one of the first of 'em."

Tibbs, a noted prankster, was at a rodeo in Puyallup, Wash., when he spied Oliver heading for a shed to take shelter from a downpour. But two girls were headed into that same shed, and the somewhat shy and proper Oliver stood outside, wondering what to do. Finally, Oliver overcame his reticence and headed to shelter. Tibbs ran over and hung a padlock in the hasp.

"You should have heard those girls. Must of thought they was locked up with a maniac," said Tibbs. "Just a-whoopin' and a-screamin' something terrible."

Dean was probably a little hysterical himself, as his event was about to begin. But Tibbs' antics helped Oliver to gain a level of acceptance among the fun-loving rodeo cowboys.

Dean weathered a few bad years after that. After winning the 1955 championship, Oliver had to retire Buck, who was no longer of service due to his injured knee. For two seasons (1956-57) Oliver was again "afoot," forced to ride other competitors' horses. He fell out of the top five finishers at the end of both seasons using other contestants' horses. In 1958, however, he found a replacement horse named Chock, who helped him re-establish his dominance in the calf roping event.

Dean captured his second world title in 1958, winning a then-record $23,269. This time around, however, he was no longer an unwanted interloper in the tight-knit calf roping society. He had become a popular and accepted competitor renowned for his formidable ground skills and his speed at tying calves.

In 1959 Texan Jim Bob Altizer had an outstanding year, eclipsing the earnings record set by Oliver. Both cowboys struggled at the inaugural National Finals Rodeo, with Altizer winning a mere $356, and Oliver failing to earn a dime in three of the ten rounds. But in those days, the NFR didn't pay nearly what it would in the years to come, and neither roper's poor performance did much to hurt his position in the world title race. Oliver, with $18,104 in earnings (including $696 in NFR money) held on to third place in the world standings.

At a time when a new pickup cost just $2,000, Oliver was making a handsome living for himself and his growing family. But despite his earnings, the two-time world champ had yet to buy a truly top roping horse. Throughout the 1950s he'd ridden mainly horses who were deemed too old to be of much use by the cowboys who had sold them, or he'd simply used the younger, faster horses owned by other calf ropers.

After the 1959 Finals Dean retired Chock, who was likewise spent and crippled, and bought an exceptional 11-year-old gelding,

With Mickey, Oliver finally had the horsepower he needed to dominate his event completely.

Mickey, from Texas calf roper Lee Cockrell. Oliver was sold on the horse after matching young Glen Franklin at a jackpot roping. That was May, and by November Dean had won more than $18,000 on Mickey to capture his third world title. He had left little to chance, finishing the season with a whopping $28,841 to regain both the world title and the earnings record.

With Mickey, Oliver finally had the horsepower he needed to dominate his event completely.

"It was such a good feeling starting out with Mickey in the trailer behind me," said Oliver some years later. "I knew I could win if I got a decent draw. He always gave me 100 percent of his ability in every run. I was so lucky to have him in his prime while I was in my prime."

Dean, who was 30 as the calendar turned to 1960, was indeed hitting his prime just as rodeo was beginning a new era with the arrival of the National Finals Rodeo. In those days the NFR didn't pay nearly as much as it would decades later and was therefore not as crucial to the outcome of the world title races. But from the start, it was regarded by the cowboys themselves as a prestigious contest that put an emphatic ending to the year-long rodeo season. In the years that followed, the NFR would play a larger and larger role in the world title chases, and Oliver would be there to take part in one of the most unusual events in the rodeo's history. But first, he had many more titles to win.

With the 1960 world title victory, Oliver initiated a championship streak that remains unprecedented in the history of calf roping. In 1961 he went into the NFR having statistically locked up the world title. Even so, he wasn't content. In an eight-round contest, Dean placed in three rounds and captured the aver-

Oliver legs down a calf at Cheyenne. Flanking calves didn't become common until the mid-1960s.

SKIPPER LOFTING/PRCA

age, totaling 124 seconds. He was second to Ronnye Sewalt in total money won at the finals, and first in the world standings with a margin of nearly $12,000 separating him from reserve champ Sonny Davis.

Surprisingly, he was also a factor in the world champion all-around race, despite the fact that he seldom competed in any event but calf roping. He'd won $47 wrestling steers at a rodeo in Canada, money that qualified him for the all-around title. His challenger, Benny Reynolds of Montana, was a genuine multievent competitor who had qualified for the NFR in bareback riding and steer wrestling.

"Trying to win the all-around was a fight all the way," said Reynolds. "I can't remember how far ahead I was, but I do remember that I was in five or six events every week and Dean only had two.

"He would darn near win more money in calf roping than any of the rest of is would win in all of our events," said Reynolds.

Indeed, while the other world champions in the standard rodeo events were earning between $15,000 and $20,000 a year, The Rope was pulling in close to $30,000. By 1962 he'd become virtually unstoppable. Throughout much of the season, Oliver not only dominated the calf roping but led the all-around title race as well. It was not until the last regular-season rodeo of the year, the Grand National Rodeo at San Francisco's Cow Palace, that timed-event ace Tom Nesmith overtook Oliver in the all-around chase.

Dean, who never really made much as a steer wrestler, succumbed to Nesmith, who also claimed the steer wrestling world title. But Dean held his formidable lead in the calf roping to close the season with $27,756 in earnings. And another world championship.

Fate, however, seemed to dictate that Dean would win the all-around crown, and so he did the following year. Up until that time, the cowboy had seldom competed in the steer wrestling.

He'd suffered a broken leg while steer wrestling some years before at the Madison Square Garden Rodeo in New York, an injury that probably cost him a great deal of money and perhaps a calf roping world title. Steer wrestling, he felt, was risky and more likely to cause injuries that would take away from his calf roping.

But after coming so close to winning the world title in 1962, Oliver decided that a run at the all-around would demand greater effort in the steer wrestling.

As he made his plans for an assault on the all-around title in 1963, his main horse Mickey injured a stifle, which forced Dean to find another horse. He'd been occasionally paying mount money to his friend and fellow roper Don Fedderson, who owned a very good horse named Vernon. In 10 runs on the horse, Dean had finished out of the money only twice, and he coveted his friend's game speedster.

Among the cowboys Vernon was highly regarded as a horse who gave anybody who rode him a fair chance at a paycheck. Such consistency was rare in a rodeo horse, which made him highly prized. There were many calf ropers who felt that the sorrel gelding was the best to ever stick his head through a halter, and Oliver wasn't one to disagree after he had won a round on the horse at the famed Cheyenne Frontier Days Rodeo. Dean knew that if he could acquire the horse, he would not only make money himself, he would finally have a chance to recapture some of the mount money he had paid over the years.

When Fedderson got injured at Cheyenne that year, he decided to give Oliver his chance. Rumor holds that Dean paid Fedderson $5,000 for the chunky 9-year-old gelding. If that is true (conflicting claims put the price at $2,500), it was probably one of the highest prices paid for a roping horse up to that time. Cowboys who claimed that Oliver could win on a donkey, or with one arm tied behind his back, now had to contend with a roper armed with a lethal weapon. Riding Vernon was akin to putting a horseshoe in Muhammed Ali's glove, or a new, longer-distance ball in Tiger Wood's golf bag.

Immediately, Dean started winning on the horse. He swept a two-head competition at Great Falls, Mont., then won back-to-back rodeos in Idaho Falls and Lewiston, Idaho. The wins proved to him that he could go on without Mickey, although he would later say that no horse would ever fit him as well as the one who'd carried him to four consecutive world titles.

Come December, Oliver returned to the NFR with Vernon, winning two go-rounds

Oliver had climbed into the rarefied air occupied by such multiple-title holders as Casey Tibbs, Jim Shoulders, and Harry Tompkins.

in the eight-round calf roping and placing in two more. He fell out of the average when his rope broke in the final round, but it hardly mattered: Dean still kept his lead in the all-around title race over Guy Weeks, who was likewise competing in only one event at the NFR, and he handily defeated Bob Wiley of California for the calf roping world title. Amazingly, Oliver had won $3 to every $2 earned by Wiley that season.

With seven world titles to his name, Oliver had climbed into the rarefied air occupied by such multiple-title holders as Casey Tibbs, Jim Shoulders, and Harry Tompkins. But unlike those '50s standouts, Dean had swung the title domination to the timed-event end of the arena.

For the next two years he dominated the all-around competition, defending rodeo's most coveted title in 1964 and again in 1965 before finally sending the gold buckle back to the rough-stock end of the arena to be worn by a young gun from Oregon—Larry Mahan.

But despite winning three straight all-around championships, Oliver would become better remembered for his amazing string of five straight calf roping world championships won from 1960 to 1964. No calf roper before or since has come close to matching that record.

Although money was always a key motivator for Dean, he says he began to think a little bit about his legacy, and about the seven calf roping world titles won by the great Toots Mansfield between 1939 and 1950.

After Oliver had won his seventh calf roping title in 1964, the sporting press began asking, "Can Oliver surpass Mansfield's record?" The answer seemed like a no-brainer. After all, Oliver was the best calf roper going down the road, wasn't he?

Well, things weren't as simple as that. Oliver began thinking about the world title as an end in itself. After finishing second to Glen Franklin in the 1965 calf roping race, he finished second again in 1966, this time to Junior Garrison. That loss was truly one for the ages, and although the story has been told a million times, it merits one more retelling here.

Dean had finished the regular season as the world standings leader, but by a very narrow margin. A mere $120 separated him from third-place Ronnye Sewalt. Sandwiched between was Garrison. That year, the NFR featured only eight rounds. After six Oliver seemed unbeatable. He'd won four of the rounds and placed fourth in another. He'd widened the gap that separated him from Garrison and Sewalt to nearly $1,000, and he led Sewalt in the average by 15 seconds, and Garrison by more than 20. In the seventh round, Sewalt went long on his calf, finally tying him tight in 27 seconds.

Although today's nylon-poly calf ropes almost never break, ropers in the mid-1960s were still using natural manila ropes. In the seventh round Dean had the bad fortune of having his calf rope break. He had to settle for a 41.9-second time, while Garrison won the round in the time of 10.8 seconds.

That set up the dramatic climax to the rodeo. Going into the final round, Garrison still trailed Oliver by $633. After Sewalt became a non-factor due to a no-time on his last calf, Garrison seemingly took himself out of contention as well when he let the clock tick off 17.6 seconds before completing his run. Oliver, roping last, only needed a run of 45 seconds to place in the average and take home his eighth world title.

Dean's run started off normally, but as Oliver dismounted and his horse hunkered down to apply the brakes to the running calf, Oliver's new rope broke, snapping backward and striking the horse. The horse bolted, and when Dean finally caught him and climbed aboard to uncoil his second loop and capture the calf, he was already past the 45-second mark. Oliver failed to earn a spot in the average. Garrison, however, finished with the second-fastest cumulative time, giving him just enough extra money to overtake Dean in the world title race. Garrison's margin of victory was $96.

"It sounded like a .22 going off when they snapped," Oliver said some 30 years afterward. "Those ropes were made of grass and it happened from time to time that they would break, but I'd never seen two of them in a row break like that before."

According to Benny Reynolds, who knew a thing or two about snatching a title from Oliver, "People at the time said that after he lost the world title, he tried to hang himself ... but the rope broke."

In 1967 Dean had a bad season (for Dean Oliver), placing seventh for the year. With his 40th birthday fast approaching, many wondered if his greatness was ebbing away. Oliver soon put their doubts to rest. Boy, did he ever put them to rest!

By March of 1969 the roper's name was again at the top of the leader board. Then, he seemed to shift into overdrive that July, having the greatest runs of his long career and one of the most memorable winning streaks in rodeo history. Dean kicked things off by winning the Calgary Stampede, following that victory by signing his name to first-place checks at Salinas, Nampa, and "the Daddy of 'Em All," Cheyenne Frontier Days. All told, he won $15,000 in a month, or an average of about $500 a day.

The world title was assured. When the NFR concluded in December, Oliver had $38,118 in his event. It was the most money ever made in a single rodeo discipline at that time.

Moreover, he'd surpassed Mansfield in calf roping titles won, setting a record that no calf roper had come close to surpassing by the end of the century.

Although Oliver would never again win a world championship, he continued on the rodeo circuit well into his 50s. He sat down once to figure out how many miles he'd traveled during his 30-year career, and the miles ran to something in excess of 2 million. He'd been there to see rodeo in general, and his favorite event in particular, go through many changes.

As his career entered its twilight years, the high school dropout increasingly faced off against college-educated ropers. One of them in particular, Roy Cooper, was taking all of the innovations he'd seen among Oliver's generation of ropers and was now using them to speed up the event.

Calf roping had taken on an all-new look. Ropers were now flanking calves instead of tripping them with a leg, and they'd switched from dismounting from the left to the right side, not having to slip under the rope to catch their calves. The calves being used were smaller, enabling ropers to snare and tie them more quickly. And, ropers were beginning to hold their slack to keep the calves on their feet, rather than "busting" the calves, as Oliver and his contemporaries had done.

Regardless, the new generation still looked up to "the Dean" as a source of inspiration. This generation, many of them raised in relative prosperity and owning college degrees gained through rodeo scholarships, knew of Oliver's impoverished upbringing. And they admired him all the more for overcoming heart-bruising obstacles to become the greatest champion the event had ever produced.

A fitness buff who never smoked nor drank, not even coffee, Oliver kept the trim, 200-pound physique he'd entered the game with well into his 50s. In 1972, at the age of 42, he came out of semiretirement to go hard after the midseason Winston $2,000 Bonus Award, which he won.

Two years later he managed to finish second to young timed-event ace Tom

Himself a child raised under difficult circumstances, Oliver often took time to brighten the spirits of handicapped and disadvantaged children.

Ferguson in the all-around title chase. And then, in 1976, he competed in a match roping against young Roy Cooper. Still mindful of Oliver's Idaho origins, the Texas crowd backed Cooper. And, just as he'd done decades before, the former dairyman humbled the proud Texans, beating the soon-to-be world champ.

Although he still enjoyed rodeo and was still capable of beating the best in the game, Oliver found a new passion: golf. Ever since taking up the game while recovering from a knee injury in 1965, he had been carrying around a golf bag and playing whenever his rodeo schedule allowed.

Eight years after taking up the sport, he was a runner-up in the Idaho Open and went on to win several Boise city championships. Had he learned the sport earlier, he might have applied himself to golf and become a leader or even a legend on the PGA Tour.

But, as he pointed out, "Rodeo's been awful good to me, so I really can't cuss it."

NE

JIM SHOULDERS

"RUTHIAN."

That's the greatest compliment you can give an athlete, no matter the sport. For Babe Ruth was more than the greatest baseball player of his era: His greatness transcended his sport.

People who wouldn't know the first thing about keeping a box score know the name Babe Ruth. Kids whose fathers weren't even born when Ruth played ball nevertheless know about the man fans and reporters called "the Bambino."

Muhammed Ali is Ruthian. So are Wayne Gretzky, Jack Nicklaus, Richard Petty, and Michael Jordan. And so, too, is Jim Shoulders.

Few athletes have dominated any sport like the Oklahoma cowboy dominated rodeo. In his career Shoulders earned an unprecedented 16 world championships, a total that 4 decades later has yet to be surpassed. From 1949 to 1959, an era of truly magnificent competitors, Shoulders garnered a record seven world titles in the bull riding and a record five world champion all-around cowboy awards. In addition, Shoulders won the bareback riding world championship four times.

Were it not for such outstanding rivals as Harry Tompkins, Jack Buschbom, and Casey Tibbs—all of whom traveled with

Shoulders—it's not inconceivable that Shoulders would have won 20 or more world titles. On no less than 10 occasions, he was the runner-up to the world champion in one or the other of his specialty events—bareback riding and bull riding—or in the all-around title race.

Shoulders was not only a fierce, fearless, and unusually gifted competitor, he was also a charismatic figure, the ultimate personification of the mythical cowboy hero. He was slight of build (a neighbor of his once said, "To look at Jim, you'd think he'd need to be anchored down with bob wire to keep from blowing away.") but also tough as bullhide.

With cornflower blue eyes, fair brown hair, and a thin-lipped smile, he was not Hollywood handsome like his stylish friend Casey Tibbs. However, Shoulders had a self-confidence and down-home charisma that made people take notice.

He spoke in the measured cadence of rural folk, yet seldom failed to deliver a cutting or humorous remark, often at his own expense. His dry wit filled many a reporter's notebook and spiced up newspaper and magazine articles from coast to coast. The attention that came with being "the greatest" eventually led to recognition far beyond the confines of the rodeo arena.

To get an idea of Shoulders' personality, listen to how he described his initiation into the rodeo game:

"It all started out kinda funny for me. My old dad was an auto body repairman in Tulsa when I was a kid, and he would have walked a mile before he would have rode a horse.

Shoulders often claimed that there was nothing to bull riding but "sticking your hand in a rope and making an ugly face for 8 seconds." Shoulders, getting ugly in Nebraska.

"We lived on a little acreage, and my older brother had done some ridin' an' rodeoin', so I thought I would give it a try. I found I liked gettin' trompled on by bulls better than beatin' out fenders."

James Arthur "Jim" Shoulders was born in Tulsa on May 13, 1928, to Joe Louis and Ellen Shoulders. He gained exposure to rural life helping out on his grandfather's farm. During the summers, Jim also drove teams of horses for his uncles.

"The bull didn't buck much, but those bells sure sounded good. I placed on a bull no one had placed on — those bells made it sound like there was more action ..."

Though not ranch-raised, the Shoulders boys nevertheless fostered dreams of one day becoming cowboys. Lacking proper riding stock, they would ride their neighbor's milk-pen calves. When the grownups were gone, they'd try their luck on the dairy cows.

When Jim was just 13, he tagged along with his older brother, Marvin, to a calf riding contest in nearby Collinsville, and thereafter, he participated in calf riding events whenever he could.

Jim rode his first bull at a rodeo in Oilton, Oklahoma. His efforts earned him a first-place check. At the time, he had been earning 25 cents an hour in the wheatfields, putting in 10 hours at a stretch.

"I won $18 and I thought that was enough money to make a man rich," said Shoulders of that fated day. "I was hooked."

To a young kid with great athleticism, rodeo indeed looked like a pretty easy way to earn money. But for every bull or bronc that he tried, Shoulders had to put up his own cash. Always the businessman, Shoulders quickly calculated that if he was going to pay to play, he'd better play to win.

"I had to learn in the arenas, and believe me, that's not the best place to do it," he said. "All we had at home was a milk cow and one old riding horse, so the practice I got was right out there in front of an audience."

At age 16 Shoulders was already contesting in professional rodeos. When he started to earn paychecks, the older rodeo hands pulled him aside and informed him that he needed to join the Cowboys' Turtle Association. Jim did so reluctantly at the Houston Fat Stock Show in 1945.

"I hardly had any money—they took $10 of my eating money to get a Turtles card. And I never even got the card — just a receipt," he recalls.

That's because, at his first meeting of the Turtles, a vote was taken to change the name of the outfit to the Rodeo Cowboys Association. Shoulders took part in that historic vote.

"I got to vote just like Ken Roberts, Dick Griffith, and all those guys who were my heroes. I didn't know what to do, so when they raised their hands, I raised mine," he said.

Shoulders ached to get on the rodeo trail full-time, but his father and mother made him stick with his schoolwork. Jim didn't mind all that much because his father would loan him the car to go to rodeos on weekends, and they didn't make a fuss if Jim missed a few Mondays at school while resting up from the all-night drives.

"I figured if Dad could hitch rides to work so I could borrow his car, the least I could do was stay in school," Jim said. There were 11 seniors in Jim's graduating class, a fact that later in life would prompt Shoulders' friend, baseball Hall of Famer Nolan Ryan to ask, deadpan, "So did you graduate among the top 10?"

Although he may not have been the school's valedictorian, Jim was something of a basketball star at Tulsa's East Central High, playing all four years and earning all-state honors. Besides school and basketball, he had one additional reason to stay close to home, at least until graduation day — his high school sweetheart, Sharron Heindselman. Later, she would play a crucial role in Jim's approach to the rodeo game.

Finally, though, it came time to leave the nest. Jim graduated in 1946 and struck out on the rodeo trail while competing as far afield as Chicago, Philadelphia, and St. Louis. But his luck and good fortune didn't always hold, and he knew hardship. At rodeos, he would tend stock or ride for "splits," borrowing his entry fee from another cowboy against the promise of a cut of any earnings. He spent cold, hungry nights curled up in his old automobile when he could afford neither bed nor board. Jim did just about anything to stay on the road, and that persistence began to pay off. By the end of his rookie season, he had won $7,000 — a sizeable sum by the measure of most people living in the postwar 1940s.

Jim's sense of showmanship was apparent from the beginning. While competing at a mud-filled arena in Springfield, Mo., in 1947, Jim wanted to make certain his bull rope would come free from his bull's muddy hide. So, he tied an extra cowbell onto the rope for added weight.

"The bull didn't buck much, but those bells sure sounded good. I placed on a bull no one had placed on — those bells made it sound like there was more action," he recalls. From then on, Shoulders always had

CAREER MILESTONES

Jim Shoulders

born: May 13, 1928
Tulsa, Oklahoma

16-Time PRCA World Champ (All-Around 1949, 1956-59; Bull Riding 1951, '54-59; Bareback Riding 1950, '56-58).

1970s Shoulders is featured with other sports celebrities in a series of commercials for Miller Lite Beer.

1966 Shoulders' bull, Tornado, is ridden by Freckles Brown at the National Finals Rodeo, bringing to an end one of the longest and most celebrated winning streaks of any animal in professional rodeo. Tornado claimed seven bucking bull of the year titles in the Pro Rodeo Cowboys Association.

1959 Competes in inaugural National Finals Rodeo in Dallas, Tex., riding nine of ten bulls to win the bull riding average along with competing in the bareback riding. Claims bull riding world title and Rodeo Cowboys Association all-around title, bringing his championship record to 16. Shoulders helps Neal Gay found the Mesquite (Texas) Rodeo.

1958 Wins third consecutive world championship triple crown in bareback, bull riding, and the all-around cowboy title. At Madison Square Garden, Shoulders wins more than $6,000.

1957 Wins his second consecutive world championship triple crown.

1956 Takes lead in Rodeo Cowboys Association world standings in bareback and bull riding, and holds both until year's end to claim both event titles and the all-around championship. Sets record for single-season earnings ($43,381) which goes unsurpassed until 1967.

1953 An arena accident in Midland, Tex., sidelines Shoulders for two months with a broken collarbone, causing him to lose position in the world title races. For the first time since 1949, Shoulders fails to win a world championship in at least one event or in the all-around.

1951 Wins Rodeo Cowboys Association bull riding world title, second in all-around title race.

1950 Wins Rodeo Cowboys Association bareback world championship, finishes second in all-around title race.

1949 At 21, becomes the youngest all-around world champion in R.C.A. history, a record that stood until Ty Murray won the all-around in 1989 at age 20.

1948 Wins first of five Calgary Stampede bull riding championships.

1947 On his honeymoon with his high school sweetheart, Sharron, he wins the bull riding, bareback, and all-around titles at New York's Madison Square Garden. The Blue Bell Co. (maker of Wrangler® Jeans) signs him as an endorsee, beginning a relationship that has made Shoulders the senior employee on the company payroll.

1946 Shoulders joins the Cowboys' Turtle Association, predecessor of the Pro Rodeo Cowboys Association.

1943 Competes in his first rodeo, in Oilton, Okla., and wins the bull riding.

Earned more than $400,000 in his career. Individual honors: *Three-time winner in bareback riding, Madison Square Garden in New York; bull riding champion, Madison Square Garden; Salinas bareback & bull riding winner; Calgary Stampede bareback & bull riding winner; Cheyenne Frontier Days bull riding and bareback winner; San Francisco Cow Palace bull riding and bareback champion; Denver Stock Show bareback and bull riding champion.*

Shoulders was among the first to endorse a new brand of rodeo wear called Wranglers®. He claims that he's been on the company payroll longer than anyone.

COURTESY WRANGLER WESTERN WEAR

the trip, and if not, the newlyweds had put aside a little money just in case. What happened surprised even the confident youth.

"I lucked out — won the bareback riding and bull riding — nearly $5,000. It was kind of a nice honeymoon," said Shoulders. "A lot of reporters over the years have asked me about what was my biggest win. And really and truly, that was the one I was tickled the most with."

Shoulders' good fortune didn't end there, however. That year at Madison Square Garden, the Blue Bell clothing company showed up with two semi-trailers full of jeans and shirts. Everyone who entered or worked in the arena received a pair of the new Wrangler® jeans, a black shirt with the Wrangler brand embroidered on it, and a Wrangler jacket.

Several world champs were signed up as product endorsers. Although Shoulders had yet to become a world champion, his wins at the Garden prompted the company to contact him the following spring.

"Their advertising man asked me if I'd like to be an endorser. And they told me it paid $150 and all the rags I could wear," he remembers. Shoulders enthusiastically signed on, going so far as to make suggestions on how the jeans could be redesigned to better suit the demands of the arena.

Over the years, Shoulders has been credited with being an original endorser of the jeans, but he disavows that. However, he is proud to say the company has sent him a check every year for more than half a century, and feels he's been in the employ of the company longer than anyone.

"Not even a janitor has been with Wrangler as long as me," he boasts. As Shoulders' accomplishments grew, he and his family figured prominently into the company's advertising, and he makes appearances on the company's behalf to this day.

In 1948 Jim Shoulders' name made its first appearance in the world standings as one of the year's top five bull riders. A sensational young rider from upstate New York, Harry Tompkins, won the bull riding world title that year, and it wasn't long before the two cowboys became traveling

an extra bell or two to enliven his rides, and perhaps influence the judges' scores.

Another trick was to ride with chaps — something that wasn't done much by bull riders and bareback riders before his era. Shoulders wore his bronc riding chaps in every event, partly because the extra padding in the knees helped protect him from chute injuries.

But the flapping chaps also helped to emphasize the vigorous leg action that characterized Shoulders' rough-stock riding style. Today, all the top bull riders and bareback riders wear chaps.

In the fall of 1947, the 19-year-old cowboy married Sharron, then 17. They decided to go to New York City for their honeymoon, and Jim entered up at the Madison Square Garden Rodeo, the biggest and most star-studded competition of the year.

Jim hoped his winnings would pay for

partners. Shoulders had first seen Tompkins ride at a rodeo in Moberly, Miss., where he was working as a judge.

"The biggest mistake I ever made in my career was not goose-egging Harry on every bull and horse he rode," Shoulders says with a chuckle. "Maybe he would have gone back to New York."

Instead, Tompkins won the rodeo's all-around title, and from there he became Shoulders' greatest rival and also a close friend. So close, in fact, that Shoulders once quipped that he was spending more time with Harry Tompkins than he was with his wife, Sharron. That's not so far-fetched when you consider that the two cowboys typically spent ten months of the year on the road, following what Shoulders liked to refer to as "the suicide circuit."

Shoulders, however, was a dedicated and devout family man. He and Sharron welcomed their first child, daughter Jamie, in September of 1948. A little over two years later, Sharron gave birth to a son they named Marvin Paul. Two more daughters, Jana and

Marcie, would follow. Fatherhood had a profound influence on Shoulders. He'd always thought of rodeo as a business, but now he felt the added pressure of supporting a family. For him, winning titles was secondary to making—and holding on to—prize money.

"You have to understand that in those days the biggest part of the guys didn't rodeo for a living. They came to a rodeo to have a party and a good time. If they won a little money, well that was a way of getting their vacation paid for," he said.

Shoulders remembers some of the old-timers arriving at the Cheyenne Frontier Days rodeo in horse-drawn wagons and camping on the rodeo grounds for a week or more. Jim and his traveling partners—bareback ace Jack Buschbom, Tompkins, and a larger-than-life bronc rider named Casey Tibbs—thought and traveled differently.

"These men were at the heart of the changing scene in rodeo. Jim and Casey and 'Buschie' and Harry were perhaps the first to realize that you didn't have to stay at a rodeo waiting three days for your

DEVERE

On the bareback bronc Roy Bean, Cheyenne, Wyo., 1960.

next ride," said rodeo reporter Gordon Hanson in an article that appeared in the *Rapid City Journal*. "Instead, they wanted to beat them all."

The cowboys would charter a plane—or whatever was available short of a pack mule—and head for the next contest, then return to the first. Traveling as hard and as fast as they could, the foursome ushered in the new era in 1949, when Tibbs won the bronc riding championship, Buschbom the bareback riding, Tompkins the bull riding, and Shoulders won the ultimate crown: world champion all-around cowboy.

He was 21 years old at the time, the youngest all-around title winner in rodeo history. It was not until 1989, when Ty Murray won the all-around title at age 20, that a younger cowboy would ascend rodeo's pinnacle at such a young age.

Shoulders shows off the loot from his triple crown victory in 1956.

DEVERE

But while Murray was fairly confident of winning that first title, Shoulders was anything but certain that he'd get the gold buckle.

According to Shoulders, the cowboys had no idea how the world titles were going to be handed out. "When it all came down to the end, it was about a half a surprise that I'd won the all-around," said Shoulders. "I really thought I had a better chance at the bareback or bull riding."

Jim's earnings that year totaled $21,495. With a portion of those earnings, he and Sharron put a down payment on a 5,000-acre ranch in Henryetta, Oklahoma.

The move made for an unusual twist: Most cowboys left their family ranches to rodeo; the city-raised Shoulders was rodeoing so that he could provide his family with a ranch. That ranch continues in the Shoulders family to this day.

In 1950 Shoulders watched the all-around crown go to the great Bill Linderman, a Montana hand and an accomplished competitor at either end of the arena. Linderman captured world titles in saddle bronc riding and steer wrestling that year, while Shoulders contented himself with a championship in the bareback riding. Although Jim failed to win the all-around, he did succeed in gathering up $7,000 more than he had in 1949.

In 1951 he ascended to the bull riding throne that had been Harry Tompkins' domain for the previous three seasons. Then, an Oklahoma-style drought struck: Shoulders had two back-to-back seasons in which he failed to win a world championship—1952 and '53. Injuries played a part in those substandard years. In 1953 a bull fell on him at a rodeo in Midland, Tex., breaking his collarbone and forcing him to convalesce for nearly two months during the busiest part of the season.

Shoulders recaptured the limelight in 1954, winning top honors in bull riding. That began an unprecedented string of six bull riding world titles through 1959. It was in 1956, however, that Shoulders would truly assert his dominance of the rodeo game, scoring a triple crown, with world championships in bareback riding, bull riding, and the all-around.

Coincidentally, that same year a young Oklahoma ball player named Mickey Mantle also scored a triple crown as the major league leader in runs batted in, home runs, and highest batting average. Howard Harris, who produced the Cowtown Rodeo in New Jersey, remarked at the time that Shoulders actually earned more money that year—$43,381—than Mantle had been paid as baseball's most valuable player.

It took 11 years and plenty of inflation before that earnings figure was surpassed by a young rough-stock hand named Larry Mahan. But such was the cowboys' popularity and drawing power in the 1950s, an era often referred to as rodeo's Golden Age.

And such was the formidable ability of Shoulders to find his way to the pay window. During the 1956 season, the cowboy managed to earn paychecks at more than 70 percent of the rodeos he contested at, a formidable "batting average" if ever there was one.

One reason Shoulders was such a productive performer was his legendary ability to ride despite injuries that would have sidelined other men.

Take, for example, the wreck that happened at a rodeo in Midland in 1953. Just as the gate swung open and the bull made the first high, leaping jump out of the chute, the animal twisted and fell on the hapless rider. Jim's left collarbone was badly broken and doctors operated on it, installing a steel pin.

Although they urged him to quit rodeo for a while, he instead went to eight more rodeos. Finally at Cheyenne, he came out on a sunfishing bareback bronc and bent the steel pin, forcing another operation.

At another rodeo in Lewiston, Ida., a powerful bronc gave his right arm a wrenching pull, breaking the end of his other collarbone. Jim completed the ride, winning the event despite what must have been excruciating pain.

During his career Shoulders broke his pelvis twice, broke his hip, broke both arms several times, and injured both knees. He was the Evel Knievel of his day—there's scarcely a bone he hasn't broken. At one

DEVERE

Shoulders didn't always ride pretty, like his friend Harry Tompkins, but he was always the last guy to let go of his rope. Getting it done on Knight's #85 at Cheyenne, 1961.

point, the American Medical Association did a feature story on the cowboy, using a chart to indicate all the places he had been injured.

Shoulders rode with leg casts, arm casts, face masks. He kept a bottle of ethyl chloride in his war bag to freeze parts of his injured anatomy, and he had a close relationship with the rodeo clowns, who kept an ample supply of whiskey "for medicinal purposes." If his riding arm was broken or injured, he switched to his left. The cowboy's ability to tolerate pain was quite remarkable to the many physicians who treated him.

At Houston in 1959, he had his face smashed in by a bull, a hit that resulted in reconstructive surgery to move his broken nose back into the middle of his face. Jim was released to convalesce at his ranch. Almost immediately, he called the surgeon to inform him he'd entered a rodeo in Phoenix.

"Good God, man, you can't ride with a nose like that!" the surgeon blurted out.

"Hell, Doc, I don't hold on with my nose," was the cowboy's sharp reply. Though a hemorrhage preempted Shoulder's Arizona plans, he donned a protective face mask and mounted a bull in Lubbock, Tex., just three weeks after the surgery. To this day, Jim likes to crack wise about his nose job.

"I broke my nose in seven places—but I don't go to those places anymore," he says.

Long after he'd quit rodeo, Shoulders was in the company of some professional athletes who were curious to know why he rode in spite of such seemingly catastrophic injuries.

"I'll tell you one damn thing," he said. "In rodeo, if you don't enter and win, you don't get nothing. Being broke will make you heal a lot quicker when you've got a wife and kids to feed."

Through it all, he always found the will to win. But there's little doubt that as the years passed, Shoulders grew weary of the

As a spokesman for Miller Lite, Shoulders toured the country with his sidekick, a bull named Buford T-Lite.

travel, the pain, and the time spent away from his family.

But, as he admitted, he could think of no other way in which an Okie with nothing but a high school education could earn $40,000 a year. Though he often said he intended to retire to his ranch when he reached the age of 30, when he reached that age in 1958, he kept right on competing.

One reason may have been the inauguration of the National Finals Rodeo, which debuted in Dallas in 1959. Casey Tibbs had enthusiastically supported the idea of a rodeo "World Series" as early as 1956,

although Tibbs probably got the idea from others. Shoulders and a few other members on the R.C.A.'s board of directors were enthusiastic about such an event, and the contest began to take form in 1958.

Around that time, Shoulders had formed a partnership with saddle bronc rider Neal Gay to take over an amateur rodeo in Mesquite, Texas. In addition to his interest in Gay's Mesquite Championship Rodeo, Jim had his own string of bucking stock that he contracted to outside rodeos under the Jim Shoulders' Rodeo Company name.

New York's Madison Square Garden had been the biggest rodeo for decades, and its fall dates and big prize purse made it the de facto championship-deciding event. But Shoulders didn't feel that it promoted the cowboys as the main attraction. He recalled one year when Lassie was the featured star.

The following year, he overheard a couple of New Yorkers in a restaurant. One asked the other if he was going to the rodeo, and his buddy replied, "I hear Roy Rogers is the star, and he don't put on as good a show as the Lassie show. So, I ain't goin'."

With the NFR the cowboys and the bucking animals would be the stars. Furthermore, it was set to take place in Dallas, in the heart of cowboy country. In the months leading up to the competition, the bull riding event shaped up as the closest contest. Shoulders was in a season-long race with fellow Oklahoman Bob Wegner, and as the December rodeo approached, Wegner held a slim lead in the standings.

Because of his involvement with the Mesquite rodeo, Shoulders was well-known to the media in Dallas and Fort Worth. John Van Cronkhite, NFR production manager, asked Shoulders to drum up some publicity for the National Finals, and Shoulders attended a flurry of press conferences, including a publicity trip to Washington, D.C., to present President Eisenhower the first ticket to the inaugural rodeo.

On December 26, the first NFR got under way. As the leading money-winner, Jim Shoulders led the large Oklahoma contingent of competitors into the arena for the historic event. Shoulders had qualified

BILL LAWLESS

in both his events, which called on him to make four rides for each of the five days of the competition.

On his third bull, with 14 head of stock yet to ride, Shoulders felt the palm of his riding hand tear, exposing the raw muscle below. In order to keep going, he froze his hand with ethyl chloride and stuck a surgical glove on under his riding glove.

The lead in the bull riding changed hands several times during the 10-round contest. When the ninth round had concluded, Wegner had bucked off two bulls but had managed to place five times, including two go-round wins. Shoulders had also placed five times, but had only one win to his credit. Significantly, however, Jim had managed to stay aboard eight of the nine bulls, setting the stage for the final round.

Shoulders swung into the arena on Harry Vold's famed bull Tiger, a bull that had dumped 46 of his previous 50 riders. Shoulders made a qualified ride, becoming the only rider to top nine bulls that year.

Next to ride was Wegner. Ironically, he'd drawn the bull Mohammed, owned by none other than Jim Shoulders. It was a tough draw, perhaps the toughest in the pen. Even Shoulders had had a difficult time with the bull. Jim had drawn the bull four times that season, and had been bucked off three times before finally besting the bull at a rodeo in Tupelo, Mississippi.

Of the bull, Shoulders said, "If that S. of a B. bucked me off one more time, I was going to make baloney out of him."

Fortunately, the bull was spared for his encounter with Wegner, who proved incapable of weathering the storm in the final round. After a few bucks, the bull reversed, leaving Wegner behind in the arena dirt and exactly $2.50 behind Shoulders after a year's competition in which each had won more than $15,700.

Jim Shoulders earned $2,345 in the NFR bull riding to finish the season with $17,021 and a seventh world championship. He also claimed $1,043 in the bareback riding to become the biggest prize-winner of the rodeo. As a bonus, Shoulders was awarded a year's proceeds from an oil well owned by a Texas fan. With combined season earnings of $33,176, Shoulders also claimed his 16th world championship as the all-around winner.

In addition to his brief stint as an oilman, Shoulders continued to enjoy success as a stock contractor. Among his famous livestock was a bull named Tornado, a Brahma cross who bucked off more than 200 riders before Freckles Brown made an historic ride on the future ProRodeo Hall of Fame bull in the first round of the 1967 National Finals Rodeo. Shoulders also opened rodeo's first rough-stock riding school. Alumni included Don and Pete Gay and Shoulders' own son, Marvin Paul.

Shoulders says he "never retired ... I just quit winning." Rodeo's favorite "has-been" salutes the crowd at Ellensburg, Wash., in 1997.

CASEY TIBBS

OUTSIDE THE ProRodeo Hall of Fame in Colorado Springs is a monumental statue by sculptor Edd Hayes entitled *The Champ*. It's a glorious piece featuring a bronc rider in perfect form — feet turned out, spurs raking along the horse's neck, arm curling the rein, body straight as a Kansas highway, an easy smile on the bronzed face. Below, etched in granite, is a portrait of the statue's real-life model and inspiration, Casey Tibbs, a man acknowledged as the greatest bronc rider in rodeo history.

It's appropriate that the statue is 28 feet tall, for Tibbs was truly larger than life. In his lifetime, he hobnobbed with presidents, rogues, high rollers, and Hollywood stars. He fancied purple Cadillacs, which he raced across the country at 95 miles per hour as he dashed from one rodeo to the next, occasionally slowing down to scatter the suitcases of hapless hitchhikers. Young girls pined over his photos, particularly the cover of a 1951 *LIFE* magazine that brought national attention to rodeo and its charismatic young star.

"He liked the gals, booze, good times, good cars. And the gals loved him," said rodeo historian Willard Porter. "I would definitely call him one of the best known, colorful rodeo people or characters there has ever been."

Tibbs was so colorful and exuded such charisma that articles and news stories

about the rider sometimes glossed over his amazing mastery of bucking horses. But it was the broncs who gave him a showcase for his attention-loving personality: A fiery horse was Ginger Rogers to Tibbs' Fred Astaire.

"He was tall and slender, and he just made it look easier than anyone else. He made it look like a dance," said Harry Tompkins, a contemporary who knew a thing or two about arena style. Tompkins, who traveled with Tibbs early in their careers, can recall dozens of great rides made by his friend. But one in particular stands out in his mind, perhaps because it captured that special magic that made Tibbs the most beloved cowboy of rodeo's "Golden Age."

"At Fort Worth there was a horse—Casey may have owned him—called Johnny Cake. Casey dedicated his ride to (bootmaker) John Justin—it was the classiest ride. When he jumped off, he landed on his feet and held the bronc rein. He worked the horse in a circle just like he was on a longe line. Then, he threw the rein to Slim Pickens, and took off his hat and bowed as he left the arena. The applause just rained," said Tompkins.

When Tibbs performed the same stunt at another rodeo, this time in Great Falls, Mont., in 1948, he invited Tompkins to match his feat. Tompkins vowed he'd do the same, and when his bull came near the grandstand stage, he alighted on his feet and doffed his hat too. A bull rider who was watching and had yet to ride said to

Though known as a great saddle bronc rider, Tibbs was equally impressive on the bareback horses.

Tibbs was indeed a spark plug. "If you were standing by him, he'd throw a firecracker at your feet. With Casey, there was never a dull moment," said Tompkins.

Casey Tibbs grew up in the rolling ranch country that surrounds Fort Pierre, South Dakota. He was the 10th and last child born to ranchers John and Florence Tibbs.

According to the cowboy himself, his parents had pretty much exhausted the supply of family names by the time Casey came along in March of 1929. Family patriarch John Tibbs was a baseball fan who liked to recite the poem "Casey at the Bat," and that's where the baby got his name.

"Sometimes, at home, when I'd make a good ride, dad would call me 'Mighty Casey,'" said Tibbs. Perhaps John Tibbs had an inkling that his son was destined for greatness.

As a kid Casey dreamed of being a prizefighter. In rural South Dakota a kid could sure fight, but didn't have many places where he could properly learn to box. So Casey turned his attentions to bronc busting. On the Tibbs ranch, that wasn't difficult to do. John Tibbs ran close to 1,000 horses, so there were always plenty of green colts to ride.

At just 10 years of age, Casey went to work taming 2-year-old colts.

"There was a lot of it to be done, so I used to ride broncs to the one-room schoolhouse 5½ miles away. I'd start off every morning with a wild horse and since I never knew what direction they'd take off in, I'd have to start out two or three hours early," he recalls.

Tibbs loved to ride the rough broncs and could scarcely get enough of them. At annual horse brandings, he would straddle the roped-down horses and ask for the other cowboys to turn 'em loose. More often than not, he would ride the horses to a standstill. In addition to working for his dad, Casey also tamed broncs for the vast Diamond A Ranch, earning $5 a head. By age 15 he was as accomplished a bronc rider as any grown

another contestant, 'If this is what I have to beat, I am going back and getting a job in the Fort Worth Stockyards."

Although Tompkins was one of only a handful of riders who could match Casey's arena flair and grace, he was no match for Tibbs when it came to high jinks, and he occasionally became one of Casey's victims.

On a charter flight out of Montana bound for Reno, Tompkins, who'd stayed up late the night before, confessed to Tibbs

"I'd start off every morning with a wild horse and since I never knew what direction they'd take off in, I'd have to start out two or three hours early."

that he didn't feel well. Tibbs told him that he had some airsickness pills, which he offered to Tompkins as the plane took off.

"I asked for one. He told me I needed two. Well, they turned out to be laxatives. For the whole flight, I had to go to the bathroom in a paper sack," said Tompkins, who was hesitant to fly with Tibbs from that day onward.

man in the area and ready, he felt, for the competitive arena.

On July 4, 1944, he entered his first rodeo at Fort Pierre, contesting in the calf riding, steer riding, and bronc riding. He handily won the calf riding and qualified for the finals in the bronc riding, but was bucked off his last horse.

Tibbs decided that he was good and ready to hit the rodeo trail, and so he hitched a ride to a contest in White River, South Dakota. But when he got there, the promoter told him he was too young to compete.

Fiery even at that young age, Tibbs vowed that he would one day be the world champ but would never step into the White River arena again. Years later, when Tibbs came home as the world champion, he was sought out by the rodeo's promoter, who offered to pay him more money than the prize purse for the entire rodeo just for appearing as a judge.

True to his word, Tibbs refused the work.

As a teen, Casey got a job with a bucking horse scout whose job was to go to ranches and find good bucking horses who could be sold to stock contractors. Each had to be tried before he could be sold, and Tibbs honed his skills on every one and occasionally competed in rodeos when delivery of the horses was made.

Tibbs was also buying and selling his own bucking horses and competing regularly. Veteran cowboys began to comment on Casey's extraordinary abilities. Gerald Roberts, a rough-stock rider and two-time all-around champ from Strong City, Kan., recalls the first time he saw the curly-headed Irish boy at the famed Cheyenne Frontier Days Rodeo.

"It was 1945, and Casey was entered in the amateur bronc riding. You had to get on four horses then, and he won three day moneys on his first three horses before he bucked off a horse called Wildfire," said Roberts, who was quick to take the young rider under his wing, traveling with him from 1947 to '49. "I could see he was just a natural-born bronc rider."

Among the cowboys, Casey's reputation for orneriness grew in direct proportion to his reputation as a bronc rider. Those lacking in humor and those who had a regard for their own personal property and safety quickly learned to steer clear of the red-headed hellion from South Dakota. But

CAREER MILESTONES

Casey Tibbs

born: March 5, 1929
Fort Pierre, South Dakota

Two-Time World Champion All-Around Cowboy (1951, '55); Six-Time World Champion Saddle Bronc Rider (1949, 1951-54, 1959); World Champion Bareback Rider, (1951).

1989 Tibbs' career is immortalized in bronze and stone with the unveiling of *The Champ*, a statue of Tibbs by sculptor Edd Hayes. The monumental statue stands outside the ProRodeo Hall of Fame in Colorado Springs. In 1990 Tibbs dies after a protracted battle with bone cancer.

1959 Wins his first and only saddle bronc title at the Calgary Stampede. Competing at the first National Finals Rodeo in Dallas, he sews up his sixth and last world championship in that event, setting a record for saddle bronc world titles that remained intact through the end of the 20th century.

1958 Helps organize and participate in the American Wild West Show & Rodeo in Brussels, Belgium.

1957 Tibbs returns to full-time competition.

1956 Announcing his retirement at the Denver National Western Stock Show, Casey nonetheless goes on to compete in the early-season rodeos, winning the saddle bronc riding at Fort Worth. He embarks on a film career, landing minor parts.

1955 Despite losing the saddle bronc title to Deb Copenhaver, Tibbs captures his second R.C.A. all-around title.

1954 Tibbs sets an unsurpassed record for consecutive saddle bronc world titles, with four.

1953 In July, Tibbs wins the Cheyenne Frontier Days all-around title as well as his second Cheyenne saddle bronc title.

1951 Following in the wake of Bill Linderman's 1950 Triple Crown victory (three world championships), Tibbs captures world titles in bareback riding and saddle bronc riding, and the all-around cowboy championship. His victories earn him the cover of *LIFE* magazine. En route to the title victories, the cowboy racks up wins in Salinas, Calgary, and Madison Square Garden.

1949 Wins his first world title in saddle bronc riding.

1948 Tibbs wins the saddle bronc riding at Cheyenne Frontier Days.

1947 Joins the Rodeo Cowboys Association, finishing fifth in the world in saddle bronc.

1945 Tibbs enters the amateur bronc riding at Cheyenne Frontier Days.

1944 Tibbs enters his first rodeo in Fort Pierre, winning the calf roping and qualifying for the saddle bronc finals.

that hardly mattered, for Tibbs understood the profundity of P.T. Barnum's words, "There's a sucker born every minute."

Jim Shoulders, whose rise to fame paralleled that of Tibbs, remembers the first time he met the South Dakota cowboy. "E.C. Roberts, Ken and Gerald's dad, had a brand new nylon rope, the first I or anyone else had seen. And he was pretty proud of it. Anyway, he introduced me to Casey, and Casey was showing us all that new rope.

"Casey spotted a fresh pile of bull crap and started walking toward it with the white rope. Before E.C. could stop him, he'd coiled the rope and tossed it into the pile," Shoulders recalled, adding that E.C. administered a little retribution with a bullwhip as Casey scrambled to get away. "That was my first experience with Casey Tibbs," says Shoulders with a laugh.

By age 17 Tibbs was competing full-time in the Rodeo Cowboys Association. In his

Tibbs, receiving a $2,500 check and "the world's biggest cowboy buckle" from Levi Strauss Advertising Manager Dick Cronin, San Francisco, 1954.

GEORGE W. BAKER/LEVI STRAUSS

first full year, 1947, he wound up fifth in the saddle bronc riding.

The next year he suffered a badly broken leg at a rodeo in Olathe, Kan., when the bronc he was riding tried to escape the arena by jumping sideways into a fence. With each jump, the horse drove Tibbs' body into the arena posts. Before he got loose, Casey had eight breaks from ankle to thigh. With a hip-high cast, Tibbs went back home to heal.

But as he convalesced, Tibbs couldn't help but think about the upcoming July 4th rodeo in his hometown. Just a month after the accident, no doctor was willing to remove the cast, so Tibbs did the job himself with a cold chisel and a bottle of chloroform as anesthetic. Then he split an old boot, taped it over the injured ankle, and went off to win the bronc riding event.

"John Tibbs, who had never quite forgiven his youngest son for going off to become a rodeo rider, died later that year," commented Mike Swift, a writer who worked for the Rodeo Cowboys Association. "Deeply affected by his father's death, the next year Casey rode with a new abandon to his first saddle bronc riding championship."

Whether young Tibbs felt he had to justify his decision to leave home, or whether he simply had come into his own as a competitor is hard to know. Still, his victory at 19 years of age (at the time, Tibbs was the youngest world champion in Rodeo Cowboys Association history) ushered in a new cowboy star, one who would set the style for bronc riding for generations to come.

"Casey made a big leap as far as changing bronc riding," notes Winston Bruce, who would watch Tibbs ride at Calgary and later compete against the great rider. "I would hear people talk about Jerry Ambler's style starting a new trend. But Casey took it to the next level."

What Tibbs brought to the arena was gracefulness and form. In the saddle he held his body ramrod-straight. So straight that when Tibbs drove his spurs home as the bronc kicked, you could draw a line from the gently curved fingertips extended back behind his head, through his shoulders, torso, and hips, down to his legs.

FOXIE

Tibbs' ride on Woodburn makes it clear why he is regarded as rodeo's greatest bronc rider. Porterville, Calif., 1967.

"He was just showy and good. He sat up straight, he never flopped around, and you seldom ever saw him buck off," said Gerald Roberts, who traveled extensively with Tibbs in the early days of the rider's career. "I've known a lot of guys who could ride a lot of horses. Hell, most of the good riders never bucked off. But Casey just looked better than anyone else. He was the best bronc rider there ever was, in my opinion."

Roberts may have been closer to Tibbs in the first few years of his career than any other cowboy. Ten years older than Casey, Roberts was a mentor and a traveling partner, someone Casey could look to for knowhow. But it was no easy job traveling with the young rider, and Roberts has enough stories of misadventure to fill a book.

"Bud Linderman, myself, and Casey were driving up a mountain in Klamath Falls, Oregon. Casey had this siren—I guess he got it because he would use his Cadillac as an ambulance. Well, he was trying to pass this guy, so he pulled out the siren.

When we got alongside the guy, it turned out he was a forest ranger—in other words, a law enforcement officer. Well, the guy went to chasing us, and Casey said he didn't know what to do.

"I said, 'Well, you'd better outrun him.' Casey got that car up to 100 miles an hour, and got out of sight. We pulled into Klamath, and Casey drove right into a service station, pulled into the service bay, and said, 'We'll need a lube job right quick.' We went across the street and laid low in a restaurant until dark. I was darn sure we were all going away to jail, but we got away clean. Casey learned not to use that siren anymore."

In 1950 Tibbs was unsuccessful in defending his first title, getting edged out of the year-end victory by a margin of just $177. The title that year went to Bill Linderman, one of the toughest multievent hands ever to ply his trade in the arena and a cowboy who Tibbs looked up to and considered a friend.

That year, Linderman had won championships in two events. In addition to the saddle bronc win, he captured the steer wrestling world title. In doing so, Linderman also claimed the all-around award, rodeo's coveted title conferred on the cowboy with the most money earned in two or more events. It was the first "triple crown" in rodeo's brief history.

Losing to someone he admired greatly must have lessened the sting of not winning the saddle bronc title somewhat, but Tibbs wasn't content to accept second place. The following year he dedicated himself to not only reclaiming the saddle bronc championship title, but to winning the bareback title too.

Tibbs struck gold at some of the biggest rodeos that year, including wins in both saddle bronc and bareback at the Calgary Stampede and a win in the saddle bronc event at the California Rodeo in Salinas.

His best showing, however, came at the

TOM KIMMELL

Casey Tibbs stands near Edd Hayes' monumental statue *The Champ*. Tibbs and the bronc Necktie were models for the sculpture.

biggest event of the year, the Madison Square Garden Rodeo in New York City. Roughly the equivalent of the National Finals Rodeo today, Madison Square Garden was the highest-paying rodeo and consequently the one that always drew the top riders.

In 1951 Tibbs bested them all, winning the bareback riding and the saddle bronc riding. By season's end he'd racked up sufficient earnings to secure both world titles, and his combined winnings (including some pocket change won riding bulls) totaled $29,104, enough to take the title of world champion all-around cowboy.

"Such is his skill with broncs and his passion for practical jokes that he may well have won the next triple crown...as a good-natured way of proving to the 'King,' as the cowboys affectionately call Linderman, that he wasn't so hot after all," commented a writer in the employ of the Rodeo Cowboys Association.

Winning a triple crown plus the exposure that came from doing well in New York landed Tibbs on the cover of *LIFE* magazine, then among the most popular and widely circulated periodicals in America. The article made a great deal of Tibbs' flamboyant personality exemplified by his purple shirts and purple Cadillac. Some of the other cowboys grumbled. One who did not was Jim Shoulders.

"A lot of them guys were jealous of Casey, and would bad-mouth him for grandstanding 'cause he drove those Cadillac and Lincoln convertibles, and stayed at the best hotel in town. I'd hear the complaints, and I would say, 'Look at how the media wants to put him in the paper.' A lot of media wouldn't have even have talked about rodeo without Casey," says Shoulders. "He did [a lot] for rodeo. He dressed the part. He lived up to whatever he said."

For the next three years, Tibbs did indeed live up to his hype. Although a back injury suffered in Nampa, Ida., in 1952 ruined Tibbs' chances at winning the all-around for a second consecutive year, he nonetheless won the saddle bronc championship. In 1953 he battled for the entire season with bronc rider Deb Copenhaver of the Pacific Northwest for the lead in the saddle bronc title race.

Among Tibbs' big wins that season was a victory at the famous Cheyenne Frontier Days Rodeo in Wyoming. Since his first saddle bronc win in 1948, the rodeo had been especially kind to the South Dakota bronc tamer. Tibbs capped his good fortune there by also capturing the '53 Cheyenne Frontier Days all-around title.

Although Tibbs was known primarily as a bronc rider, he'd started out contesting in five rodeo events. Demonstrating his versatility, he limbered up a stiff bull riding rope in 1953 and entered that contest for the first time in several years. At the Reno Rodeo, held over the Fourth of July, Tibbs claimed the win along with a check for $900. That bull riding victory, along with a win in the saddle bronc event, contributed to Tibb's defense of the Reno All-Around Award he'd won in 1952.

From that day forward, he would compete in the bull riding event when it suited him, never piling up enough money to show among the top 15 riders at year's end, but often finishing among the front-runners at individual rodeos.

As the '53 season came to a close, Casey spurted ahead of Copenhaver to capture his third consecutive saddle bronc world championship by a margin of just over $2,000. In 1954 he again bested Copenhaver to stretch his title streak to four. To date, no saddle bronc rider has surpassed Tibbs' four-year championship run.

In 1955 Copenhaver finally outdid his better-known rival, but Tibbs (who finished second overall in the bronc riding, a mere $174 behind Copenhaver) managed to secure his second all-around title with $42,065 in season earnings.

Throughout that stretch of his career, Casey evidenced a preference for high living. He was known as an unrepentant gambler, at one point gambling away $40,000 — including oil well shares—in a week of dice and poker in Las Vegas. Tibbs wasn't one to save for a rainy day, and he was always looking for a new way to earn a buck.

Given his popularity, his charisma, and his attention-loving personality, it was natural that he try his hand at acting.

Casey announced his retirement at the Denver National Western Stock Show in 1956. He had an agent in Hollywood and contracts to appear in movies and tele-

COURTESY PRCA

Tibbs would, on occasion, limber up a bull rope and make an outstanding ride like this one.

vision shows. Furthermore, he was developing a trained horse act that, he hoped, would help keep him close to the rodeo game while appeasing his Hollywood clients, who were fearful he'd be injured while riding rough-stock.

Those fears certainly seemed justified. At Denver Tibbs bucked off a Beutler bronc ironically named Be Careful. He suffered three broken ribs and a punctured lung. Not content to go out that way, Casey taped up his ribs and, two weeks later in Fort Worth, won the Southwestern Stock Show rodeo's saddle bronc championship.

Tibbs' horse act, which featured a trained black horse named Midnight, met with derision among the cowboys and

R.L. POUND

This famous photo proves Tibbs' assertion that he was so good, he could ride blindfolded. Tibbs on Calgary, 1958.

soon earned him the mocking title of "Captain Midnight."

Although he managed to get bit parts in some Hollywood projects, his film and television career never really took flight. At a Lions Club rodeo in Pomona, Calif., Casey agreed to ride a bronc for a documentary on rodeo. With writers, directors, acting coaches, and agents looking on, the horse leapt from the chute and promptly reared over backwards.

Accustomed as he was to troublesome broncs, Tibbs escaped unscathed. However, his supporters were horrified and reportedly never quite got over the horror of seeing their star attraction nearly crushed. When his team of advisors disbanded after a proposed television series failed to materialize, Casey returned to competition in 1957.

But he continued to work on other projects, including his horse act, and in 1958, he went overseas for the World's Fair in Brussels, Belgium, to star in the American Wild West Show & Rodeo. According to his old friend Gerald Roberts, the cowboy was

under contract to appear in the show, which featured a number of top competitors and contract acts. It was an ill-fated starring role if ever there was one.

"The promoter wasn't making any money. So, he left us all stranded over there, and we had to get the U.S. Embassy to send us all back home," recalls Roberts.

By 1959 Tibbs was deep in another project, but this time the venture succeeded. Throughout the 1950s, Tibbs had served as the vice president of the Rodeo Cowboys Association. During his tenure, he championed the idea of a season-ending rodeo championship that would decide the world titles. Although the idea for the National Finals Rodeo probably didn't originate with Tibbs (R.C.A. Secretary Lex Connelly was also credited with initiating the idea), Jim Shoulders remembers Tibbs as the most vocal supporter.

"The best I can remember, it was Casey Tibbs' idea (or dream) to have a National Finals Rodeo. He was the first person to talk to me about it," wrote Shoulders in the book, *The Finals: A Complete History of the National Finals Rodeo*. "At the time, I served on the R.C.A. board as bull riding director. Like Casey, I thought it would be great for rodeo."

According to Shoulders, support on the R.C.A. board wasn't strong. For three years, Tibbs and others hammered away at the idea until then-President Gene Pruett finally conceded that such an event would benefit the sport, and a sufficient number of board members proved willing to go along with the idea. The event was scheduled to debut in Dallas in 1959, just after the Christmas holiday.

Casey opened the season by wedding Cleo Harrington on New Year's Day.

"I been courtin' her ever since I met her at the Inaugural Ball of my friend Joe Foss when he came in as governor of South Dakota. She was Miss South Dakota then. Took me four years to wear her down," said Tibbs at the time. But the two scarcely had time for a proper honeymoon because the cowboy had his mind set on qualifying for the first NFR.

"Being a rodeo wife isn't the most pleasant thing for a girl like Cleo. So we don't know how much she'll be a-travelin' with me this year," he wrote. "Haven't figured out how she's gonna haul." Cleo, it seems, was sturdier than Tibbs had thought, for she joined him on the road and was instrumental in helping him launch several rodeo productions.

By season's end Tibbs was again atop the world standings in the saddle bronc event. When he arrived at the NFR on December 26, the cards were stacked in his favor. Winston Bruce, the only opponent with a prayer of catching Tibbs, needed a flawless performance, while Tibbs only had to stay aboard a few of the 10 broncs to clinch the championship. When Bruce bucked off in the first round, Tibbs' sixth world title was certain.

Tibbs posted scores in the first four rounds, sharing the fourth-round win with Lyle Smith. But Casey's performance waned as he bucked off three of his last six mounts and failed to spur his horse out during the final round, a mistake that earned him zero points. Though other riders, including Winston Bruce, earned more money than Tibbs at that first NFR, all the glory belonged to the South Dakota rider, who picked up his record sixth world title in saddle bronc riding and extended his gold buckle count to nine.

Although he kept competing until 1964, Tibbs' greatness ebbed after that first NFR. He suffered a broken leg during the 1960 season that hampered his ability to remain at the top. Tired of life on the road, he returned to Hollywood to restart his film and television career. When lead roles were not forthcoming, the cowboy served as a technical advisor, a bit-part player, and a stuntman.

In 1967 he auditioned for a part in a television commercial that was to feature a cowboy. According to Tibbs, the director informed him that he "didn't look like a cowboy." But he was interested in using Tibbs' name. Insulted and incensed, Tibbs returned to the arena briefly during the 1967 season.

"I was so mad, I entered the first rodeo I could find. I won it and won the next nine," he said. Tibbs said that he placed in 20 of the 27 rodeos he entered, but he never finished the season and so failed to contend for another world title.

At that time, Tibbs was busy with a documentary film he was producing called *Born To Buck*. The feature-length film involved a bucking horse roundup on the Lower Brule Sioux Indian Reservation. During the filming, Tibbs nearly drowned while trying to swim 400 horses across a flooding river. It was a little ironic that the project brought Tibbs back to the same White River arena where, in his youth, he'd refused to compete. He used the arena to film some bucking horse sequences for the film.

In February of 1989, doctors revealed that Casey Tibbs had contracted bone cancer. The discovery prompted many of his friends and admirers to expedite the creation of the monumental statue that now graces the ProRodeo Hall of Fame. Tibbs was present in Colorado Springs in August of 1989 for the dedication of *The Champ*. Just prior to the unveiling, the sculpture's creator Edd Hayes revealed a secret: While casting the statue, he'd placed a heart-shaped bronze plaque inside the rider's chest that bore the words, "Ride, Cowboy, Ride."

Tibbs addressed the crowd, saying, "Thank you all for making me look good." Then he paused and said, "Hell, I was good."

He died five months later at his home in Ramona, California.

JJJ PHOTO/JIM SVOBODA

HARRY TOMPKINS

THIS PHOTO says more about Harry Tompkins' ability as a rough-stock rider than any scribe could possibly write. The photo was taken at a rodeo in Eureka, Calif., in the 1950s by legendary rodeo photographer DeVere Helfrich.

Tompkins is aboard a leaping Brahma bull, his legs outstretched as comfortably as if he were reclining in a lounge chair. His left arm is high in the air, his palm open and waving in greeting. He grips his bull rope with his right hand as casually as a woman might palm a shopping bag. Tompkins, dapper in a pressed cotton shirt, is flashing a grin for the camera.

"DeVere told me the bull would turn back, and when it did, to look his way. I could see him there, and when it was just right, I turned to him and said, 'How's this?'" recalls the cowboy.

Whether he was riding broncs or bulls, Tompkins made it all look easy. And for him, it was. An admitted natural athlete, Tompkins possessed an enviable package of skills that would have made him a standout in any number of sports: coordination, quick reflexes, timing, and balance. Legendary balance.

"I can't remember exactly when I realized I had that talent," recalls the cowboy. "But I could easily walk wood planks, fence rails, even a cable strung across swimming pools." An often-told tale

among old rodeo hands recalls the time Harry performed his low-wire act at a pool party thrown by some of his cowboy friends. Soon, the pool was filled with rodeo cowboys (many of them admittedly a little drunk) who tried to emulate Tompkins' feat.

"I wasn't trying to embarrass anyone by outdoing them, or trying to show off by doing those things—it was just something that came very easily," he explained.

Biologists who debate nature versus nurture might want to study Tompkins, who clearly falls in the nature camp. For who could have predicted that a city kid raised amid the stately Victorian houses of prosperous Putnam County, N.Y., would go head-to-head with ranch-raised cowboys from out west—and beat them at their own game?

But that's where Harry was raised, in the sleepy bedroom community of Peekskill, along the east bank of the Hudson River about 40 miles upstream from New York City.

Harry Tompkins was born October 5, 1927, in Furrance Woods, N.Y., to Frank Tompkins, an itinerant waiter, and his wife, Ethel. Neither of his parents owned horses or ever rode a horse in their life. But Harry was enchanted with horses, so much so that as a growing boy he followed along behind a local plowman so he could be around the horses.

Harry also liked ice skating, and on weekends he was often seen on a pond near his house, skating from dawn to dusk. "I was always the first to fall into the pond in

Tompkins' amazing athleticism and balance show in this classic shot taken at Eureka, California.

rode long after the stable closed in the evening, sneaking into the pastures and catching mounts. And he wasn't above a little mischief.

"I really liked to jump them over fences. After so long of this, you know, those horses just wouldn't stay in the pasture. The owner never could figure out why all of a sudden his gentle horses acquired an intense desire to jump all the fences they could," he recalls with a laugh.

By his late teens, Tompkins had found full-time employment at the Cimarron Guest Ranch, a popular retreat for New Yorkers who wanted to escape the city.

Though he again started at the bottom, he quickly worked himself up in rank and eventually became one of the senior wranglers entrusted with riding the new horses and sanding the rough edges off the sour ones. According to Harry, that often meant riding 150 horses over the course of a season. Adding challenge to the chore was the fact that the ranch wranglers often ran out of saddles in their efforts to accommodate guests, so Harry was usually forced to ride bareback.

Although ranch-raised cowboys might look down on the dude-wrangling profession, Tompkins is convinced that it was one key to his later success in rodeo.

"Riding so many horses taught me good balance. If (rodeo) cowboys today rode as many horses, and rode them bareback like I did, they'd be better riders for it," he says.

It was at Cimarron that Tompkins got his first taste of rodeo, and that on a dare. On Sundays the ranch owner sometimes held small rodeos for his guests. Harry was watching one of the shows while sitting on a fence with the boss's daughter. Harry hadn't really thought much about competing. Instead, he'd been roughhousing with the young lady.

"We were just kids, and sometimes kids play a little rough. So in the course of the afternoon we were scuffling, and she fell

the fall, and the one who broke through the ice when it melted in the spring," he recalls.

But his career as a hockey player (or perhaps a figure skater, for he was always very slight of build) was cut short by his desire to be a horseman.

Tompkins began in the lowliest job, working as a stable hand at a county riding stable. All of 12, he willingly cleaned stalls and groomed horses all day long for two weeks until the stable owner finally

Because bucking bulls were in short supply back east, Tompkins trained himself for that event by riding white-faced steers.

allowed him to ride for half an hour. It was his first time on the back of a horse.

He remembers that his first ride left his skin chapped and his knees sore, and that he had to hold his trouser legs up away from the reddened skin on the long walk home. But discomfort did nothing to discourage him. A few hours of trail riding a week wasn't enough for Harry. He often

off the fence," he recalls. "Her father was watching, and he came over to me and said, 'Boy, if you are going to play so rough and be so tough, you had better get in the rodeo competition.' So I did. But by that time, I wasn't so sure that I was so tough."

But Tompkins cowboyed up, making the bell on his steer. And in that moment, a rodeo career was born. Tompkins continued to ride in the ranch rodeos on weekends, and he gained some pointers from the ranch foreman, Mike Hastings, who was a seasoned bulldogger, a veteran of 30 years on the rodeo trail, and later an inductee into the Cowboy Hall of Fame in Oklahoma City.

Although you might expect that most of the horses Harry rode were pretty tame, he related how the foreman would make them into full-fledged bucking horses.

"They had the rodeo on Sunday, and if the horses didn't buck, they'd put High Life on them. High Life was a liquid that would heat up, like to burn them. Once you put some on the horses, they'd buck like they'd go through a fence," he said.

Because bucking bulls were in short supply back east, Tompkins trained himself for that event by riding white-faced steers. At night, he would go out and load the steers into a bucking chute, flank them, and pull his own rope. He had a gate rigged so that he could pull the latch by himself and push the gate open. Often Harry rode 40 steers in a session, alone. But as any rodeo hand will tell you, a steer is to a bull what a kitty cat is to a mountain lion. Tompkins was ready for his next test.

It wasn't long before Harry got his chance to ride in a real rodeo, and the biggest rodeo event of its day, at that. As a promotion, the 1946 Madison Square Garden Rodeo gave New York dude ranchers an opportunity to send local entries. But to weed out ringers, the designated riders had to have worked for the guest ranch for at least 90 days prior to the rodeo.

Tompkins was the lone qualifier from the Cimarron. The ranch only wanted him to ride bareback horses, but Harry insisted that they let him try the bulls.

As you might expect, the quiet but earnest New Yorker didn't exactly cause the hard-core cowboys from out west much concern, or even much thought. They pretty much ignored the young cowboy.

A few did take note of the slender-faced boy, commenting that if he stuck with it, he'd be "tough as a boot." But probably not one of them realized that the future was right there in front of their eyes — in two

CAREER MILESTONES

Harry Tompkins

born: October 5, 1927
Furrance Woods, New York

World Champion All-Around Cowboy (1952, '60;) World Champion Bareback Rider (1952); World Champion Bull Rider (1948-50, '52, '60).

1997 Tompkins is honored by the Professional Bull Riders as one of the sport's greatest performers.

1968 Career earnings stand at more than $380,000.

1961 Tompkins dislocates his elbow; his riding declines as a result, though he continues contesting throughout most of the decade.

1960 Claims his second all-around title with $32,522 in earnings — the largest single-season earnings of his career. At the NFR, he places on but three of ten bulls yet still manages to claim the bull riding world title; in the bareback event, Tompkins trails his old traveling partner, Jack Buschbom, claiming the reserve world title.

1959 A bull falls on Tompkins' leg, damaging his knee. It is the first "serious" injury in his career, causing him to miss six months of competition. Despite this, Tompkins qualifies for the inaugural National Finals Rodeo, placing in three of ten rounds of bull riding, including a fifth-round win. He supplied the bucking chutes for the rodeo, pioneering the portable steel bucking chutes now commonly used by rodeo stock contractors.

1953-1958 Tompkins never fails to place among the top five riders in the world standings in at least one of his two specialty events.

1952 Wins the Triple Crown with world titles in bareback riding, bull riding, and the all-around.

1950 Claims third consecutive bull riding world title.

1949 He and his travel partners Jim Shoulders, Jack Buschbom, and Casey Tibbs all win world championships, Tompkins claiming the bull riding world title for the second straight year. Wins the bull riding at Cheyenne Frontier Days Rodeo.

1948 In only his second year of pro rodeo competition, the 19-year-old cowboy wins the Rodeo Cowboys Association world champion bull riding title. He becomes one of the original Wrangler® Jeans endorsees. In his first full season, he claimed victories at Denver's National Western, the Houston Livestock Show, and the Fort Worth Stock Show.

1946 Enters the Madison Square Garden rodeo as a local entry and wins $316. Prior to that, he'd tried riding only two bulls in his life.

MOSS

Rides like this one at the Colorado State Fair Rodeo in Pueblo helped Tompkins to win the bareback riding title in 1952.

years, everyone would know the name and face of Harry Tompkins.

At that contest, Tompkins bucked off all the bulls he tried except one. But he won the round on that one, and pocketed $316.

"I remember it exactly, because I would count it every day, maybe take $5 with me to live on for the day. At the dude ranch, I was only making $9 a week, next to nothing once I paid my soda pop tab," he said. Needless to say, Harry had been bitten by the rodeo bug.

While still working for the guest ranch on weekends, Tompkins was conscripted by the U.S. government, serving an 18-month hitch in the Army on New York's Staten Island. When he entered the military, he weighed scarcely 100 pounds.

Near the end of basic training, a grueling program designed to whip the troops into shape, Harry got sick with the mumps and was forced to return to basic training and start anew. Those months and months of physical training helped him to bulk up— Tompkins added 40 pounds to his 5-foot 8-inch frame. On top of that, Harry constantly kept a rubber ball in his right hand, squeezing it to develop the strength he'd

need to ride bulls. His forearm grew so much that Harry could hardly roll up his shirt sleeve. That added strength would play an important role in his rodeo career, for as he said, "In rodeo, you've got to be strong for your size."

Tompkins rose to the rank of sergeant before his military service ended in 1947.

Although some accounts say that Madison Square Garden in 1946 was Harry Tompkins' first professional rodeo, Tompkins admits it wasn't so, even at the risk of spoiling a pretty good legend.

His first contest rodeo was in fact at Moberly, Mo., and was judged by Jim Shoulders. Though they never talked at that event, Shoulders was soon to become Tompkins' good friend ... and biggest rival.

It was at the 1946 Madison Square Garden Rodeo that Tompkins joined the Rodeo Cowboys Association. And that began what must be the most meteoric rise to fame in rodeo history, for in just two years (most of which were spent in military service), Harry rose from a lowly dude wrangler to champion of the world.

Traditionally the rodeo season kicked off with the National Western Stock Show, held each January in Denver, Colorado. In 1948 Tompkins was at Denver, ready to ride. Astoundingly, the city boy from back east won the bull riding. The victory prompted Ken Roberts, a great bull rider of the day, to say to the easterner, "If you don't get hurt, you'll be the next champion."

Over the course of the winter, Harry won at some of the biggest rodeos of the season, including the Houston Stock Show, the Fort Worth Stock Show, and at a major rodeo in Phoenix, Arizona. It wasn't long before the other cowboys had given him the nickname, "Uppy," a reference to his upstate New York roots. They also took advantage of the young rookie, albeit unintentionally.

At the time, it was a common practice for cowboys to share a percentage of their earnings with their fellow cowboys as insurance against future cold streaks. The system was fair, so long as all the cowboys were making roughly the same amount of prize money over the season. But Tompkins quickly tipped the scales in the other cowboys' favor by winning or placing at nearly every contest.

"One way that you know that you are going to do pretty good in rodeo is if a lot of the better cowboys come around and want to split with you on your percentage of the winnings. To me, I just thought it was a big thing to have all the good cowboys split with me," he remembers. "But after a while, I realized that I was paying them more than they were paying me, so I quit that too."

By the end of the 1948 season, Uppy was not only a recognized rodeo rider, he'd risen to its highest title: world champion.

Although such a rapid climb to the top may have taken the other cowboys by surprise, it was no surprise to Harry.

"I always knew I could ride," he said in his matter-of-fact manner.

Tompkins began his career traveling with Jack Buschbom, another all-around contender who was especially competitive in the bareback bronc riding. Soon the duo was joined by several up-and-coming cowboys who were to change the nature of the rodeo game. Among them were Casey Tibbs, a fun-loving prankster from the South Dakota Badlands, and Jim Shoulders, a cagey gamesman and son of a Tulsa auto body mechanic.

According to Skipper Lofting, who often documented the group's exploits, the general consensus among Tibbs, Shoulders, and Buschbom was that it was better to have Tompkins close by, where they could watch him, than have him sneak off and beat them any worse than he already had.

Together, the gang developed a strategy that would prove unbeatable: They would fly.

Because commercial planes were scarce in the 1940s and early '50s, especially in the smaller cities of the West, the cowboys employed private pilots. They used private planes — sometimes charters, sometimes planes owned by cowboys or their families.

Flying enabled them to get to more rodeos, thus giving them more chances to win money. But the flying was often bumpy, and the danger could be graver than the risks they faced in the rodeo arena.

DEVERE

"Uppy" riding chapless on #557 at La Fiesta de los Vaqueros in Phoenix, 1962.

"We had some close calls," said Tompkins. "Once we were flying from Cheyenne to Kansas City in this old military surplus plane. We got low on fuel and this warning buzzer came on, which meant we had about 20 minutes of flying time before we ran out. It was nighttime, and we saw some lights ahead. Figuring it was Kansas City, we headed for them—this was already 30 minutes after the buzzer started. The airport was right on the river. Both the engines had quit, but the pilot managed to glide us to the

"Most cowboys don't see the animal after the first jump—they see them three jumps later."

touchdown. I remember the airport officials wanting to lock up the pilot."

Another time, Harry had to get to a rodeo in California, but heavy fog prevented flights from arriving or departing. He and his pilot decided that, if they followed the railroad tracks all the way, they could get close enough to the airfield for the cowboy to make the rodeo.

"We'd fly along, and suddenly there'd be a tunnel ahead. The pilot would aim the plane straight up, and then straight down, and we'd hope that we'd spot the tracks on the other side. We finally got to the airfield, and the pilot left me off there to get a ride. Since no one was there, I went to the airport hangar. I told 'em I needed a ride to the rodeo, and they asked me where I'd come from. I said we'd just flown in. They all thought I was kidding," he said.

When commercial airlines became more widespread in the mid-1950s, Tompkins and his crowd were able to fly between big cities and get to most of the important rodeos. Tompkins says he didn't miss the small puddle-jumper flights aboard rickety old private planes.

"It scared us every time we got into a plane, but we figured if we'd quit the plane,

the others would get to more rodeos. So we stayed with the plane.

"When Jack Buschbom got his [pilot] license, I'd decided to never get in a plane with him," Harry said. "The way he drove cars was bad enough."

Despite the danger, the strategy helped to outdistance competition. In 1949 Tibbs won the saddle bronc world championship, Buschbom the bareback title, Tompkins the bull riding, and Shoulders the all-around. In so doing, they laid the foundation for today's jet-set rodeo stars.

Harry blazed some other trails for the top professional riders of today. Unlike many of the cowboys of the 1940s and '50s, Tomkins seldom drank alcohol. "I am sure it was an advantage for me—most of the guys I traveled with drank like everyone else," he said.

He was also among the first cowboys to receive corporate sponsorship. In 1948 the Blue Bell Company asked the champion to endorse a new brand of jeans called Wranglers® that they'd invented for cowboys. Photographers took pictures of the cowboy wearing the jeans in a basement room at Madison Square Garden. Soon after, his traveling partner, Jim Shoulders, also became an endorser of Wrangler Jeans.

Signing up Tompkins and Shoulders was an astute business decision for Wrangler, for the two were to dominate the bull riding and bareback riding events for the better part of the 1950s. Within a decade, nearly every cowboy in rodeo adopted the jeans as their standard competition wear.

Shoulders and Tompkins shared some similarities and also some stark contrasts. Both of them were raised in cities: Tompkins in Peekskill, Shoulders in Tulsa. Both began competing seriously in 1948, winning 11 bull riding championships between them in 13 years. Both rode bareback horses—Tompkins won the world title in that event in 1952, and Shoulders won it four times in his career. And, both were phenomenal natural athletes.

But whereas Shoulders had a reputation for never letting go of a bull or bronc, Tompkins jumped ship when he sensed that his Wrangler pockets were heading south. Some cowboys might have questioned Harry's "try," or willingness, but the fact was that he avoided injury and seldom rode hurt. Tompkins was so adept at dismounts that he could jump off a bull at the end of a ride and land on his feet, a trick more common to bronc riders, but seldom seen in the bull riding event. As one would expect, that dismount saved the cowboy from major wear and tear.

The same couldn't be said for Shoulders, whose legend is filled with stories of how he rode despite injuries that would have sidelined lesser men. Rodeo writer Skipper Lofting once commented that you only needed to see how Shoulders walks today to realize that his strategy may not have been as wise as Tompkins'.

But no one questions Harry's bravery. When he needed to, he stuck it out. At one rodeo his bareback horse jumped the arena fence and took a detour through the parking lot. Tompkins remained cool.

"I just hung on while the horse ducked and dived through all those cars," said the cowboy in a story that appeared in the *Pro-Rodeo Sports News*. "I kept looking, but there wasn't a place to hit besides bumpers and windshields. So I waited until he got out the back end of the lot, where there was open ground and a safe place to land. This situation scared me, but riding and thinking got me out of it."

Riding and thinking. Rodeo announcer Bob Tallman once called the bull riding event "action and reaction." But for Tompkins, the reactions were instantaneous, not requiring conscious thought. That enabled him to study the animals and play to the judges while he rode.

"Most cowboys don't see the animal after the first jump—they see them three jumps later. I could see the animal all the time I was riding," he said. Such visual acuity gave Tompkins an edge.

"Harry figures out bulls better than anybody else," noted bull rider Bill Rinestine. "All of us watch 'em. But Harry sees more."

Tompkins wasn't just perceptive and quick-thinking, he was cagey. While Shoulders was the consummate gamesman, doing things like adding bells to his rope so that it would make more noise to impress judges and wearing chaps to enhance the action, Harry had a few tricks of his own to psych-out the competitors. Because of his extraordinary balance, Tompkins didn't need to cinch his bull rope tight like many of his fellow riders. He used this to his advantage.

"I would have girls pull mine, just to hear the other cowboys bitch," he said. "Guys would ask if I needed help, and I'd say 'No, I've got a helper.' Then I'd go get some gal to come over and help me out."

Of course, there were always young

Tompkins displays the treasures he amassed as the all-around and bull riding champ in 1960.

DEVERE

DEVERE

women available to aid the handsome cowboy from New York. But rather than play the field, Harry settled into domestic life rather early in his career, marrying Rosemary Colborn, the daughter of stock contractor Everett Colborn.

The couple met in Salt Lake City in 1949. The bull rider topped two of Rosemary's father's best bulls, which had both been unridden to that point. Rosemary turned to her friend Berva Dawn Sorensen (now Taylor) and asked, "Who is that cowboy?"

And Berva Dawn replied, "Why, he's my boyfriend." Well, so she thought.

Tompkins had his first date with Rosemary three months later at a rodeo in Great Falls, Montana. That fall they saw each other again in New York City, where their romance blossomed.

The couple married January 5, 1950, in Rosemary's hometown, Dublin, Tex., where they settled and started a family. A daughter, Martha, was born in 1951. She was soon followed by two sons: Mark in 1954 and Neal in 1956. Martha went on to become Martha Wright, a two-time NFR-qualifier in barrel racing and a top barrel horse trainer, but

according to Harry, neither of the boys was particularly successful in following their father into the arena.

"They tried, but they didn't have the talent for it," said Tompkins.

Harry enjoyed his best season in 1952, when at 25 years of age he was named the Rodeo Cowboys Association world champion all-around cowboy. An Associated Press article that appeared in newspapers all across the country ran the (incorrect) headline, "Hadn't Been on a Horse Five Years Ago — Texas Rodeo Performer Wins Top Cowboy Title." Still, the idea of a former New Yorker defeating the best hands of the West was a sweet story for the sports reporter, even if he bent the truth a little in writing the story's lead paragraph.

Tompkins says winning the all-around that year, along with his fourth bull riding title and first bareback championship, was his proudest accomplishment as a rodeo competitor. And it was a rare accomplishment, as well. In the more than 70 years that world titles have been awarded by the Professional Rodeo Cowboys Association and its predecessors, only nine men won the all-around plus two world titles in the same year.

Harry never managed to repeat that feat, but he did capture the all-around again in 1960, finishing with yet another championship in bull riding and a reserve world championship in the bareback event behind his old traveling partner Jack Buschbom.

Tompkins had, up to that time, largely avoided serious injury — a torn knee cartilage suffered at Calgary in 1958, some broken toes, a few broken ribs. But nothing that had hampered his riding, or that hadn't healed. But in 1961 he dislocated an elbow while on track for another all-around title. It was the beginning of the end to Tompkins' storied career.

"My arm never did get straight, to this day. When you can't go to the end of your arm, when you don't have the snap to get back — that's it," he said.

Despite the injury, Harry continued to ride in the R.C.A. until 1968. However, he was never the threat he had been when he was barnstorming with his buddies Jim Shoulders, Jack Buschbom, and Casey Tibbs in the 1940s and '50s.

From 1948 to 1958, Tompkins never failed to place among the top five riders in at least one of his two events. After 1960 he never placed among the top five riders again. He came closest in 1965, placing 12th overall in the bareback event, 6th in the bull riding, and 10th in the all-around. Still, Tompkins continued banking arena checks, amassing $380,454 over a 21-year career.

But it wouldn't be fair to say how much Tompkins took away from the arena without mentioning how much he gave back.

While competing at Madison Square Garden in the 1950s, Tompkins helped solve a problem that had vexed stock contractor Everett Colburn: setting up the bucking chutes. Crews would arrive a week before the event to build corrals and construct the bucking chutes. Tompkins wondered why the entire bucking chute couldn't be built as a unit, then stored for the following year's contest.

While laid up with a knee injury, he designed a portable bucking chute made of welded steel pipe that soon became standard equipment in the big indoor arenas throughout the country. His bucking chutes were used for the first National Finals Rodeo, held in Dallas in 1959. He also made chutes for stock shows in San Antonio and San Angelo and for stock contractors Everett Colburn and Tommy Steiner.

Harry didn't bother to patent the design. He even went so far as to donate chutes to some of the rodeos.

"I didn't do this for the money; I did this for the cowboys and to make rodeo a little safer," he'd say later.

Additionally, Tompkins helped revise the scoring system. In the old judging system, cowboys were awarded fewer points than the animals, thus giving more weight to a good animal than to a good effort by the cowboy. Often the bull riding came down to the luck of the draw.

Tompkins advocated a system in which each of two judges scored the riders up to 25 points, and the bulls on the same scale. That system is used for all rough-stock events today.

Tompkins never really quit the rodeo business; he just quit winning. Each year, he makes the pilgrimage to the National Finals Rodeo. He and his wife, Rosemary, divorced after 25 years, so he makes the trip with his second wife, Melba. These days, he's working on an invention that he thinks will make rough-stock events safer — a radio-controlled release mechanism that would free the rope or riggin' when a rider gets hung by the hand.

A few years ago Tompkins attended the Professional Bull Riders Finals in Las Vegas, where he accepted an award as the Greatest Bull Rider of the Century. He's also been inducted into the ProRodeo Hall of Fame in Colorado Springs, the Cowboy Hall of Fame in Oklahoma City, and the Texas Cowboy Hall of Fame in Hico.

"In 22 years of bull riding, with about 60 rodeos a year, I've been on something like 4,000 of the meanest bulls anywhere. It was a good, exciting life. It was what I wanted to do more than anything," Harry said. "I've had fun and made friends in the rodeo business. I am a lucky man."

FRED WHITFIELD

BESIDE THE obvious, Fred Whitfield isn't like most rodeo cowboys. No "aw shucks" humility masks his emotions. When Whitfield is elated, you know it, and when he is angered, you had best stay out of his way.

Although he prefers to let his rope do the talking, his mouth serves equally well when a loop isn't near at hand. Like a Stetson-clad Muhammed Ali, Whitfield isn't afraid to proclaim "I am the Greatest!" Such proclamations have occasionally drawn the ire of other rodeo cowboys, such as the steer wrestler from Whitfield's hometown who said, "Fred thinks he's better than all the rest of us."

However, the athletically blessed Texan's ability to back up his words with breathless performances and cliff-hanging championship victories has tended to silence his critics. And even if his stoical fellow cowboys don't always appreciate Whitfield's emphatic statements and jubilant arena behavior, the fans at least love this cowboy, whose charisma radiates to the highest coliseum seats.

Whitfield might have been right at home in the National Football League or the National Basketball Association, and with his work ethic and his abilities, neither would have been out of the question. But he didn't grow up wanting to juke linebackers ala Jerry Rice or feed no-look passes to the open man like Magic Johnson.

Like a lion poised to pounce, Whitfield sets up for a winning run at La Fiesta de los Vaqueros Rodeo in Tucson.

Instead, he dreamed of roping for the world title, like his hero Roy Cooper.

Fred Whitfield wasn't raised on a ranch, like most timed-event competitors, but his upbringing was decidedly rural. When he was 9, his mother and father separated. Because his mother worked, Fred spent a good deal of his time at his grandfather Elwood's place, which was always stocked with chickens, hogs, and a few cows. His grandpa (who lived to be more than 100) encouraged his grandsons to ride and rope. But it didn't take a great deal of coaxing for either Fred or his younger brother, Anthony.

As kids, the Whitfield brothers would rummage through a junkyard to find ropes with which to play cowboy. They'd rip cords off old vacuum cleaners and tie hondas out of the ends of extension cords. Anything was fair game—the mailbox, a stray chicken, their mother's legs. "I'd be walking by and sometimes he'd rope me," remembers his mother, Joyce. "Rodeo was in his blood." In the summer time, the two boys would ride the Welsh ponies their grandfather had given them several miles to the local 7-Eleven store. Then, after returning home, the two would get bored and go riding back to the 7-Eleven.

"We'd make at least three trips a day. We'd hang out and drink Slurpees, then, right before dark, we'd ease back to the house. We didn't have a worry in the world. We were carefree," Fred remembers.

"Once we got those ponies, we never thought for a moment about bicycles," adds Anthony. After all, you couldn't rope a goat

now a family man who manages Moffitt Oil, a lubricant distribution company. "It got to the point where I made sure I had enough to pay his entry fees before mine. He was 15 and winning events with guys a lot older."

Moffitt's financial support was a huge boost to a boy of decidedly modest means. It was Moffitt's belief in Fred that spurred the cowboy to excel. "Roy had a lot to do with Fred's success. He put pressure on Fred, pushed him to do better. But Fred pushed himself too. He always wanted to rope, and he hated to lose," remembers Anthony, now a successful businessman who owns a trucking company in Houston.

The Whitfield boys had a bull riding cousin, Ronnie, who once enticed Fred to try that event. Fred remembers kissing the first bull between the horns, then successfully riding the second bull but catching a spur in his behind after dismounting. "Since then, I've never had any desire but to rope calves," he said. A brief stab at a football career while at Cypress-Fair-banks High ended much the same way — Fred had missed some practices due to his rodeo schedule, and the coach took him aside and said, "You have to choose between football or that hick sport." Whitfield quit the squad, perhaps denying the NFL a future fullback. As he said, "Guess I got into rodeo too early."

off a bicycle. Of course, Fred eventually began to outgrow the pony, but he found a helpful patron in his friend Roy Moffitt, a member of the family for whom Fred's mother, Joyce, cleaned and ran errands. Moffit was 7 years older than Fred, but the two shared a brotherly bond through their dreams of becoming rodeo cowboys. Fred went to his first competition at age 9, a Little Britches Rodeo in Tomball, Texas. He roped a calf and rode a steer, winning the first

Indeed, by age 16, Fred had already established himself as a serious competitor in Texas, the toughest proving ground on the planet for calf roping talent . He entered a Texas Calf Ropers Association event at Giddings, where world champion Roy Cooper was also competing. Cooper won the first round; Fred answered by winning the second. That event opened his eyes, made him realize that he could rope on the same level with the world's best. But it would take some soul searching before he was ready to commit himself to a professional career.

"I learned early how quick the world of rodeo changes ... It was the biggest letdown of my life."

round in both events. Then, in the finals, he missed his calf and bucked off his steer.

"I learned early how quick the world of rodeo changes," he said of the experience. "It was the biggest letdown of my life." By the time he was a teen, Fred was competing against adults in amateur rodeos and jack-pots. For Moffitt, it was apparent that he had a prodigy on his hands.

"He'd rope in (jackpots) once in a while, and I saw how good he was," said Moffitt,

After high school, Whitfield continued competing in amateur rodeos and took a job helping Moffitt. But the lure of professional rodeo pulled him in, and Fred bought his Pro Rodeo permit in 1988. One of his first experiences taught him a lesson about just how tough the pro ranks could be. After driving all night to a rodeo with roper Alan Branch, Whitfield caught some sleep in the truck cab. He awoke to an incessant rainstorm and a flooded arena. He walked over to another roper, Dan Taylor, and said "Are they planning to rope in this?"

"Son, I don't know what you're gonna be doing at 8 o'clock tonight, but we're gonna be roping calves," Taylor replied.

"It was like, 'This is the PRCA, the Big Leagues'. They go on come hell or high water," said Whitfield.

Although he could have made 1989 his first full season as a rookie, Whitfield chose to sit out another year and get his head together. In addition to grieving the loss of an older sister who died in a car accident, Fred had his own personal tribulations. At a Bill Pickett Invitational Rodeo in Hayward, Calif., Whitfield had a run-in with a cowboy who'd tried to pick up Fred's girlfriend a few weeks before in Austin, Texas. The two got into a scuffle outside a bar and a knife was pulled. The other cowboy ended up in jail; Fred ended up in the hospital with a deep gash across his face. The cut required 36 stitches and left a deep scar. Although plastic surgery might have hidden the disfigurement, Whitfield's friends convinced him that it added character to his face.

Despite his woes, Whitfield still managed to win more than $35,000 in amateur events in 1989, money that helped launch him on his quest to win the PRCA top rookie honors.

Fred began the 1990 PRCA season by placing at the first calendar event, the American Royal in Kansas City, Missouri. Then he hit a cold streak that lasted through 10 rodeos and had him wondering if he'd made the right decision. His horses weren't working well for him, so Whitfield was forced to pay "mount money," and ride other ropers' horses. Despite this difficulty, Whitfield's season began clicking. At the

San Antonio livestock show, the rookie placed in two rounds and was third overall in the rodeo's average, toting up more than $8,000. Soon after, he claimed top honors at La Fiesta de los Vaqueros in Tucson, to take the lead in the rookie standings.

In March, Fred and a vanload of Texas calf ropers traveled north of the border, and Whitfield captured the first outright win of his pro rodeo career at Canada's Rodeo Royale in Calgary. The $3,836 win boosted Whitfield to within a few hundred dollars of the lead in the world standings. Whitfield was on a roll, placing at more than half the rodeos he competed in. Then he did an astonishing thing by

CAREER MILESTONES

Fred Whitfield

born: August 5, 1967
Houston, Texas

PRCA World Champion All-Around Cowboy (1999); Five-time World Champion Calf Roper (1991, '95-96, '99-2000).

2001 Wins Calgary's $50,000 bonus for the second time, becoming one of only a handful of repeat winners of "rodeo's richest hour."

2000 On the strength of wins at Cheyenne, San Antonio and Houston, Whitfield sets a regular season earnings record with $129,516, then goes on to win his fifth world title in calf roping.

1999 Championship earnings in calf roping plus money won team roping propel Whitfield to a first all-around world title. At the NFR, he wins his third NFR average title.

1997 Roping at the NFR, Whitfield sets a calf roping average record (84 seconds).

1996 Defends his 1995 calf roping world title and claims the Texas Circuit Finals calf roping title for the second time.

1995 PRCA world champion calf roper.

1994 Wins his second of three Cheyenne Frontier Days calf roping titles.

1993 Wins the Calgary Stampede $50,000 bonus.

1991 In his second year as a pro, Whitfield claims the calf roping world title.

1990 After a resounding victory at Cheyenne Frontier Days, Whitfield goes on to become the PRCA/Resistol overall and calf roping rookie of the year and competes for the first time at the NFR.

Three-Time Original Coors Showdown calf roping champ; three-time Cheyenne Frontier Days calf roping champion; more than $1.5 million in arena earnings, $500,000 in National Finals Rodeo earnings; winner of three NFR calf roping averages ('91, '97, '99), and holder of two NFR calf roping average records.

MIKE COPEMAN

Whitfield raises the roof and spreads the joy with a signature gesture that has endeared him to the NFR spectators.

winning the most venerated rodeo on the summer schedule.

Whitfield had bought a roping horse named Ernie in April, but the punishing travel schedule and constant competition weakened the horse, who contracted pneumonia and had to be rested. By July, however, Fred felt that Ernie was sufficiently rested, so he hauled him to Cheyenne, Wyo., for the famous Frontier Days Rodeo.

With a long score that gives calves a substantial headstart, Cheyenne is among the toughest rodeos anywhere, particularly if your horse isn't seasoned. Many good cowboys have gone their entire careers and never won a Frontier Days belt buckle. Any win there is epic.

Fred and Ernie looped their first calf in 14 seconds, then caught their second in 12 to take control of the average competition. In the finals, the duo combined for a 12-second time (a respectable mark in the Frontier Park arena), and Fred and his buddy Roy Moffitt, who had flown up just for the finals, looked on as the competition withered in the Wyoming sunlight.

Whitfield left the arena $13,174 richer, while Moffitt also banked money, having bet on his protegé to win in the rodeo's Calcutta auction. Fred would long remember winning his first Frontier Days Rodeo as one of the greatest accomplishments of his life.

Whitfield's storybook year ended with the overall and calf roping rookie of the year titles and his maiden trip to the National Finals Rodeo in Las Vegas. Fred was dazzled by the bright lights and non-stop action; he checked into the Mirage Hotel, rented a limo, and partied it up with friends, new and old.

Looking back, he admitted that his high-rolling ways took a toll on his roping. His arena performance was scarcely memorable; he finished a desultory 10th in the calf roping average as a result of running eight calves in double-digit figures and slipped from fourth to seventh in the world standings.

But careful observers might have noticed a few flashes of brilliance that foreshadowed Whitfield's world championship potential. In round five, the roper trussed a calf in 9.3 seconds to finish in a three-way tie for second place. He won the next round with a 9-second run. Then, roping in round seven, Fred missed his first toss.

As his horse skidded to a stop, Whitfield's hand slipped down to his side and pulled up a second loop. He spurred his horse forward, drawing tight on the calf just as it reached the far end of the arena. Fred slid off his horse and tried the calf, stopping the clock in just 14.5 seconds. Whitfield's run didn't result in a paycheck, but the cowboy's display of athleticism and competitiveness connected with the crowd in a way that would become legend in the years to come.

Like Joe Beaver, another tough roper raised in the Texas amateur circuit, Fred Whitfield was destined to rise rapidly in the pro ranks. But even the cowboy himself had no idea just how rapid and overwhelming that rise would be. At 23, Whitfield entered his second season determined to win the world championship, and he progressed through the year like a man possessed.

Fred again won the American Royal Rodeo to grab the lead in the early season standings, then came very close to winning the National Western Stock Show in Denver, the first major event of the year, leading the average into the final round only to miss his calf. Later that winter, he regained the world standings lead at a rodeo in Jackson, Miss.; then the lead see-sawed among several calf ropers during the hectic summer season.

Whitfield's season was hot, then cold. By fall, Fred had slipped from the top spot in the world standings, ceding the lead by a huge margin to Joe Beaver. If he was to win the world, it was going to take a massive effort at the National Finals to rise from his seventh-place ranking in the world standings. Double-digit times weren't going to cut it. Fred vowed to himself to concentrate on the task at hand and save the party for the evening following the final round.

Whitfield roped his first two calves out of the money, but from then on, he took possession of the calf roping. In the next six rounds, Whitfield strung together three second-place finishes and won two rounds outright, clocking his fastest time in round eight with a 7.8-second effort. He rushed the barrier night after night, but drew not a single penalty, and his quick dashes down the rope and lightning-quick wraps kept him in the lead in the 10-round average.

Fred closed out the 10-day run with a 9.2-second time to set an NFR arena record for the fastest time ever on 10 calves: 91.7 seconds. It was an astounding feat — Whitfield had trimmed the previous record by more than 10 seconds. The win helped push his NFR earnings to a record level as well. All told, the cowboy banked $70,609 in Vegas, handily defeating Beaver for the world title by a nearly $10,000 margin.

With the win, Fred joined a vanguard of calf ropers who were to revolutionize the event. Like Whitfield, most of them had grown up watching Roy Cooper set new

standards of skill while also presenting a hip new sensibility to what had been one of rodeo's least appealing events.

The generation that came in Cooper's wake was arguably the best, most competitive group of calf ropers in rodeo history. During the 1990s, ropers Joe Beaver, Whitfield, Herbert Theriot, Brent Lewis, Blair Burk, Troy Pruitt, and a young upstart named Cody Ohl (who was to give Whitfield fits in his pursuit of world championships) transformed calf roping from the event during which fans flocked the concession stands to the one that had

MIKE COPEMAN

Whitfield excels when all the chips are on the table — such as at the 2000 NFR, where he clinched his fifth calf roping world title in the final round with only one second to spare.

them sitting on the edges of the bleachers. Their most epic battles were fought at the National Finals.

After his first title win, Whitfield bobbed along among the top 10 ropers in the world for the next 3 seasons, never finishing lower than seventh, as Joe Beaver and Herb Theriot divvied up the world titles.

Then, in 1995, the always volatile and sensitive cowboy hit a bump in the road that truly tested his desire to continue in the sport. In April, Whitfield went through a painful split with his girlfriend of four years. It was rumored that the champ was contemplating hanging up his rope. At the time, he'd won a scant $7,500 and wasn't even ranked among the top 50 ropers.

But he vowed that he would not go down in flames. He pulled himself together and began a long climb "from worst to first," as he told the editor of the *ProRodeo Sports News.* As the season closed out in November, Whitfield was indeed ranked No. 1 going into the NFR, the championship title his to lose. But the battle would prove to be close. Fred led Joe Beaver by a mere $2,906 going into the 10-round bout, and Beaver was known to deal more than a few knock-out punches in Las Vegas.

Whitfield leapt to the fore in the first round with a 7.6-second winning run that would stand up as the fastest of the competition (Ricky Canton, another outstanding Texas roper, would tie the time in round seven). Fred placed in the next round, then grabbed another first-place finish in round nine. Meanwhile, Beaver floundered.

Although Whitfield's performance was

"He's blessed with ability, but he's also a person who's worked very hard at it."

— *Roy Cooper*

nowhere near as flawless as it had been in 1991 (he broke two barriers), he never relinquished his world standings lead during the entire ten rounds, earning more money than any other competitor, and defeating Beaver by a hefty margin—$44,000.

By this time, Whitfield had become a certifiable rodeo superstar. Always a flashy dresser (one woman remarked to him, "Fred, I want your shirts when you outgrow them"), the roper hooked up sponsorships with Ariat Boots® and the new upstart jeans company, Cinch®. Whitfield's appeal helped both of the fledgling companies to

gain market share from established rivals. And at the NFR Whitfield had become a fan favorite, enervating the crowd after a successful run with his trademark palms-to-the-sky invitation to blow the roof off the Thomas & Mack Center.

In 1996 Fred set his mind on defending his world title. He was out to prove wrong the few remaining skeptics who considered his first world title a fluke. Now squarely in the limelight, Fred began to address the issue of racial prejudice that had dogged him throughout his career. Reporters invariably asked Fred about his experiences as a black rodeo star, and the cowboy put a positive spin on the subject by stressing that his talents had brought African-Americans closer to the sport and emboldened many young black cowboys to pursue careers in the rodeo game.

Whitfield had earned the respect of the rodeo community, not merely as a talented black roper, but as the one of the best ropers of his or any other generation.

"He's blessed with ability," said Roy Cooper, the eight-time world champion whom Fred had looked up to as a kid, "but he's also a person who's worked very hard at it. He's put in the hours practicing to get where he's at. He's the type who can win on anything. If Fred's got everything together, he's tough to beat."

In 1996, Whitfield had everything together. Over the course of the season, he swept titles in every series championship (set up by sponsors to reward cowboys competing in a particular group of rodeos), including the Texas Circuit calf roping championship, the Wrangler World of Rodeo title, the Copenhagen/Skoal series championship, and the Dodge Truck series championship. Wins at top-20 rodeos in Pendleton, Salt Lake City, Redding, Calif., Reno, and Hermiston, Ore., helped to put the cowboy in the lead in the world title race by December. But that lead was certainly vulnerable; his margin was a mere $10,000.

Whitfield asserted his dominance by

winning the the second and third rounds. Then, seemingly out of nowhere, Cody Ohl of Orchard, Tex., looped three straight wins and a second-place finish to pressure Whitfield as the rodeo ground to its conclusion. The audience picked up on the growing battle between the two rivals, and Whitfield went gunning for arena records rather than sticking with his game plan of consistent roping. He missed his calf in round seven as Ohl took top honors for a 7.3-second time. "If he can win five straight rounds, he deserves to be the champion," said Whitfield, obviously upset with his own performance.

But as Ohl gunned for the win every night, inevitably his luck took a turn for the worse. The cowboy missed his last two calves, and the back-to-back goose eggs kept him from succeeding in his run at the defending champ. When the dust settled, Whitfield's consistency carried the day, and the champ finished the year with his third world title and $155,336 in earnings.

The following year, it was Whitfield's turn to put a scare into Ohl. At the 1997 NFR, Fred handled his 10 calves with consummate skill, downing them in an amazing 84 seconds to set yet another arena record—one that would survive the century. Meanwhile, Ohl held onto his lead in the world standings with a near-flawless performance in which he snared 10 calves in 87 seconds. A single slip-up and Ohl would have lost to Whitfield. Many will remember 1997 as one of the toughest roping matches in the rodeo's history.

In addition to Whitfield's stirring victory in the average competition, he played a part in one of the most memorable events in the 40-plus year history of the NFR. In round eight, calf roper Ronnie Hyde ripped a 7.1-second run to set an arena record. Fast times had been the order of the day, but that mark set the stage for what was to come in round eight. First, Blair Burk looped and trussed his calf in 7-seconds flat. Pandemonium reigned as Whitfield backed into the box, and the cowboy fed off the energy of the audience. Whitfield blasted out of the roping box and downed his calf

Whitfield chatting with Joe Beaver just prior to the final round of the 1997 NFR.

in 6.9 seconds—the first sub-7-second time in NFR history.

His record, however, was a brief one; only seconds after Whitfield left the arena, roper Jeff Chapman tied his calf in 6.8 seconds—just one-tenth of a second off the all-time PRCA record mark of 6.7 seconds set by Joe Beaver at a rodeo in West Jordan, Utah, in 1986.

Whitfield had scarcely dreamed of scaling such heights as a roper, but he'd always been a goal-setter and a fierce competitor. In 1999, with little left to win that he'd not already won, he decided it was time to set his sights on the PRCA all-around title. It was a lofty goal indeed: Whitfield had always focused on calf roping. Realistically, the only events he could hope to succeed in were team roping or single steer roping, events that he'd never seriously practiced. But with the discipline that he'd applied with such great success in the calf roping, Whitfield decided to master another event.

Early in the season, Whitfield partnered with Arles Pearce, a PRCA rookie permit-holder who'd grown up near Whitfield. The combo clicked, and by March, Fred had astounded the team roping fraternity by reaching the top 15 in that event. Meanwhile, he was laying the calf roping field to waste, cashing $63,000 in checks by the time the bluebonnets blossomed in his native Texas.

Whitfield's "marriage" to Pearce fell apart, and he headed for a host of other ropers: Trevor Brazile, Mike Beers, Marty Becker, and Nick Rowland. Although he failed to qualify for the NFR as a team roper, Whitfield did amass $25,690 in team roping earnings, a war chest that put him in the top spot in the all-around title race

With a chauffeured limo available 24/7, Whitfield enjoys the VIP treatment in Las Vegas.

come December. As it turned out, he would need every penny to win rodeo's most coveted award.

Fred's game plan for the 1999 NFR was, as one might expect, to remain consistent. With a considerable lead in both the all-around and calf-roping title races, he knew that gunning for wins and arena records every night was a risky proposi-

tion. But playing your cards conservatively in Las Vegas is also risky. As Whitfield held back, careful not to make mistakes but not capturing any first-place go-round wins either, Cody Ohl chipped steadily away at his all-around and calf roping leads. Joe Beaver, sidelined by injuries and working as a commentator for the ESPN broadcast of the rodeo, foresaw the danger of Whitfield's strategy.

"Blair (Burk) broke a barrier early on, and that relaxed Fred. Then Cody (Ohl) two-looped a calf, and that relaxed Fred even more. So, those two go gunning for him every round and pretty quick, they've made it up and passed him by," said Beaver, summarizing the events leading up to the final-round showdown between the trio.

Burk had a legitimate chance at stripping Whitfield of the calf roping title, and Ohl was in position to claim the all-around. Whitfield seemed unworried, however, telling a *Wall Street Journal* reporter on the eve of the final round, "I'm still in the driver's seat. It's all mine to win now."

Beaver remained skeptical. "Today's gonna be either the toughest day of Fred's career or the easiest," said Beaver, speaking from personal experience.

Whitfield charged the barrier on his final run and slipped the loop on quickly. But as he tied the calf, an extra piggin' string attached to his belt got tangled up with the one he was using to tie the calf and precious seconds ticked away as he dealt with the fouled lines.

"I didn't panic," said Whitfield. "I knew I had time to spare."

Cagily, Whitfield had figured that Ohl's calf would present problems for him. "I'd run that same calf earlier and I knew it would try him. I didn't have to run at the day money."

And indeed, Ohl's calf was a devil. The calf ran up the rope, and the stocky Texan fell gracelessly atop the startled animal. Although Ohl righted the animal, the delay enabled Whitfield to maintain a 1.4-second lead in the crucial average. Having

GAVIN EHRINGER

Fans line up for a city block when Whitfield signs autographs.

iced the world all-around championship, Whitfield looked on as Burk missed his final calf, which assured that Whitfield would take home not one but two world championships.

With the all-around championship, Whitfield became the first African-American to win rodeo's most prestigious title. Although he'd remained almost mute on the topic of race throughout his rise to the top, Whitfield finally felt free to speak out on the subject. And he gladly assumed the responsibility of being a role model for other ropers, black and white.

"You can't imagine the number of African-Americans who've been to the NFR since I started roping here," he said. "I think people who see me will realize they can accomplish this, too, and I will be the inspiration that drives them."

Within days of his victory, Whitfield was off to the Caribbean to do stunt work for R&B singer Montel Jordan. Fred came back to win another calf roping world title in 2000, setting an all-time record for regular-season earnings ($129,215) in any rodeo event. Following his Hall-of-Fame rodeo career, Whitfield says he hopes to do more stunt riding work and teach young kids to ride and rope.

Taking full advantage of a "bye" that allows the current world champion to compete for Calgary's famed $50,000 bonus round, Whitfield returned to Alberta in 2001 with high hopes of reclaiming the award he'd won there in 1993 — a bonus he'd used to purchase his ranch outside Houston. And, in typical Whitfield fashion, he didn't mince words with the press.

"They don't give you a dime for second place, and I didn't drive all the way up here to go home empty-handed," said Whitfield just prior to the bonus round. And, as might be expected, Whitfield added another page to his legend. Having lost the lead in the world standings to his rival Blair Burk at the Wrangler® Pro Tour Finale in Las Vegas, Whitfield entered the finals with a score to settle. The cowboy had drawn a fiery, difficult calf, forcing Fred to rope him fast if he hoped to contain it in the large arena. This he did, but not as quickly as he might have hoped. After reaching for the calf, Whitfield had to hustle down the rope and make a quick tie to earn the sub-10-second time he felt he needed to claim the win.

With the clock ticking, Whitfield tied off and fretted as his horse dragged the calf a few feet as it struggled up and tried to break free from the piggin' string. Mounting his horse hastily, Whitfield watched as the calf continued to struggle, finally breaking free — but only after the necessary 6-second waiting time had passed. Burk and another roper had no such luck; both watched in dismay as their calves broke free prior to the 6 seconds required. Whitfield had won again.

"I came here in 1993 and won it, and that gave me the money I needed to buy my place. Now, I'll use the money to buy me some more land," said Whitfield of his second Calgary bonus. "I've always said I was a big event player. And this proves it again."

AUTHOR PROFILE

WRITER GAVIN EHRINGER is one generation removed from ranching. His father, William Joseph, "Bill" Ehringer, was raised in the desert ranching community of Nogales, Ariz., on the Mexican border. Ranching there in the 1950s was fashionable among the Hollywood crowd and business executives, who wanted to shelter their money and hob-nob with film stars.

Ranching provided them all with great money-losing tax shelters. William Ehringer Sr., a horticulturist, and his crews landscaped the showcase ranches. His son, Bill, worked as a ranch hand.

Bill Ehringer attended the University of Arizona, which had an excellent rodeo program at the time. Although he was not an active rodeo competitor, he did rope some, and he enjoyed riding a great deal. An enthusiastic rodeo fan, he met some of the great riders of the day, including Casey Tibbs and Jim Shoulders.

After serving as an officer in the U.S. Army, Bill returned to Nogales, where the movie *Oklahoma!* was being filmed at the time. Given a bit part as a townsperson, he followed the director around for days, telling him, "I want to be a cowboy!"

When it turned out that the Hollywood stuntmen hired for the film couldn't actually ride horses, the director turned to Bill and said, "Okay, Ehringer, here's your chance." He appeared as an extra in numerous scenes.

Bill Ehringer left that life behind to pursue a career in business. The Ehringer family settled in a dairy community south of Tacoma, Washington.

In 1980 son Gavin moved to Colorado to attend college. A trip to a local guest ranch led to a summer job, which he held for nearly 6 years. Having always admired his father for his "cowboy" heritage, Gavin set out to acquire those skills and experiences, as well.

As a wrangler and then a cowboy, Gavin rode from dawn to dusk, 6 or 7 days a week, and learned basic horse-training, horse-packing, team-roping and other skills. He also helped neighbors with haying and ranch chores, eventually taking additional work as a ranch hand on a cow-calf operation.

Gavin briefly entertained the idea of trying his hand at rodeo. He rode practice broncs as a rodeo club member at the University of Colorado, and even entered one amateur rodeo. But he concluded that he'd joined the game a bit late and didn't foresee much chance for success. After seeing his college coach hung up on a bareback horse at a rodeo in Canon City, Colo., Gavin realized how much he valued his personal safety, and became an enthusiastic rodeo fan instead.

The ranch where he worked, more than 100 years old, hadn't seen many improvements; there was no electricity except for a generator that seldom ran. The only running water flowed from a spring box to a horse trough. And the cabins all had dirt floors. The experience wasn't that different from what a cowboy a century ago might have known, which made visitors curious about how ranchhands make do with so little.

To answer their questions, Gavin began writing stories about living with 65 horses and 300 cow-calf pairs in the Colorado high country. Photography, a passion of his since junior high school, became a way to illustrate his stories.

Around 1987 Gavin left the ranch and moved to Colorado Springs to work on a project supported by *Western Horseman*. Through the years he's received a great deal of support from the people he met at *Western Horseman*, who were impressed with his writing skills, knowledge and willingness to learn and improve.

Gavin eventually found work in the Professional Rodeo Cowboys Association media department, where he worked for 2 years. In 1991, he left PRCA to pursue a free-lance writing and photography career. Gavin was (and still is) the "Rodeo Arena" columnist for *Western Horseman.*

Reporting for *Western Horseman*, the writer has attended all but one National Finals Rodeo since 1991. In addition, he's reported on nearly every major rodeo in the West, including Cheyenne Frontier Days, Houston Livestock Show, Calgary Stampede, Denver's National Western Stock Show, Dodge City Days in Kansas, the Greeley (Colo.) Independence Stampede, and many more. Around 1997, Gavin co-authored the book *Rodeo in America* with Dr. Wayne Wooden, Ph.D., of the California Polytechnic Institute, Pomona.

In addition to writing about rodeo, Gavin has also covered a broad spectrum of horse and western-lifestyle subjects for *The Quarter Horse Journal, Horse & Rider, Paint Horse Journal, NRHA Reiner, Cowboys & Indians, American Cowboy* and others. He's written sports articles for *Encyclopedia Britannica* and personality profiles for *PEOPLE Weekly.* In addition, Gavin covers the winter ski and sports scene for the *Rocky Mountain News* in Denver, and has written for numerous outdoor-lifestyle magazines about skiing, rodeo, horses, adventure sports and travel.

As a writer, Gavin has won three AQHA Steel Dust Awards for outstanding editorial accomplishment, as well as several photographic awards.

Western Horseman, established in 1936, is the world's leading horse publication.
For subscription information: 800-877-5278. To order other *Western Horseman* books: 800-874-6774.
Western Horseman, Box 7980, Colorado Springs, CO 80933-7980. Web site: **www.westernhorseman.com**.

Books Published by *Western Horseman*

ARABIAN LEGENDS by Marian K. Carpenter
280 pages and 319 photographs. Abu Farwa, *Aladdinn, *Ansata Ibn Halima, *Bask, Bay-Abi, Bay El Bey, Bint Sahara, Fadjur, Ferzon, Indraff, Khemosabi, *Morafic, *Muscat, *Naborr, *Padron, *Raffles, *Raseyn, *Sakr, Samtyr, *Sanacht, *Serafix, Skorage, *Witez II, Xenophonn.

BACON & BEANS by Stella Hughes
144 pages and 200-plus recipes for delicious western chow.

BARREL RACING, Completely Revised by Sharon Camarillo
128 pages, 158 photographs, and 17 illustrations. Teaches foundation horsemanship and barrel racing skills for horse and rider, with additional tips on feeding, hauling and winning.

CALF ROPING by Roy Cooper
144 pages and 280 photographs covering roping and tying.

CUTTING by Leon Harrel
144 pages and 200 photographs. Complete guide on this popular sport.

FIRST HORSE by Fran Devereux Smith
176 pages, 160 black-and-white photos, about 40 illustrations. Step-by-step information for the first-time horse owner and/or novice rider.

HELPFUL HINTS FOR HORSEMEN
128 pages and 325 photographs and illustrations. *WH* readers and editors provide tips on every facet of life with horses and offer solutions to common problems horse owners share. Chapters include: Equine Health Care; Saddles; Bits and Bridles; Gear; Knots; Trailers/Hauling Horses; Trail Riding/Backcountry Camping; Barn Equipment; Watering Systems; Pasture, Corral and Arena Equipment; Fencing and Gates; Odds and Ends.

IMPRINT TRAINING by Robert M. Miller, D.V.M.
144 pages and 250 photographs. Learn to "program" newborn foals.

LEGENDS by Diane C. Simmons
168 pages and 214 photographs. Barbra B, Bert, Chicaro Bill, Cowboy P-12, Depth Charge (TB), Doc Bar, Go Man Go, Hard Twist, Hollywood Gold, Joe Hancock, Joe Reed P-3, Joe Reed II, King P-234, King Fritz, Leo, Peppy, Plaudit, Poco Bueno, Poco Tivio, Queenie, Quick M Silver, Shue Fly, Star Duster, Three Bars (TB), Top Deck (TB), and Wimpy P-1.

LEGENDS 2 by Jim Goodhue, Frank Holmes, Phil Livingston, Diane C. Simmons
192 pages and 224 photographs. Clabber, Driftwood, Easy Jet, Grey Badger II, Jessie James, Jet Deck, Joe Bailey P-4 (Gonzales), Joe Bailey (Weatherford), King's Pistol, Lena's Bar, Lightning Bar, Lucky Blanton, Midnight, Midnight Jr, Moon Deck, My Texas Dandy, Oklahoma Star, Oklahoma Star Jr., Peter McCue, Rocket Bar (TB), Skipper W, Sugar Bars, and Traveler.

LEGENDS 3 by Jim Goodhue, Frank Holmes, Diane Ciarloni, Kim Guenther, Larry Thornton, Betsy Lynch
208 pages and 196 photographs. Flying Bob, Hollywood Jac 86, Jackstraw (TB), Maddon's Bright Eyes, Mr Gun Smoke, Old Sorrel, Piggin String (TB), Poco Lena, Poco Pine, Poco Dell, Question Mark, Quo Vadis, Royal King, Showdown, Steel Dust, and Two Eyed Jack.

LEGENDS 4
216 pages and 216 photographs. Several authors chronicle the great Quarter Horses Zantanon, Ed Echols, Zan Parr Bar, Blondy's Dude, Diamonds Sparkle, Woven Web/Miss Princess, Miss Bank, Rebel Cause, Tonto Bars Hank, Harlan, Lady Bug's Moon, Dash For Cash, Vandy, Impressive, Fillinic, Zippo Pine Bar, and Doc O' Lena.

LEGENDS 5 by Frank Holmes, Ty Wyant, Alan Gold, and Sally Harrison
248 pages, including about 300 photographs. The stories of Little Joe, Joe Moore, Monita, Bill Cody, Joe Cody, Topsail Cody, Pretty Buck, Pat Star Jr., Skipa Star, Hank H, Chubby, Bartender, Leo San, Custus Rastus (TB), Jaguar, Jackie Bee, Chicado V and Mr Bar None.

PROBLEM-SOLVING by Marty Marten
248 pages and over 250 photos and illustrations. How to develop a willing partnership between horse and human to handle trailer-loading, hard-to-catch, barn-sour, spooking, water-crossing, herd-bound, and pull-back problems.

NATURAL HORSE-MAN-SHIP by Pat Parelli
224 pages and 275 photographs. Parelli's six keys to a natural horse-human relationship.

REINING, Completely Revised by Al Dunning
216 pages and over 300 photographs showing how to train horses for this exciting event.

RODEO LEGENDS by Gavin Ehringer
Photos and life stories fill 216 pages. Included are: Joe Alexander, Jake Barnes & Clay O'Brien Cooper, Joe Beaver, Leo Camarillo, Roy Cooper, Tom Ferguson, Bruce Ford, Marvin Garrett, Don Gay, Tuff Hedeman, Charmayne James, Bill Linderman, Larry Mahan, Ty Murray, Dean Oliver, Jim Shoulders, Casey Tibbs, Harry Tompkins, and Fred Whitfield.

ROOFS AND RAILS by Gavin Ehringer
144 pages, 128 black-and-white photographs plus drawings, charts, and floor plans. How to plan and build your ideal horse facility.

STARTING COLTS by Mike Kevil
168 pages and 400 photographs. Step-by-step process in starting colts.

THE HANK WIESCAMP STORY by Frank Holmes
208 pages and over 260 photographs. The biography of the legendary breeder of Quarter Horses, Appaloosas and Paints.

TEAM PENNING by Phil Livingston
144 pages and 200 photographs. How to compete in this popular family sport.

TEAM ROPING WITH JAKE AND CLAY by Fran Devereux Smith
224 pages and over 200 photographs and illustrations. Learn about fast times from champions Jake Barnes and Clay O'Brien Cooper. Solid information about handling a rope, roping dummies, and heading and heeling for practice and in competition. Also sound advice about rope horses, roping steers, gear and horsemanship.

WELL-SHOD by Don Baskins
160 pages, 300 black-and-white photos and illustrations. A horse-shoeing guide for owners and farriers. The easy-to-read text, illustrations, and photos show step-by-step how to trim and shoe a horse for a variety of uses. Special attention is paid to corrective shoeing techniques for horses with various foot and leg problems.

WESTERN HORSEMANSHIP by Richard Shrake
144 pages and 150 photographs. Complete guide to riding western horses.

WESTERN TRAINING by Jack Brainard
With Peter Phinny. 136 pages. Stresses the foundation for western training.

WIN WITH BOB AVILA by Juli S. Thorson
This 128-page, hardbound, full-color book discusses traits that separate horse-world achievers from also-rans. World champion horseman Bob Avila shares his philosophies on succeeding as a competitor, breeder, and trainer.